Computational Intelligence for Cybersecurity Management and Applications

As cyberattacks continue to grow in complexity and number, computational intelligence is helping under-resourced security analysts stay one step ahead of threats. Drawing on threat intelligence from millions of studies, blogs, and news articles, computational intelligence techniques such as machine learning and automatic natural language processing quickly provide the means to identify real threats and dramatically reduce response times.

The book collects and reports on recent high-quality research addressing different cybersecurity challenges. It:

- explores the newest developments in the use of computational intelligence and AI for cybersecurity applications
- provides several case studies related to computational intelligence techniques for cybersecurity in a wide range of applications (smart health care, blockchain, cyber-physical system, etc.)
- integrates theoretical and practical aspects of computational intelligence for cybersecurity so that any reader, from novice to expert, may understand the book's explanations of key topics.

It offers comprehensive coverage of the essential topics, including:

- machine learning and deep learning for cybersecurity
- blockchain for cybersecurity and privacy
- security engineering for cyber-physical systems
- AI and data analytics techniques for cybersecurity in smart systems
- trust in digital systems

This book discusses the current state-of-the-art and practical solutions for the following cybersecurity and privacy issues using artificial intelligence techniques and cutting-edge technology. Readers interested in learning more about computational intelligence techniques for cybersecurity applications and management will find this book invaluable. They will get insight into potential avenues for future study on these topics and be able to prioritize their efforts better.

Computational Intelligence for Cybersecurity Management and Applications

Edited by
Yassine Maleh, Mamoun Alazab,
and Soufyane Mounir

CRC Press
Taylor & Francis Group
Boca Raton London New York

CRC Press is an imprint of the
Taylor & Francis Group, an **informa** business

First edition published 2023
by CRC Press
6000 Broken Sound Parkway NW, Suite 300, Boca Raton, FL 33487-2742

and by CRC Press
4 Park Square, Milton Park, Abingdon, Oxon, OX14 4RN

CRC Press is an imprint of Taylor & Francis Group, LLC

ISBN: 978-1-032-33503-2 (hbk)
ISBN: 978-1-032-33507-0 (pbk)
ISBN: 978-1-003-31991-7 (ebk)

DOI: 10.1201/9781003319917

Typeset in Times
by MPS Limited, Dehradun

Contents

Section I Big Data and Computational Intelligence for Cybersecurity Management and Applications

Section II Computational Intelligence for Cybersecurity Applications

Section III   Blockchain and Computational Intelligence for Cybersecurity Applications

Preface

There is a growing demand for automated solutions to supplement human analysis as cyberattacks on vital infrastructure rise and adapt. Finding the sources of the breaches is akin to finding a needle in a haystack. When dealing with such a massive business, it might be challenging to know where to begin when trying to find useful information among the mountains of data. Traditional intelligence analysis is a repetitive, largely manual procedure using an infinite quantity of data to deduce attackers' complex patterns and actions. Furthermore, most detected incursions only offer a bare minimum of attributes on a single stage of an assault. We share multiple parts of an attack, so we have accurate and timely knowledge of each step. We could better assist our cyber-detection and prevention skills, improve our awareness of cyber-threats, and simplify the instant sharing of information on threats. New research in cyber-threat hunting, statistics on cyber dangers, and analyses of crucial data are only some of the things that this book hopes to convey.

Since even a single cyberattack may result in lost data and considerable damages, protecting computer systems from cyberattacks is one of the most critical cybersecurity jobs for individual users and organizations. Extremely high stakes mean that reliable and rapid detection procedures are essential. In particular, current static and dynamic approaches fail to detect zero-day attacks effectively. Because of this, we may employ methods based on machine learning and big data analytics.

Computational Intelligence for Cybersecurity Management and Applications comprises many state-of-the-art contributions from scientists and practitioners working in cybersecurity. The book's goal is to serve as a reliable resource for students, researchers, engineers, and professionals in the field, as well as anyone interested in learning about the many dimensions of cybersecurity and the cutting-edge developments in artificial intelligence for cyber threat management. This book contains 11 chapters divided into three sections. Section I: Big Data and Computational Intelligence for Cybersecurity Management and Applications. Section II: Computational Intelligence for Cybersecurity Applications. Section III: Blockchain and Computational Intelligence for Cybersecurity Applications.

This book discusses the current state-of-the-art and practical solutions for the following cybersecurity and privacy issues using artificial intelligence techniques and cutting-edge technology. Readers interested in learning more about computational intelligence techniques for cybersecurity applications and management will find this book invaluable. They will get insight into potential avenues for future study on these topics and be able to prioritize their efforts better.

Maleh, Mamoun & Mounir

Editor biographies

Yassine Maleh (http://orcid.org/0000-0003-4704-5364) is a cybersecurity professor and practitioner with industry and academic experience. He received a PhD degree in computer sciences. Since 2019, he has been working as a professor of cybersecurity at Sultan Moulay Slimane University, Morocco. He worked for the National Port agency (ANP) in Morocco as a senior security analyst from 2012 to 2019. He is the founding chair of IEEE Consultant Network Morocco and founding president of the African Research Center of Information Technology and Cybersecurity. He is a senior member of IEEE, member of the International Association of Engineers, and the Machine Intelligence Research Labs. Dr. Maleh has made contributions in the fields of information security and privacy, Internet of Things security, and wireless and constrained networks security. His research interests include information security and privacy, Internet of Things, network security, information system, and IT governance. He has published over 70 papers (book chapters, international journals, conferences/workshops), 12 edited books, and 3 authored books. He is the editor-in-chief of the *International Journal of Information Security and Privacy (IJISP)* and the *International Journal of Smart Security Technologies (IJSST)*. He serves as an associate editor for *IEEE Access* (2019 Impact Factor 4.098), the *International Journal of Digital Crime and Forensics*, and the *International Journal of Information Security and Privacy*. He was also a guest editor of a special issue on "Recent Advances on Cyber Security and Privacy for Cloud-of-Things" of the *International Journal of Digital Crime and Forensics*, Volume 10, Issue 3, July–September 2019. He has served and continues to serve on executive and technical program committees and as a reviewer of numerous international conferences and journals such as Elsevier Ad Hoc Networks, *IEEE Network Magazine, IEEE Sensor Journal*, ICT Express, and Springer Cluster Computing. He was the publicity chair of BCCA 2019 and the general chair of the MLBDACP 19 symposium and ICI2C'21 Conference.

Mamoun Alazab (https://orcid.org/0000-0002-1928-3704) is an associate professor in the College of Engineering, IT and Environment at Charles Darwin University, Australia. He received his PhD degree in computer science from the Federation University of Australia, School of Science, Information Technology and Engineering. He is a cybersecurity researcher and practitioner with industry and academic experience. Dr Alazab's research is multidisciplinary and focuses on cybersecurity and digital forensics of computer systems including current and emerging issues in the cyber environment like cyber-physical systems and the Internet of Things, by taking into consideration the unique challenges present in these environments, with a focus on cybercrime detection and prevention. He looks into the intersection use of machine learning as an essential tool for cybersecurity, for example, for detecting attacks, analyzing malicious code, or uncovering vulnerabilities in software. He has more than 100 research papers. He is the recipient of short fellowship from the Japan Society for the Promotion of Science (JSPS) based on his nomination from the Australian Academy of Science. He has delivered many invited and keynote speeches; 27 events in 2019 alone. He convened and chaired more than 50 conferences and workshops. He is the founding chair of the IEEE Northern Territory Subsection: (Feb. 2019–current). He is a senior member of the IEEE, Cybersecurity Academic Ambassador for Oman's Information Technology Authority (ITA), Member of the IEEE Computer Society's Technical Committee on Security and Privacy (TCSP), and has worked closely with government and industry on many projects, including IBM, Trend Micro, the Australian Federal Police (AFP), the Australian Communications and Media Authority (ACMA), Westpac, UNODC, and the Attorney General's Department.

Soufyane Mounir has been an associate professor in the National School of Applied Sciences of Sultan Moulay Slimane Slimane, Beni Mellal, Morocco, since 2014. He received his PhD in electronics and telecommunication from University Hassan 1st, Morocco. His research is multidisciplinary and focuses on telecommunications, VoIP, signal processing, embedded systems, and cybersecurity. He is an active member of LaSTI Laboratory, ENSA Khouribga.

Contributors

Izzat Alsmadi
Texas A&M University
San Antonio, TX, USA

V. Arulkumar
Sri Krishna College of Engineering
and Technology
Coimbatore, Tamilnadu, India

Pinky Bai
School of Computer & Systems
Sciences
Jawaharlal Nehru University
New Delhi, India

Mustapha Belaissaoui
ENCG
University Hassan 1er
Morocco

Mohan Babu Chowdary
Dept. of CSE
Sir C.R.Reddy College of Engineering
Eluru, India

Upasana Dohare
Department of Computer Applications
School of Computing Science &
Engineering
Galgotias University
Greater Noida, Uttar Pradesh, India

Francesco Flammini
University of Applied Sciences
and Arts of Southern
Switzerland (CH)

Aswin G
Full Stack Developer
Zealbots in Chadura Tech
Tiruchirappalli, Tamilnadu, India

Harinahalli Lokesh Gururaj
Department of Information Technology
Manipal Institute of Technology
Bengaluru
Manipal Academy of Higher Education,
Manipal, India

Jean Claude Kamgang
Department of Mathematics and
Computer Science
Faculty of Science
The University of Ngaoundéré
Ngaoundéré, Cameroon

Amer Kareem
University of Bedfordshire
United Kingdom

B.H. Khoi
Industrial Univ of Ho Chi Minh City
Vietnam

Cédric Tala Kuate
Department of Mathematics and
Computer Science
Faculty of Science
The University of Ngaoundéré
Ngaoundéré, Cameroon

Sushil Kumar
School of Computer & Systems Sciences
Jawaharlal Nehru University
New Delhi, India

Swathi Lakkineni
University of The Cumberlands
USA

Nandini Nagaraj
Department of CSE
Vidyavardhaka College of Engineering
Mysuru, Karnataka, India

Musarrat Saberin Nipun
University of Bedfordshire
United Kingdom

Nidhi Pandey
Department of Computer
Science & Technology
SRM University
Delhi-NCR, Ghaziabad, India

Chhabi Rani Panigrahi
Department of Computer Science
Rama Devi Women's University
Bhubanewar, Odisha, India

Bibudhendu Pati
Department of Computer Science
Rama Devi Women's University
Bhubanewar, Odisha, India

B.V. Quang
Industrial Univ of Ho Chi Minh City
Vietnam

Sunil Kumar Byalaru Ramesh
Department of CSE
Vidyavardhaka College of Engineering
Mysuru, Karnataka, India

Mamata Rath
Department of Computer Science
and Engineering DRIEMS
(Autonomous)
Cuttack, Odisha, India

Balakrishnan S
Sri Krishna College of Engineering
and Technology
Coimbatore, Tamilnadu, India

Oshin Sharma
Department of Computer Science &
Technology
SRM University
Delhi-NCR, Ghaziabad, India

Rejwan Bin Sulaiman
University of Bedfordshire
United Kingdom

Beekanahalli Harish Swathi
Department of CSE
Vidyavardhaka College of Engineering
Mysuru, Karnataka, India

Lo'ai Tawalbeh
Texas A&M University
San Antonio, TX, USA

Franklin Tchakounte
Department of Mathematics and
Computer Science
Faculty of Science
The University of Ngaoundéré
Ngaoundéré, Cameroon

Niva Tripathy
Department of Computer Science and
Engineering DRIEMS (Autonomous)
Cuttack, Odisha, India

Subhranshu Sekhar Tripathy
Department of Computer Science and
Engineering DRIEMS (Autonomous)
Cuttack, Odisha, India

N.V.T. Truong
Industrial Univ of Ho Chi Minh City
Vietnam

Section I

Big Data and Computational Intelligence for Cybersecurity Management and Applications

1 Big Data and Blockchain for Cybersecurity Applications: Challenges and Solutions

Swathi Lakkineni
University of The Cumberlands, USA

Lo'ai Tawalbeh and Izzat Alsmadi
Texas A&M University, San Antonio, TX, USA

CONTENTS

DOI: 10.1201/9781003319917-2

1.1 INTRODUCTION

Internet of Things slowly raised from consumer usage to usage in the manufacturing process. Because of IoT's benefits (Internet of Things) in manufacturing, industry owners are fostered to implement them. Although the generated data from MIoT (manufacturing Internet of Things) adds value to the industrial process, there are challenges encountered in analyzing the collected and stored data. Also, the uncertain nature of big data further affects the results of big data analytics and uncovers different challenges. Computational intelligence techniques are discussed that can help overcome uncertainty challenges.

Integrating big data with business intelligence leverages vast amounts of accumulated information. As a part of the exploration of this fact, two case studies have been considered: the application of business intelligence transformed companies and earned profits.

Bitcoin is one of the many applications of blockchain (Tadaka, S.M., 2020). A case study is explained about Switzerland, where Bitcoin was legalized, and other countries where Bitcoin was not legalized. In addition to that, advantages and disadvantages of Bitcoin were also studied. Cybersecurity is another area where blockchain is applied. Cybersecurity can be improved in different areas like IoT, networking, etc., by using blockchain. Gaps in blockchain and various attacks that happened with blockchain were also discussed. Finally, a few use cases of blockchain in cybersecurity are discussed, which organizations can leverage. The following table illustrates the challenges facing integrating blockchain in IoT systems (Table 1.1).

There are five different concepts where blockchain and big data can be applied. It starts with discussing the application of big data and blockchain in e-governance. The advantages and challenges are discussed. The second is about health care, and the third is about personal big data management, where a prototype is discussed to overcome the challenges of blockchain when storing big data. The fourth is about the importance of big data and blockchain in

TABLE 1.1

Challenges Facing Blockchain and IoT Integration

	IoT	Blockchain
Privacy	No privacy	High
Security	Not secure	Secure
Latency	Low	High
Scalability	Highly scalable	Poor scalability
System structure	Centralized	Decentralized
Bandwidth	Limited	High

cryptocurrency. The last concept discussed is the application of big data and blockchain in fog-enabled IoT devices.

1.2 BENEFITS OF BIG DATA ANALYTICS FOR MANUFACTURING INTERNET OF THINGS

The widespread use of IoT has resulted in a deluge of information hitherto unseen in human history. There is a tremendous increase in the complexity of the data being generated by consumer wearables and self-driving vehicles. Data from the Internet of Things has far-reaching consequences for industries as diverse as manufacturing, transportation, and retail, with hundreds of sub-segments that provide unique risks and issues that the current IT infrastructure cannot address.

Applying big data to manufacturing the Internet of Things provides us with many advantages. Below discussed are some of the benefits.

1.2.1 IMPROVING FACTORY OPERATIONS AND PRODUCTION

Through predictive analysis of manufacturing data, predicting the customer demand, and then keeping machinery and raw materials ready for manufacturing is possible (Dai et al., 2020). For example, manufacturing down coats can be ready to forecast a cold wave. Due to this, factory operations and machinery are best utilized.

1.2.1.1 Reducing Machine Downtime

Sensors deployed all over the assembly line collect data related to the machines' status (Dai et al., 2020). By analyzing the root cause of a machine failure, steps can be taken to avoid failures to reduce machine downtime. It also helps to detect if any machines are overloaded to balance the load among other machines.

1.2.1.2 Improving Product Quality

Analyzing manufacturing data makes it possible to identify defective goods and eliminate the root cause to improve product quality (Dai et al., 2020). Further, the product design can be enhanced by analyzing marketing data and customer requirements.

1.2.1.3 Enhancing Supply Chain Efficiency

The inventory supply can be arranged based on analyzed supplier data (Dai et al., 2020). A lot of data gets are generated from an increasing number of sensors, RFID, and tags, which on analysis can help reduce the holding time of supplies and meet the customer demand.

1.2.1.4 Monitoring Manufacturing Process

IoT-based sensors combined with big data processing proved to be sufficient to monitor and detect faults in the manufacturing process (Syafrudin et al., 2018). The data generated by IoT devices is enormous, and without a big data processing capability, it is hard to analyze and retrieve useful information. Fault detection is essential in manufacturing to ensure everything is running fine. By applying DBSCAN to the collected data, outliers can be removed. The random forest method is further used to predict the faults in the manufacturing process.

1.2.1.5 Reduction in Energy Consumption and Energy Costs

Data collected through IoT sensors in the energy-intensive manufacturing process is further analyzed by big data technologies to identify wastages in energy (Zhang et al., n.d.). Thus, identified waste can be eliminated, reducing energy consumption and costs.

1.2.1.6 Reduction of Scrap Rate

Every manufactured product goes through a series of tests to determine whether the product meets the desired standard (Lade et al., 2017). Suppose if it does not, then the product is scrapped. By analyzing the data generated during the manufacturing process, it is possible to reduce the scrap rate.

1.3 BIG DATA ANALYTICS RESEARCH IN IOT: ISSUES AND CHALLENGES

Many challenges are encountered when applying big data analytics to MIoT data (Muheidat & Tawalbeh, 2021). The authors (Dai et al., 2020) classified the challenges into three groups. They are challenges in data acquisition, data preprocessing and storage, and finally, generating data analytics.

1.3.1 DATA ACQUISITION CHALLENGES

Data acquisition deals with collecting data from different sources and representing and transmitting it (Dai et al., 2020). As data comes in heterogeneous forms representing the vast data in a standard format is not easy. Similarly, transferring enormous volumes of data to a storage system is also challenging as it requires high bandwidth and industrial wireless sensor networks have to be highly efficient.

1.3.2 DATA PREPROCESSING AND STORAGE

The collected data should be integrated and cleaned to perform analytics (Dai et al., 2020). Below are some of the challenges encountered in this phase.

1.3.2.1   Data Integration

Data collected from multiple sources in multiple formats is challenging to integrate (Yu et al., 2020). The data can be in many forms, structured, unstructured, and semi-structured data (H.-N. Dai et al., 2020).

1.3.2.2   Redundancy Reduction

Data collected from different devices might have temporal and spatial redundancy that might affect the analytics (H.-N. Dai et al., 2020). Therefore, eliminating data redundancy is not easy.

1.3.2.3   Data Cleaning and Data Compression

Due to defects in the machinery or sensor errors, the collected data might have noise and errors (Dai et al., 2020). Therefore, it is crucial to clean the data accurately before performing the analytics. But the volume of data generated through manufacturing IoT devices is vast. Therefore, efficient schemes must be designed to compress the data and then clean the data for analytics purposes. Further discussed are the challenges in data storage.

1.3.2.4   Reliability and Persistence of Data Storage

One of the big data analytics requirements is the reliability and persistence of the data (Dai et al., 2020). It is challenging to meet the requirement because storing tremendous amounts of data also has a cost.

1.3.2.5   Scalability

As data is generated by various machines, sensors are in huge numbers, and the storage to save the data is always expanding (Yu et al., 2020). In addition to the storage, the tools and techniques applied to big data should also be scalable. For example, machine learning techniques and open-source tools should also be scalable.

1.3.2.6   Efficiency

A prodigious number of queries access the data concurrently (H.-N. Dai et al., 2020). Therefore, the data storage should be efficient, reliable, and persistent in supporting analytics.

1.3.3   Data Analytics

After collecting data, preprocessing, and storing, the last phase is to generate data analytics, which further presents the below challenges.

1.3.3.1   Data Temporal and Spatial Correlation

The data from conventional data warehouses are different from the MIoT data. MIoT data is spatially and temporally correlated (Dai et al., 2020). Extracting valuable information from such data is challenging.

1.3.3.2 Efficient Data Mining Schemes

The conventional data mining schemes may not apply to MIoT data because of its volume and nature (Dai et al., 2020). Efficient data mining schemes must be designed to manage the tremendous volume and uncertainty of MIoT data.

1.3.3.3 Privacy and Security

It is also essential to ensure the data's privacy and security while generating analytics (Dai et al., 2020). The conventional schemes cannot be applied to MIoT data due to its volume, heterogeneous structure, and spatio-temporal correlations. Although multiple challenges are encountered while generating the analytics, the benefits add value to the industrial process. Next comes big data's challenges, primarily due to uncertainty. Computational intelligence techniques that help mitigate the challenges are discussed further.

1.3.4 UNCERTAINTY CHALLENGES AND COMPUTATIONAL INTELLIGENCE TECHNIQUES

A separate set of challenges encountered in big data analytics due to uncertainty.

Uncertainty is a condition that represents unknown or imperfect information (Hariri et al., 2019). Each of the "V" that represents big data introduces many sources that bring uncertainty to the data. Because of the uncertainty lot of challenges are introduced. When dealing with big data, security is also considered another challenge (Iqbal et al., 2020). Discussed below are some of the challenges introduced by each "V."

1.3.4.1 Volume

It is impossible to specify a specific limit to big data size (Hariri et al., 2019). Generally, exabyte (EB) or zettabyte (ZB) data is considered big data. But challenges exist for smaller data sets too. For example, Walmart collects 2.5PB of customer data every hour. Continuous storage of this data presents scalability and uncertainty problems because the data storage technologies may not handle infinite amounts of data. Data analysis techniques are designed mostly for smaller data sets and may fail when applied to extensive data.

1.3.4.2 Variety

Variety refers to different forms of data like structured, semi-structured, and unstructured data (Hariri et al., 2019). Structured data is a relational form of data and is very easy to analyze. Unstructured data, for example, refers to images and videos that are challenging to explore and to analyze semi-structured data, the data has to be separated from the tags. Uncertainty is introduced when converting unstructured data to structured data.

1.3.4.3 Velocity

It refers to the speed at which a vast volume of data arrives (Hariri et al., 2019). The processing speed of the big data must match the incoming rate of the data.

The velocity presents itself as a challenge because it is crucial. For example, IoT (Internet of Things) devices continuously generate data. When used in health care, if the processing speed does not match the incoming rate of the data, then a delay in sending the results to the clinicians might injure the patient.

1.3.4.4 Veracity

Veracity refers to data quality and is categorized as good, bad, and undefined (Hariri et al., 2019). Low quality of data adds unnecessary processing costs. Due to that, accuracy and trust in big data analytics are hard to achieve. For example, when performing analytics to mitigate disease, any ambiguities in the data might affect the data analytics process's accuracy.

1.3.4.5 Value

The value represents the usefulness of the analyzed data in making decisions (Hariri et al., 2019). The prior V's deal with the challenge of representing big data. Companies like Facebook, Amazon, and Google leverage analytics and use them to make decisions. For example, Amazon collects user data and analyzes it, sending product recommendations to its customer, thus increasing sales. Similarly, Google uses the location services data to improvise Google maps services. Facebook analyzes users' activities to send target advertisements and also friend recommendations. Computational intelligence techniques can be applied to mitigate the challenges.

1.4 COMPUTATIONAL INTELLIGENCE TECHNIQUES

Computational intelligence (CI) consists of nature-inspired algorithms designed to imitate human information processing and reasoning to deal with complex and uncertain data (Iqbal et al., 2020). Computational intelligence is also a subclass of machine learning approaches. To handle the growing class of real problems, fuzzy logic (FL), evolutionary algorithms (EAs), and artificial neural networks (ANNs) form a triad of core CI techniques. Further discussed are each one in detail.

1.4.1 FUZZY LOGIC

Fuzzy logic uses linguistic quantifiers, which are fuzzy sets, and provides an approximate reasoning approach, qualitative modeling data, and adaptive control (Iqbal et al., 2020). Linguistic quantifiers are also used to represent the uncertain real world, user- and data-defined concepts, and human interpretable fuzzy rules. Thus, defined data is further used for decision-making purposes. Due to big data's nature, collecting from different sources has many uncertainties, noise, and outliers. Fuzzy logic systems are capable of handling uncertainties; for example, creating models to predict the users' emotions has to deal with many ambiguous data.

In addition to dealing with uncertainty, fuzzy logic systems can deliver results in a reasonable amount of time (Iqbal et al., 2020). Fuzzy logic is used to analyze big data generated by social networks to analyze public opinion. The experiments conducted to analyze Twitter data resulted in a high prediction rate and good performance. Similarly, fuzzy logic–based matching algorithms and MapReduction helped in clinical decision support. Further discussed are evolutionary algorithms that deal with another type of challenge.

1.4.2 EVOLUTIONARY ALGORITHMS

As mentioned earlier, one of the challenges of big data is its high dimensionality and sparseness due to high volume and variety (Iqbal et al., 2020). Evolutionary algorithms are another CI technique applied to explore the search space and meet high dimensionality. They are also used in machine learning problems in big data analysis, such as clustering, feature selection, etc. EAs discover an optimal solution to a complex problem by imitating the evolutionary process and slowly developing the solutions (Hariri et al., 2019). For example, using a parallel genetic algorithm for medical image processing using the Hadoop system brings effective results. Artificial neural networks also play a vital role.

1.4.3 ARTIFICIAL NEURAL NETWORKS

Artificial neural networks are based on the parallel processing and information representation of neurons like animals and the human brain (Iqbal et al., 2020). They help to perform feature extraction and learning from experimental data. Feature extraction is essential as it helps to identify critical input parameters that affect the output. Therefore in big data analytics, it is vital to determine spatial co-relations between input variables at a given instant. At the same time, it is also essential to determine temporal co-relations between input parameters that change over time.

Feature learning methods are based on supervised approaches such as deep neural networks, convolutional neural networks, recurrent neural networks (Iqbal et al., 2020). There are also unsupervised techniques, such as deep belief networks. Deep learning approaches leverage supervised and unsupervised training. They are based on the principle of artificial neural networks with multiple hidden layers. First, unsupervised (bottom-up) training produces a higher-level representation of sensory data. It can be further used for training classifiers (top-down) based on a standard supervised training algorithm.

Three types of computational intelligence techniques, fuzzy logic, evolutionary algorithms, and artificial neural networks, are designed based on human interpretation and reasoning. Therefore they seem to overcome the challenges that occur due to uncertainty. The next part discusses the integration of big data with business intelligence.

1.5 INTEGRATION OF BIG DATA WITH BUSINESS INTELLIGENCE

Integrating big data with business intelligence leverages vast amounts of accumulated information. As a part of the exploration of this fact, two case studies have been considered. One is Bikers Haven Restaurant, where migration happened from a manual way of storing data as receipts to a business intelligence system. The second one is ChangQing Drilling Company, whose information systems were scattered, and data was distributed in different locations. The application of business intelligence transformed these two companies and earned profits. The case studies are elaborated further.

1.5.1 BIKERS HAVEN RESTAURANT CASE STUDY

Bikers Haven has become a popular restaurant in Tagaytay and Amadeo to serve authentic dishes to its customers (Alday & Rosas, 2019). But its success was affected due to its inefficient way of managing and manually storing the data. The way Bikers Haven does business is the manual way. That means all the transactions are done physically without retaining the data using technologies like data warehouse. Decision-making regarding sales is based upon assumption and not based upon data. Some of the existing problems are reasons for inefficient data management.

1.5.1.1 Problem

The existing system problems can be classified into three types (Alday & Rosas, 2019). One is data storage. The data is currently stored in different locations physically and is not accessible to everyone. The second is data retrieval. Due to the way the information is stored, data retrieval is time-consuming. And the last one is data management. There is no way to use the data and get useful information, resulting in data wastage.

1.5.1.2 Solution

Researchers proposed a few solutions to avoid the wastage of the data and efficiently use it (Alday & Rosas, 2019). An efficient design for a big data solution is needed for data storage problems. For the data retrieval problem, a data warehousing solution is necessary so that business owners can access it from anywhere. And to solve the data management problem, data mining resources and tools are needed. In addition to the mentioned solutions, efficient forecasting methods are required to solve the business intelligence problem so that data can be used efficiently and effectively.

1.5.1.3 Methodology

As part of this research, a web design-based platform is used for data storage purposes where employees can track the data from the business into the system (Alday & Rosas, 2019). A mobile platform is connected to the web design for business owners to retrieve data from anywhere. GSuite's sheets and Microsoft's Excel address the data management problems. Finally, Google Analytics addresses business intelligence problems aligned with Rapid Miner for complexity and technological forecasting.

Using Google sheets made it easy for the employees to input the data (Alday & Rosas, 2019). Data owners could also view the data from anywhere, anytime, thus providing transparency. Using a web-design platform and connectivity to mobile devices enabled employees and data owners to view data on any device from any location. Security has to be implemented for data access based on the business owner's requirements.

1.5.1.4   Results

Results are gathered through the employee's contribution and collecting data logs (Alday & Rosas, 2019). Thus, gathered core information would be transitioned and cleaned for further migration to a data warehouse. Thus, migrated data can be used for forecasting as data grows big. Forecasting the data helped the data owners visualize peaks in the sales. They were able to visualize sales hourly. The data owners could identify the periods when sales are low and then decide upon replenishing the supply. They could also develop ideas to boost sales during downtime, like introducing combos. With the help of this prototype, the owners of the restaurant were able to survive the competition.

1.5.2   CHANGQING DRILLING COMPANY CASE STUDY

ChangQing Drilling company has information systems built as needed and scattered (Xiang & Fang, 2017). The data is distributed among servers and in databases such as SQLServer, Oracle, MYSQL, Microsoft Access, and Microsoft Excel. If the information is gathered, cleaned, and analyzed, it could help decide on new drilling projects. For this reason, the first step is integrating the distributed and heterogeneous data into a data warehouse.

1.5.2.1   Data Integration

A data integration tool called Kettle Management is used along with ETL (Extract-Transform-Load) to construct a data warehouse (Xiang & Fang, 2017). There are three modules in the construction of the drilling data warehouse. The Metadata Management module drives the entire ETL process and plays a significant role in the overall data process. The ETL management module is the core of the ETL process and handles the extraction, transformation, and loading of the data from the source to the target database. The task management module records configuration information.

1.5.2.2   Implementation of Business Intelligence

Once the data warehouse is ready, it needs to be integrated with OLAP (Online Analytical Processing) and data mining techniques to generate data visualization reports (Xiang & Fang, 2017). The company could view data related to the drilling speed through data visualization. The company also identified critical factors that can enhance the drilling speed. The company could enhance its return on investment by improving the drilling speed.

1.5.2.3   Discussion

The idea behind the prototype used in Bikers Haven Restaurant was good, but the selection of tools might be better. GSuites have incompatibilities in the automation of input that further connects to the data warehouse (Alday & Rosas, 2019). The whole prototype combines the employee input data with data warehouse, data mining, and business intelligence. Before data goes into the data warehouse, it has to be extracted, transformed, and loaded, and the whole process is called the ETL process (El Bousty et al., 2018). The researchers did not mention the tool they used for the ETL process. It is one of the significant steps in integration.

Identifying patterns through data mining also needs efficient algorithms not mentioned by Alday and Rosas (2019) in their paper. There might be a scope for improvement at that point. However, Google Analytics and Rapid Miner provided the required analytics to the business owner to improve the restaurant business.

Improvement in the return of investments was experienced by ChangQing Drilling company after using the business intelligence (Xiang & Fang, 2017). In this case study, implementing a data warehouse was one of the challenges because of the existing data's distributed nature in different databases. However, the data warehouse implementation was handled efficiently. Another good thing done in the ChangQing Drilling case study was improving data retrieval speed.

With the help of materialized squares and constructing the OLAP index structure, the data is retrieved faster from the data warehouse (Xiang & Fang, 2017). The data visualizations were also valuable as the factors influencing the drilling speed can be identified. It is important because the drilling speed can be enhanced by taking care of the influential factors. The only thing not specified here is the selection of a data mining algorithm. The visualizations result from applying a data mining algorithm, showing an increase in the return of investments to the company. Data warehouse, OLAP, data mining, and visualization tools are the essential components that can help to integrate big data with business intelligence. Thus, the case studies prove that big data can be integrated with business intelligence, and no separate system is again needed. Besides integrating big data with business intelligence, combining big data with blockchain is possible. Bitcoin is a well-known application of blockchain (Saldamli & Razavi, 2020).

1.6   BITCOIN ADOPTION AND REJECTION

Bitcoin is not accepted everywhere in the world. A case study is explained about Switzerland, where Bitcoin was legalized, and other countries where Bitcoin was not legalized. For example, Bangladesh, Vietnam, etc., are some of the countries where Bitcoin was not legalized.

1.6.1   BITCOIN ADOPTION

Zug's canton was the first public institution to accept Bitcoins as a payment mechanism in 2016 (Kondova, 2018). The finance minister of Switzerland, Mr. Johann Schneider-Ammann, wanted the country to be a cryptocurrency leader. He also praised Canton of Zug as a model of making Switzerland a crypto nation. Many blockchain companies worldwide were attracted to the Canton of Zug. It is also the foundation of another cryptocurrency called Ethereum. Although the value of Bitcoin was on the rise for some time, it slowly declined.

In 2018, due to the investors' theft that has stolen cryptocurrency, the Bitcoin value decreased (Kondova, 2018). However, with the support of the police and politicians, Zug of Canton got its image back. Last year there was an announcement that the tax payments for Feb 2021 could be accepted as Bitcoin payments (Zug/db, n.d.).

In 2016, Canton of Zug accepted payments for government services (Kondova, 2018). But it was only up to $220. The Bitcoin payment amount for taxes now has a limit of 111,226.20$, which is CHF 100K. With this move, the Switzerland government encourages citizens to get used to Bitcoin payments. Additionally, Zermatt in Switzerland will accept tax payments in unlimited Bitcoin amounts starting this year. Italy, too, has started accepting a limited amount of Bitcoins for tax payments. Although Switzerland embraced Bitcoins, some other countries rejected them.

1.6.2 BITCOIN REJECTION

Despite many advantages of Bitcoin-like decentralization, security, and speed, there is also a negative side of Bitcoin due to which some governments do not encourage Bitcoins in their countries (Sahoo, 2017). For example, Mt. Gox (Magic: The Gathering Online eXchange) has suffered from fraud due to hackers accessing the user's credentials (Sahoo, 2017). Before that, Mt Gox was an online exchange for cryptocurrencies where users could buy and sell their Bitcoins. But after the fraud hit the exchange, it was closed. Similarly, Silk Road is another example.

Silk Road is a website for illegal activities (Sahoo, 2017). Its activities started in 2011. Money transactions for illicit activities such as drugs, malicious software, weapons, etc., were done in a cryptocurrency called Bitcoin. These transactions were quickly done as the parties involved were unknown. In 2013, the FBI captured Ross William Ulbricht, the creator of the Silk Road, and after that, the website was shut down. The FBI seized a lot of money in this process; a large amount came from Ross William Ulbricht's computer. Thus, generated Bitcoins between 2011–2012 were further exchanged with Bitcoin exchanges.

Due to these fraudulent activities, the trust in cryptocurrencies is decreased (Sahoo, 2017). Many governments did not legalize Bitcoins or any form of cryptocurrency because of fraudulent activities. Below are some of the countries that restrict the use of Bitcoins.

1.6.2.1 Bangladesh

In 2014, Bangladesh Central Bank banned cryptocurrency usage (Sahoo, 2017). It also mentioned that anyone caught using virtual currency will be punished under the 2012 ACT for being involved in unapproved money laundering activities.

1.6.2.2 Bolivia

In Central South America, Bolivia banned cryptocurrency and made using virtual currency illegal (Sahoo, 2017). The money that is approved by a central authority is only considered legitimate.

1.6.2.3   Russia

Russia also banned cryptocurrency usage but did not ban blockchain as it can enhance many online services (Sahoo, 2017).

1.6.2.4   Vietnam

Vietnam's government did not legalize Bitcoins and announced individuals and financial institutions not use Bitcoins (Sahoo, 2017). It also mentioned that usage of cryptocurrency would increase money laundering activities.

1.6.3   ADVANTAGES AND DISADVANTAGES

There are both advantages and disadvantages of Bitcoin that made some countries accept it while others still reject them.

1.6.3.1   Advantages

Further discussed are the advantages, followed by the disadvantages of Bitcoin.

1.6.3.1.1   Personal Data Protection

If the retailer or another partner's transaction is hacked and a hacker gets access to the financial and personal information, other users' personal information is still confidential (Dumitrescu, 2017). Until the private key is safe, the hackers will not gain access to the other Bitcoin users' data.

1.6.3.1.2   Lower Transaction Fee

The processing fee of a transaction is much lesser with Bitcoin than with a credit card (Dumitrescu, 2017). For a $100 fee, a merchant pays a $3.37 transaction fee, and when the same amount is processed using Bitcoin, it would only cost a $0.61 transaction fee. Therefore some countries like China, Ethiopia, and Denmark would like to use blockchain technology to improvise their public services.

1.6.3.1.3   Protection through Speed of Transfer

Transfers through Bitcoin are much faster than through the banking system (Dumitrescu, 2017). It takes 10 minutes to 30 minutes to confirm a Bitcoin payment, whereas banks might take several days. Due to that merchant can have his payment even before delivering the goods. Once a transaction is done, it cannot be reversed unless both parties agree. Due to the speed of transfer in Bitcoin payments, merchants are protected from chargeback fraud.

1.6.3.1.4   Immunity to Inflation

Bitcoin is immune to inflation. Its monetary inflation decreased from 2010 to 2017 as the Bitcoins increased (Dumitrescu, 2017). The inflation is expected to decrease until the maximum limit of 21 million Bitcoins is reached. It is predicted to happen in 2060. Therefore, all these advantages made some countries like the USA and the United Kingdom allow Bitcoin currency.

1.6.3.2 Disadvantages

In addition to the previously discussed example, further discussed are the disadvantages.

1.6.3.2.1 Lack of Solid Anonymity

The flooding protocols used in Bitcoin technology do not guarantee a hundred percent anonymity (Dumitrescu, 2017). Therefore, every fifth user considers leaving the Bitcoin network.

1.6.3.2.2 Prone to Scams

Every Bitcoin user will have a private key (Dumitrescu, 2017). If he/she loses that private key, they will lose their Bitcoin amount. Many fraudsters scammed innocent cyber customers. Between 2011 and 2014, there were 10 million dollars scammed from Bitcoin deposits. Such scams include Mining Investment Scams, where customers pay for mining equipment but never receive one. Similarly, exchange scams that promise a higher rate but never deliver the money.

1.6.3.2.3 Trust

It might take some time for people to accept Bitcoin as everyone is used to regular payment systems like cash and credit cards (Dumitrescu, 2017). Older people are especially hesitant to invest in this new technology and be frightened about the virtual wallet. Some younger generations might be coming forward to experiment with the latest technology but may not entirely invest in Bitcoin currency. Because of the Bitcoin's advantages and disadvantages, some countries accept Bitcoin, but some reject Bitcoins. But blockchain technology is not limited to Bitcoin. The benefits of blockchain technology are leveraged into several other areas like cybersecurity.

1.7 BLOCKCHAIN IN CYBERSECURITY

Cybersecurity can be improved in different areas like IoT, networking, etc., by using blockchain. A few use cases of blockchain in cybersecurity are discussed, which organizations can leverage.

1.7.1 IMPROVING CYBERSECURITY THROUGH BLOCKCHAIN

The current techniques that are available in cybersecurity offer a centralized storage system to authorize access (Taylor et al., 2020). However, blockchain uses distributed ledger technology, which gives it additional power to not get compromised quickly. Below are some areas where blockchain can be applied from a cybersecurity perspective.

1.7.2 IOT DEVICES

Blockchains can track data and malicious activity on the IoT devices connected to the network (Taylor et al., 2020). In addition, firmware deployment can also happen securely on IoT devices through peer-to-peer propagation. It also ensures device identification, authentication, and continuous, secure data transfer.

1.7.3 DATA STORAGE AND SHARING

Blockchain uses hashing techniques to ensure that data stored anywhere, including the cloud, is not tampered with and secured (Taylor et al., 2020). Since blockchains are decentralized networks and have client-side encryption, changes to the data must be approved through consensus and shared across the network.

1.7.4 NETWORK SECURITY

Software-defined networks security can be improved by authenticating stored data in a distributed and robust manner (Taylor et al., 2020). Public and private blockchains can be used to handle secure communication between the nodes in the network.

1.7.5 NAVIGATION AND UTILITY OF THE WORLD WIDE WEB

Wireless connection points can be validated by storing and monitoring the ledger's access control data (Taylor et al., 2020). Also, the DNS record information can be stored, which helps in safely navigating the webpages. Furthermore, blockchain has some direct applications in cybersecurity.

1.7.6 APPLICATION OF BLOCKCHAIN IN CYBERSECURITY

Blockchain achieves trust among the users by applying cryptographic and mathematical algorithms and does not depend on any third party (Dai et al., 2017). The characteristics of blockchain technology like authenticity, transparency, and immutability made it applicable to various other sectors. For example, it is applied in the financial sector, medical, IoT, education, and cybersecurity. Further discussed are some of the cybersecurity problems addressed by blockchain.

1.7.7 SECURE DOMAIN NAME SERVICE

The centralized domain name service (DNS) is susceptible to attacks as the core functions of resolving the domain name etc., are located in a centralized location (Dai et al., 2017). A map can be established between DNS and hash using blockchain. Users can register, transmit and revise domain names. Each block represents domain owners' public and private keys and resolved domain names. Since the information is distributed across the nodes, there is no centralized location to attack. Unlike a centralized DNS system, even if a node is attacked, there is no harm to other nodes in the network.

1.7.8 KEYLESS SIGNATURE INFRASTRUCTURE

Authentication schemes that rely on keys suffer from the problem of key distribution, key update, and key revocation (Dai et al., 2017). Recent blockchain research resolves this problem using key signature infrastructure (KSI). Each node in the blockchain stores the state of the data, network, and hash. KSI will constantly monitor the hash value with a timestamp. Any change in the data changes the hash value and helps to detect unauthorized access. Using a timestamp-based monitoring system does not need to distribute, maintain or revoke keys. KSI-based security protection systems have been applied in England's nuclear power and flood-control systems.

1.7.9 SECURED STORAGE

Information regarding finances, and medical is usually stored in a centralized location, and unauthorized access to the information brings various problems to the organizations and the users (Dai et al., 2017). Using the hash value concept of blockchain, the data can be stored efficiently. Apart from the areas discussed, there are other IoT equipment certification areas, cloud data desensitization, and secure data transmission. Though there are advantages of using blockchain in cybersecurity, gaps are identified.

1.7.10 GAPS AND RESOLUTIONS OF SECURITY ISSUES IN BLOCKCHAIN

The frauds in a cryptocurrency network are increasing (Al-Dherasi & Annor-Antwi, 2019). The increase in fraud each year is slowing down the cryptocurrency market. Weak security systems and lack of government regulations are blamed for it. Another gap is the increase of quantum power. An increase in quantum power will make hackers break the key used for encryption in the blockchain. It is therefore feared to be a cybersecurity threat.

Similarly, one more gap identified is inexperienced users in the blockchain networks (Al-Dherasi & Annor-Antwi, 2019). Users who are unaware of safe practices in the blockchain are prone to get attacked by scammers. They thereby provide insecure access to the blockchain network. Further discussed are three solutions to handle the security gaps identified in the blockchain.

1.7.11 QUANTUM COMPUTING

The gap related to quantum computing can be overcome by using a key with a higher number of bits (Al-Dherasi & Annor-Antwi, 2019). Because quantum computers can crack keys with a lower number of bits quickly. Therefore, it is better to offer packages with 64-bit, 128-bit, and 256-bit cryptography so that users can choose depending on their requirements.

1.7.12 DEALING WITH INEXPERIENCED USERS

Proper training has to be provided for inexperienced users not to give away their keys to scammers (Al-Dherasi & Annor-Antwi, 2019). Similarly, it is better to add two or three layers of authentication for verification purposes. Another solution is to track transactions using network features, alerting users, and confirming access to their systems.

1.7.13 User Anonymity

The user identity in the blockchain network is hidden. Due to this, scammers and hackers are taking advantage of it (Al-Dherasi & Annor-Antwi, 2019). When a public key gets flagged, there should be a possibility to track the user's identity. The tracing also should be enabled for government agencies that deal with cybersecurity. This feature would create fear among scammers, so the probability of fraud might be reduced. Although blockchain has many features to improve cybersecurity, some attacks happened on the blockchain.

1.8 CYBER SECURITY ATTACKS IN BLOCKCHAIN

According to Mishra (2019), some attacks happened in public blockchains. Even though the decentralized nature of blockchain offers security, there are loopholes that hackers and scammers target. Mentioned below are some of those attacks.

1.8.1 DAO Attack

Reentrancy vulnerability was exploited in decentralized autonomous smart contracts (Mishra, 2019). The attacker deployed withdraw function code into the contract, and that function was executed every time the contract was executed, allowing the hackers to steal US $6 million.

1.8.2 Liveness Attack

Bitcoin and Ethereum networks were hacked by a Liveness attack where the attacker prevents confirmation of a transaction (Mishra, 2019). It is done in three phases where a group of miners collide and store a transaction in a private block. The attacker will then propose a transaction to create a separate chain with more loyal miners. Thus, another transaction is again selected, ensuring denial of validation for selected transactions.

1.8.3 Eclipse Attack

The attacker takes control of a node's incoming and outgoing requests and isolates them with the blockchain network (Mishra, 2019). Then the attacker utilizes the computational power of that node. The eclipse attack gives way to attacks like selfish mining, engineering block races, etc.

1.8.4 Distributed Denial of Service Attack

In this attack, the attacker generates malicious transactions with a higher transaction fee, and miners will pick that transaction and waste their computational power on it

(Mishra, 2019). It, in turn, makes valid transactions to be waited to be validated by miners. Organizations should deploy private blockchains with limited accessibility to overcome these attacks. Next discussed are the use cases of blockchain in cybersecurity.

1.9   USE CASES OF BLOCKCHAIN IN CYBERSECURITY

Despite attacks, there is a lot of scope for applying blockchain in organizations with limited accessibility. Discussed below are some of the use cases.

1.9.1   BLOCKCHAIN EMAIL

Phishing attacks are prevalent and can lure employees into clicking a button and downloading malicious code (Vance & Vance, 2019). A blockchain-based email system will have a record of each transaction and can enhance the chance of non-repudiation. Besides, modifying the blockchain-based email system was proven tamper-resistant.

1.9.2   ENDPOINT SECURITY

Endpoint security can no longer depend on centralized protection (Vance & Vance, 2019). Employees of an organization trying to access the company's resources from any electronic device. Therefore, blockchain's distributed nature gives more security and protects a company's assets.

1.9.3   PRIVACY

Organizations that want to keep the customer's data, like personally identifiable information, can use blockchain technology and ensure that the data is secure (Vance & Vance, 2019).

1.9.4   SMART CONTRACTS

Blockchain-based smart contract system provides encryption when sharing information in a distributed manner. It was not possible before without blockchain technology (Vance & Vance, 2019). Having discussed big data and blockchain's applications, the final section of this paper discusses combining big data and blockchain in various concepts.

1.10   INTEGRATION OF BIG DATA AND BLOCKCHAIN

Five concepts are explored where blockchain and big data can be applied together. They are using big data and blockchain in e-governance, health care, personal big data management, cryptocurrency, and blockchain in fog-enabled IoT devices.

1.10.1 BIG DATA AND BLOCKCHAIN IN E-GOVERNANCE

Hou (2017) elucidated in "Guangdong Province Big Data Comprehensive Experimental Area" where the Chancheng district was the first to implement blockchain technology for China's e-governance. It collaborated with a software company called 21ViaNet China Inc to build a blockchain-based system for e-governance. Citizens can then find a one-stop solution to obtain government services securely.

1.10.1.1 Advantages

Further discussed are some advantages of applying blockchain for e-governance (Hou, 2017).

1.10.1.1.1 Enhancement in Quality

The quality of government services can be enhanced (Hou, 2017). Documents like certificates, property papers, public and personal records can be obtained on one platform. Each document can be provided with a digital identity. Since blockchain has immutability, all the documents stored in the blockchain are free from tampering. It would also help the government process the requests faster because it will rely on individual credit rather than considering various other conditions.

1.10.1.1.2 Ease of Access

The storage of citizens' records is not centralized (Hou, 2017). For example, identity records, and permanent registered records are stored separately. Similarly, educational and employment records are preserved at the respective institutions. Due to that, citizens should go to multiple places to collect documents necessary for any public service. With blockchain's help, each citizen is given a digital identity that can help them access all their information in one place.

1.10.1.1.3 Strengthening Trust

Once citizen's documents are managed by blockchain technology, there is transparency between the government and the public since any transaction to their data is visible (Hou, 2017). It also helps respective governments to manage better and govern.

1.10.1.2 Framework for Secured E-Governance

Although there are advantages of blockchain-based e-governance systems, there are a few challenges like scalability, flexibility, and security (Assiri et al., 2020). A framework was proposed to protect the e-governance system from internal and external attacks. The framework uses a combination of firewalls and intrusion monitoring systems to avoid suspicious traffic from entering the network.

The framework is comprised of different layers. One end of the framework represents users on the internet and is denoted as an untrusted network (Assiri et al., 2020). The other end is semi-trusted, where the connection has to be made to other user systems to serve the requests made by customers or citizens in an untrusted network. It is called a semi-trusted network. The zone between untrusted and semi-trusted networks is DMZ (de-militarized zone). There is another secure intranet layer that contains various government services-related apps.

Placing the blockchain between a secure intranet and DMZ, a high level of confidentiality, trust, privacy, and access control are obtained (Assiri et al., 2020). This framework was proposed for Saudi Arabia. The proposed framework supports three kinds of access very securely. They are consumer to government (C2G), government to business (G2B), and government to government (G2G). Since the blockchain technology sits between DMZ and secure intranet, all three access types are done securely.

1.10.2 BIG DATA AND BLOCKCHAIN IN HEALTH CARE

Many sectors like banking and retail use big data (Bhuiyan et al., 2018). Health care also is one of the industries that can leverage big data. The data that gets generated every day is increasing. Healthcare data generated by healthcare devices, providers' computer systems, and wearable devices can be structured and unstructured. When transformed into big data, the data can help in clinical decision making. Traditionally doctors used to depend on their judgment in providing treatment. With big data, decision making takes into consideration of the best available information. However, there are concerns regarding the privacy and security of big data in health care.

Blockchain is considered a solution for privacy and security. There are different types of blockchains: public, private, and hybrid (Bhuiyan et al., 2018). For healthcare purposes, a patient can choose a private or hybrid blockchain where he/she can decide whom to give access to their medical information. For example, to the healthcare provider, family, etc. In this way, the patient will have complete control over his/her health information. Otherwise, if a patient goes to four different providers, then he/she will have his medical information at four different places and cannot control any modification to his medical information.

In the case of blockchain, adding information, needs the approval of at least half of the blockchain participants (Bhuiyan et al., 2018). The blockchain proposed for healthcare data consists of three layers. The first layer is the interface to the blockchain and is called the application layer. The second layer is the private blockchain, which consists of nodes and an essential authoring entity responsible for generating public and private keys. The third layer is the encrypted database layer, where all the protected health information is saved.

When a health record gets created, it will be encrypted and stored in the database (Bhuiyan et al., 2018). Every time a new record is inserted, a pointer is made in the blockchain along with the creator information. The patient would also get notified. The patient can access his health records from anywhere in the world. He/she can control who gives access to their health records.

1.10.3 PERSONAL BIG DATA MANAGEMENT USING BLOCKCHAIN

The data collected by companies and organizations is growing daily, leading to big data (Chen et al., 2019). Such data must be efficiently stored and secured to avoid data leakage and tampering. Traditionally all the data is stored in a centralized system and is more prone to attacks. The distributed ledger technology, consensus mechanism, and encryption technology of blockchain provide an efficient and secured way to store data. However, blockchain has limited storage space makes storing big data a challenge.

The two ways to solve this problem are to increase the memory inside each block from 1MB (Chen et al., 2019). It would further expand as blockchain starts to synchronize and bloat the whole system. Another way is to reduce the block's size, increasing the speed, but the storage problem still exists. The solution to this problem is to store the data represented in each block in a database. A prototype is built based on the idea that can resolve the capacity problem of the blockchain.

The prototype is developed based on the Hyperledger Fabric blockchain (Chen et al., 2019). It is an open-source blockchain structure with a throughput of 2,000 transactions per second. More than 250 companies use it, including IT companies like IBM, Intel, Accenture, etc. The prototype runs on Ubuntu virtual machine, an Intel processor with 8 GB RAM and MYSQL Ver 14.14 simulation central database. With this, the personal data is ready to be stored.

The idea is to store only the personal data's core information in the blockchain and create a hash of the remaining data using SHA 256 (Chen et al., 2019). Core information refers to a person's first name, last name, date of birth, etc. Each block in the blockchain will then contain core information and the hash value of the remaining data. The hash value is further stored in the database. A comparison is performed with the hash value present in the blockchain and the hash value in the database. If the hashes do not match, then the data has tampered, and the information is reliable if matched. This way, the blockchain's performance does not go down, and the storage problem is also resolved.

The performance difference is seen more when the data size grows (Chen et al., 2019). The performance is very slow if all personal data is stored on the blockchain. If only the core data is stored and the rest is stored in the database increases the performance. Only core data is stored without additional information; the performance was even better. But the problem with the last approach is that not all the data is stored; similarly, in the first approach, where all the information is in blockchain, the performance was very slow. Therefore the prototype not only ensures security through hashing but also improvises performance.

1.10.4 BIG DATA, BLOCKCHAIN, AND CRYPTOCURRENCY

Blockchain is the technology behind cryptocurrency (Hassani et al., 2018). The distributed ledger technology, immutability, and consensus protocol make blockchain ideal for cryptocurrency. In a Google trend analysis, the top searches were related to blockchain and cryptocurrency. Although blockchain is ideal for cryptocurrency, preserving the anonymity attracted cybercriminals that hacked blockchains. The other problem with the blockchain is the performance. Verification of a new transaction requires an acknowledgment from more than 50% of the participating nodes. All the processing requires high computational power and storage space.

Two technologies can be used to overcome the limitations (Hassani et al., 2018). One is TANGLE based on IOTA protocol, does not need a transaction fee, and is much faster in machine-to-machine micropayments. The other is Hashgraph, which uses gossip for consensus. The first one may not be widespread because there is no transaction fee, and miners might be discouraged. The second is a patented technology that cannot be validated in a public setting. Besides its limitations, blockchain has extensive applications in different sectors like banking, health care, IoT, AI, cryptocurrency, etc.

The nature of cryptocurrency makes it ideal for big data analytics (Hassani et al., 2018). The data keeps increasing as new transactions keep adding to the blockchain to generate cryptocurrency. Thus, generated data in a blockchain is structural and accurate and is ideal for big data analytics. Two main areas where big data and cryptocurrency interact are security and privacy, analysis and prediction. Research in the area of improving safety and privacy is progressing. Due to that, the application of blockchain in various sectors like banking and health care also is increasing. The same is repeated for analysis and prediction as well.

1.10.5 BIG DATA AND BLOCKCHAIN IN FOG-ENABLED IoT APPLICATIONS

A device connected to the internet with processing and storage power is called an IoT device (Tariq et al., 2019). IoT devices collect a lot of information, including personal data. Hence there comes a need to store and protect the information efficiently. Cisco expects to be 500 billion devices connected to the Internet by 2025, and the data thus generated is enormous. Companies depend on cloud computing which provides an on-demand solution to processing and storage requirements. However, there are a few limitations like low latency, insufficient bandwidth, mobility support, and location unawareness. Fog computing emerged to overcome the problems.

Unlike cloud computing, fog computing puts storage, computation, control, and management on the network side rather than creating channels to store in a centralized location (Tariq et al., 2019). However, there are still privacy and security concerns in fog computing. There is no standard architecture for fog computing. The proposed architecture has three distinct layers: the core network and service layer, datacenter layer, and the device layer.

The core layer provides functionalities to the end-user (Tariq et al., 2019). It comprises devices such as routers, bridges, switches, etc. They are also called fog nodes and can be deployed anywhere in the network. Datacenter layer is responsible for scalability, flexibility, computation, and resource sharing. The device layer refers to mobile IoT devices such as smart mobiles and fixed IoT devices such as sensors and RFID tags. As mentioned earlier, security and privacy are of significant concern.

Blockchain technology can be applied to address privacy and security concerns (Tariq et al., 2019). The immutability, decentralization, and security make it ideal for fog-enabled IoT devices. Another essential feature of blockchain is smart contracts. They define rules based on which authentication is carried out. Thus privacy is preserved. Smart contracts are also able to sense malicious actions and breached blockchains reject updates. Besides, a unique GUID is provided along with a symmetric key pair for each IoT device connected to the blockchain network. However, there are also challenges in blockchain as the data starts to grow bigger. Therefore, further research is needed to overcome the challenges of blockchain. Using a database to handle enormous amounts of data and linking blockchain might overcome the difficulties of storing big data in a blockchain.

1.11 CONCLUSION

This paper discussed some challenges and issues in big data, focusing on the fields and applications of machine learning in blockchain and IoT. The advantages of integrating big data with machine learning are studied. Case studies related to the integration of those fields are discussed. We discussed in this chapter the integration of those three fields in the scope of cybersecurity, cybersecurity concerns, and challenges.

The applications of IoT around us are increasing rapidly. Most of the applications and the "things" around us are now connected to the Internet. They have IP addresses; they can be reached and communicated with through the Internet. While this comes with lots of services and opportunities, no doubt in terms of security, this comes with lots of threats and challenges. The fact that serious utilities that we used in our daily life, like water, electricity, security controls, smartphones, etc. can be accessed and controlled remotely can open a plethora of threats and possible attacks. There is a dire need to find solutions and mechanisms to ensure authorized users only access those systems.

We examined five different concepts to use blockchain for storing big data. Although the solutions presented are feasible, there is still a lot of scope for research.

REFERENCES

Alday, R. P., & Rosas, M. F. (2019). Business intelligence solution for Bikers Haven Restaurant. *2019 IEEE 10th Annual Ubiquitous Computing, Electronics Mobile Communication Conference (UEMCON)*, 1204–1210. 10.1109/UEMCON47517.2019.8992956

Al-Dherasi, A. A. M., & Annor-Antwi, A. (2019). *Dependence on blockchain technology for future cybersecurity advancement: A systematic analysis*. 15. Available at SSRN: https://ssrn.com/abstract=3472774. or 10.2139/ssrn.3472774

Assiri, H., Nanda, P., & Mohanty, M. (2020). *Secure e-Governance using blockchain*. (No. 4252). Preprint EasyChair.

Bhuiyan, M. Z. A., Zaman, A., Wang, T., Wang, G., Tao, H., & Hassan, M. M. (2018). Blockchain and big data to transform the healthcare. *Proceedings of the International Conference on Data Processing and Applications – ICDPA 2018*, 62–68. 10.1145/3224207.3224220

Chen, J., Lv, Z., & Song, H. (2019). Design of personnel big data management system based on blockchain. *Future Generation Computer Systems*, *101*, 1122–1129. 10.1016/j.future.2019.07.037

Dai, F., Shi, Y., Meng, N., Wei, L., & Ye, Z. (2017). From Bitcoin to cybersecurity: A comparative study of blockchain application and security issues. *2017 4th International Conference on Systems and Informatics (ICSAI)*, 975–979. 10.1109/ICSAI.2017.8248427

Dai, H.-N., Wang, H., Xu, G., Wan, J., & Imran, M. (2020). Big data analytics for manufacturing internet of things: Opportunities, challenges and enabling technologies. *Enterprise Information Systems*, *14*(9–10), 1279–1303. 10.1080/17517575.2019. 1633689

Dumitrescu, G. C. (2017). Bitcoin – A brief analysis of the advantages and disadvantages. *Global Economic Observer*, *5*(2), 9.

El Bousty, H., krit, S., Elasikri, M., Dani, H., Karimi, K., Bendaoud, K., & Kabrane, M. (2018). Investigating business intelligence in the era of big data: Concepts, benefits and challenges. *Proceedings of the Fourth International Conference on Engineering & MIS 2018 - ICEMIS '18*, 1–9. 10.1145/3234698.3234723

Hariri, R. H., Fredericks, E. M., & Bowers, K. M. (2019). Uncertainty in big data analytics: Survey, opportunities, and challenges. *Journal of Big Data*, *6*(1), 44. 10.1186/s40537-019-0206-3

Hassani, H., Huang, X., & Silva, E. (2018). Big-Crypto: Big data, blockchain and Cryptocurrency. *Big Data and Cognitive Computing*, *2*(4), 34. 10.3390/bdcc2040034

Hou, H. (2017). The application of blockchain technology in E-Government in China. *2017 26th International Conference on Computer Communication and Networks (ICCCN)*, 1–4. 10.1109/ICCCN.2017.8038519

Iqbal, R., Doctor, F., More, B., Mahmud, S., & Yousuf, U. (2020). Big data analytics: Computational intelligence techniques and application areas. *Technological Forecasting and Social Change*, *153*, 119253. 10.1016/j.techfore.2018.03.024

Kondova, G. (2018). The "Crypto Nation" Switzerland 2018. *CARF Luzern 2018. Controlling, Accounting, Risiko, Finanzen. Konferenzband*, *10*.

Lade, P., Ghosh, R., Llc, R. B., & Srinivasan, S. (2017). Manufacturing analytics and industrial internet of things. *IEEE Intelligent Systems*, *32*(3), 74–79.

Mishra, V. K. (2019). Cyber security in blockchain based system. *Scholastic Seed*, *1*(1), 3.

Muheidat F., & Tawalbeh L. (2021) Artificial Intelligence and blockchain for Cybersecurity Applications. In Y. Maleh, Y. Baddi, M. Alazab, L. Tawalbeh, & I. Romdhani (Eds.), *Artificial intelligence and blockchain for future cybersecurity applications. Studies in big data*, vol 90. Springer, Cham. 10.1007/978-3-030-74575-2_1

Sahoo, P. K. (2017). Bitcoin as digital money: Its growth and future sustainability. *Theoretical and Applied Economics*, *XXIV*, 53–64.

Saldamli, G. & Razavi, A. (2020, October). Surveillance missions deployment on the edge by combining swarm robotics and blockchain. In *2020 Fourth International Conference on Multimedia Computing, Networking and Applications (MCNA)* (pp. 106–112). IEEE.

Syafrudin, M., Alfian, G., Fitriyani, N., & Rhee, J. (2018). Performance analysis of iot-based sensor, big data processing, and machine learning model for real-time monitoring system in automotive manufacturing. *Sensors*, *18*(9), 2946. 10.3390/s18092946

Tadaka, S. M. (2020, December). Applications of blockchain in Healthcare, Industry 4, and Cyber Physical Systems. In *2020 7th International Conference on Internet of Things: Systems, Management and Security (IOTSMS)* (pp. 1–8). IEEE.

Tariq, N., Asim, M., Al-Obeidat, F., Zubair Farooqi, M., Baker, T., Hammoudeh, M., & Ghafir, I. (2019). The security of big data in fog-enabled IoT applications including blockchain: A survey. *Sensors*, *19*(8), 1788. 10.3390/s19081788

Taylor, P. J., Dargahi, T., Dehghantanha, A., Parizi, R. M., & Choo, K.-K. R. (2020). A systematic literature review of blockchain cyber security. *Digital Communications and Networks*, *6*(2), 147–156. 10.1016/j.dcan.2019.01.005

Vance, T. R., & Vance, A. (2019). Cybersecurity in the blockchain era: A survey on examining critical infrastructure protection with blockchain-based technology. *2019 IEEE International Scientific-Practical Conference Problems of Infocommunications, Science and Technology (PIC S&T)*, 107–112. 10.1109/PICST47496.2019.9061242

Xiang, G., & Fang, W. (2017). The research of Data Integration and Business Intelligent based on drilling big data. *Proceedings of the 9th International Conference on Information Management and Engineering – ICIME 2017*, 64–68. 10.1145/3149572.3149603

Yu, W., Dillon, T., Mostafa, F., Rahayu, W., & Liu, Y. (2020). A global manufacturing big data ecosystem for fault detection in predictive maintenance. *IEEE Transactions on Industrial Informatics*, *16*(1), 183–192. 10.1109/TII.2019.2915846

Zhang, Y., Ma, S., Yang, H., Lv, J., & Liu, Y. (2018). A big data driven analytical framework for energy-intensive manufacturing industries. *Journal of Cleaner Production*, *197*, 57–72.

Zugdb, C. (n.d.). *"Crypto Valley" canton to accept Bitcoin for tax payments*. SWI Swissinfo.Ch. Retrieved February 6, 2021, from https://www.swissinfo.ch/eng/-crypto-valley-canton-to-accept-Bitcoin-for-tax-payments/46010364

2 Deep Learning Techniques for Cybersecurity Applications

Balakrishnan S
Sri Krishna College of Engineering and Technology,
Coimbatore, Tamilnadu, India

Aswin G
Full Stack Developer, Zealbots in Chadura Tech,
Tiruchirappalli, Tamilnadu, India

Mohan Babu Chowdary
Dept. of CSE, Sir C.R.Reddy College of Engineering,
Eluru, India

V. Arulkumar
Sri Krishna College of Engineering and Technology,
Coimbatore, Tamilnadu, India

CONTENTS

DOI: 10.1201/9781003319917-3

2.1   INTRODUCTION

Cybersecurity includes shielding information with various gadgets analyzed by cyber threats. This is a crucial enterprise part of gathering an enormous data set of customer information, a social stage where individual data is submitted and the public authority associations play a mystery role in politics, governments, and defense; thus, we must safeguard all important data that is taken into count. This helps secure the data from cyberattacks or dangers with exceptional information, which threatens various applications, organizations, and gadgets. The number of people accessing the data online is increasing daily with dangerous threats. This information is expanded with the expense of online violations that are measurable in billions. Digital protection, i.e., cybersecurity, is the collection of advanced tools that shield the computer, project organization and important data from cyberattacks that have unauthorized access and destruction. The organization of cybersecurity helps host the idea of security and privacy. Everything about privacy is safeguarding (Adamou Djergou et al., 2022). This includes an intrusion detection system (IDS), antivirus PC code, firewalls, and an interruption recognition framework. This review sums up the significance of network protection over deep learning procedures.

The DL procedure has been utilized by specialists lately. Deep learning might be used close by the common mechanization ways like the principle of heuristics generally based on AI procedures. This investigation helps comprehend the upside of deep learning calculations to characterize and relate pernicious exercises apparent from the changed sources like DNS, email, URLs, etc. Dislike antiquated AI draws various techniques over deep learning algorithm calculations with delineation phases. They will separate most ideal choices without help from anyone else. In any case, further space-level alternatives had the opportunity to examine deep learning routes in data science errands. The network safety occasions considered during this investigation are encased by messages (Alazab & Tang, 2019).

To incorporate deep learning, the text is changed over genuine esteemed vectors, various semantic correspondence cycles and numerous text mining methods. Lately, the expansion in the event of recurrence of the organization tackles possesses significant issues identified with online protection. The rise in modern organization innovations needs an improvement in online protection. Cybersecurity is a vital process with a basic foundation on virus attacks and unwanted access to the software. Network protection incorporates numerous advancements and operations. These operations involve security on application, security on data, security over the network, security on operational research, catastrophe recovery, and user end client. These securities are a few classes of online protection, so-called cybersecurity. Network protection hazards represent the absolute most genuine monetary and public security difficulties of the 21st century, and these need to be comprehended. The inspiration for network protection and its privacy is incredible. The cyberattack is a cutting-edge battle of malicious weapons that prompts by cyber software and leads to individual business data, upsetting basic tasks, ongoing weaknesses, unapproved and unlawful admittance to gadgets and programming, forcing significant expenses on the national economy. Network protection is an enduring issue for most rumored associations; for example, banks, retail locations, foundations like SCADA, power lattices, etc. (Gollmann & Krotofil, 2016).

Here, an attack is a feature of hostile targets on software PCs. This framework consists of data with its organization gadgets. The cyberattacks are utilized by countries, peoples, gatherings, and associations. This may start from an unidentified destination. The cyberattack takes time to change and eradicate the predefined data by managing the defenseless framework even though there is an adequate number of accessible attack identification frameworks and fast expansion on fraudulent activity to increase the abilities of research advancements in cybersecurity. DL strategies have been effective in many late years; these techniques face incredible challenges in recognizing cyberattacks in huge dispersed conditions and the versatility of these techniques over a huge organization is nearly nothing. One of the disadvantages of conventional DL is using handmade highlights for acknowledgment tasks. However, actual machines help in preventing software from the discovery in cyberattacks (Maleh et al., 2021).

At present, DL assists in escalating the recognition pattern of man-made consciousness and widely opens up the conquering occasions with imperative customary AI strategies. In conventional DL algorithms, the highlights are removed by people. There is an extraordinary exploration heading that includes feature engineering. However, a huge amount of information is handled by DNN, which works with human extraction ideas. Here, deep learning gives accurate, quicker, and exact preparation in refinement and self-training ability to learn the process. The accomplishment of DL poses different controls, which impedes the customary methodologies in cybersecurity that require the examination of DL applications for security purposes. DL can be effectively applied to network protection, for example, cyberattack recognition. However, DL techniques are effectively concerned with pictures, discourses, voice detections, entity analysis, and item acknowledgment. These strategies are sought to identify virtual attacks and fraudulent activities (Chowdhury et al., 2016). Cybersecurity powerlessness adapts in developing elements for cyberattacks, inability to recognize new dangers, troubles in the identification process, intricate occasions, and impediments of viable versatility by expanding the volume of information. The attacks are the fundamental difficulties in front of the new online protection arrangements making territory. The deep learning strategy application kills the key issues of methodology, which are under analysts' consideration. Deep learning strategies are fruitful applications with broad abilities over online protection issues, for example: recognition of attacks, conduct irregularities location, malware analyzer, conventions discovery, CAPTCHA codes identification, botnet discovery, and recognizable proof of the individual by voice. Here, the cybersecurity techniques depend on different DL structures, which are broken down into essential methodologies of investigations with their favorable circumstances and issues of strategies that are depicted. This study focuses on the DL approach for cybersecurity network protection from attack operations.

2.2 ARTIFICIAL INTELLIGENCE WITH MACHINE LEARNING AND DEEP LEARNING

As its name shows, the design is to direct a machine so it can learn, tackle issues and settle on choices dependent on measurable models. To accomplish this, model info or upgrade is introduced as data parsing handled by the algorithms to remove a model utilized as the reason for settling on choices. The way to progress will pick the proper improvement in the input information. This clear model includes Google's search engine. Many individuals do specific searches depending on their location, real-time skyline, etc. As they click on connections of interest, the Internet search engine can build up its model to foresee a wide range of patterns. Here, the subcategory of ML is deep learning, a specialization in DL algorithms that learn on their own using various method standards to arrive at their own choices (Bhalekar & Shaikh, 2019). At present, DL assists in escalating the recognition pattern of man-made consciousness and widely opens up the conquering occasions with imperative customary AI strategies. In conventional DL algorithms, the highlights are removed by people. There is an extraordinary exploration heading that includes feature engineering. These algorithms depend on neural network organizations and layers. To incorporate deep learning, the text is changed over genuine esteemed vectors, various semantic correspondence cycles, and numerous text mining methods. Lately, the expansion in the event of recurrence of the organization tackles possesses significant issues identified with online protection. The rise in modern organization innovations needs an improvement in online protection. Here, cybersecurity is a vital process with a basic foundation on virus attacks and unwanted access to the software. Network protection incorporates numerous advancements and operations. Deep learning performs incredible execution in various zones of network protection like cybersecurity (Kolosnjaji et al., 2016). This works on the cerebrum of the small brain. The way to progress lies in characterizing the engineering model by enhancing the brain. For instance, today this is utilized to improve expectations of seismic tremors or their potential greatness. This outlines rapid perception of what innovation is being examined (Fig. 2.1).

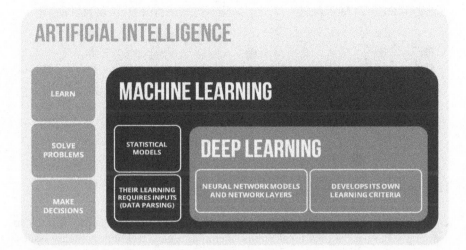

FIGURE 2.1 DL within ML and ML within AI.

2.3 DEEP LEARNING AND NEURAL NETWORK

"Deep learning is a sub-field of machine learning dealing with algorithms inspired by the structure and function of the brain called artificial neural networks." Let's see what that means: In other words, deep learning mirrors the functions of our brain (Sutskever, 2013). The deep learning algorithm is almost identical to the nervous system's structure, where every neuron is linked and progresses various data. The magic part of deep learning is the layer system. A huge variation in AI is categorized as machine learning (ML) and deep learning (DL). Machine learning models have a saturation point that automatically stops after improving.

In contrast, deep learning models tend to operate on an infinite data set that improves by itself. Moving forward, the other difference is feature extraction areas. In ML, the feature engineering is assisted by humans, and in DL, the models it structures out themselves.

Deep learning is a process of handling large data sets with the help of neural networks. This stage of operations provides the most acceptable solution to many issues in image recognition, speech recognition, and natural language processing. In the process of deep learning, computation power is more important. It depends on our layers; if the layer is convenient, then a feasible amount of GPU and CPU is needed. Otherwise, it's hard to get the result after a day or month or maybe a year. The capability to process large amounts of features makes deep learning extremely powerful when dealing with unstructured data. However, deep learning algorithms can be excessive for less convoluted issues because they require entry to a huge bulk of data that needs to be more effective. As a result, deep learning models are not as powerful compared to other system techniques (such as linear models and boosted decision trees) for more significant practical work problems such as the realization of client churn, exposing fraudulent negotiations, and in alternative cases with lesser data sets and lean features. Whereas in assured cases like multiclass

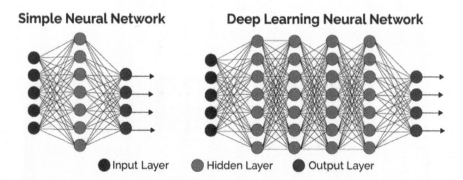

FIGURE 2.2   Deep learning and neural network.

analysis, deep learning can work for minor processes and deliberate data sets. Deep learning (DL) has various focal points, including quick tackling, complex issues, enormous computerization, and high-caliber results. Neural network is an inter-connection of nodes and artificial neurons. Here, every neuron performs an instruction towards the hidden layers. Here, the human brain acts as an associate node that transmits data over each other. The nodes interact to share information, where every node takes the input and functions some operations before passing it onwards. The work is activated with the help of the activation function. That could convert and transfer the input flow into the output, which could be pre-owned as the input nodes (LeCun et al., 2015) (Fig. 2.2).

2.4   CYBERSECURITY

Cybersecurity includes all types of innovation assortments, identification process, and practices that intend to secure organizations, gadgets, projects, and information from attacks, harm, or unapproved access. Cybersecurity network protection is known for data innovation security. Network safety is significant for military, administration, monetary, corporate, and clinical unions to organize the process, and save uncommon estimation of the information on personal computers and different gadgets. The inspiration of cyberattackers is incredible. Cyberattacks are a cutting-edge battle of malicious prompting uncovering that leads to individual business data, upsetting basic tasks, ongoing weaknesses, unapproved and unlawful admittance to gadgets and programming, and forcing significant expenses on the national economy. Network protection is an enduring issue for the vast majority of the rumored associations, for example, banks, basic foundations like SCADA (Zhu et al., 2011), power lattices, and so any kind of cyberattack is a hostile move that is against PC gadgets or PC data with a huge part of the details could have data of delicate that is regardless of the licensed innovation, personal data, different sorts or budgetary information of data for which openness or is unapproved access could have thrown the negative results. Associations transfer sensitive data across the global networks and various gadgets throughout organizations and network protection. The frameworks are used to store or calculate it (Maleh et al., 2019). As refinement and the volume of cyberattacks develops, organizations and associations with particularly entrusted defending data that identifies public security, monetary records, or health care need to discover a way to ensure their delicate data for their business and workforce. The top country's authorities of insight advised that computerized spying and cyberattack are the principal danger to public security, which obscures the level of illegal intimidation.

2.4.1 Elements of Cyber Encompass

For network protection of cybersecurity, an association is required to facilitate its attempts throughout its overall data framework system. The following are the cyber encompass elements:

- Network Security: Toward shielding away the organization from assaults, interruptions, and undesirable clients.
- App Security: Applications need consistent updates/upgrades and testing to ensure these projects are guaranteed from attacks.
- Endpoint Security: The remote examining is a fundamental phase of the marketing business, yet it could also be a powerless point for information—endpoint security to ensure the distance of admittance to an organization.
- Security in Data: Within organizations and apps is the information. To ensure client data and organizations are the most specified layer of security.
- Identity management: This is a process of grasping the entry with every individual of an association.
- Infrastructure Security: Everything in an organization includes data sets and actual gear. Secure these gadgets is similarly dominant.
- Security in Cloud: Numerous documents are in advanced smart conditions or else "the cloud."
- It is ensuring data in a 100% online phase that gives a bulk of obstacles.
- Mobile Security: Tablets and phones contain certain kinds of issues in security on their own, which face many challenges.
- Business Continuity Planning: Occasion information or catastrophic event should be secured, and business should go on in case of a break.
- End User: Clients signing on to an organization application or users may be workers getting to the organization software. Instructing great propensities is a significant level of network protection in the cybersecurity system.

The most annoying test in cybersecurity is easily the steadily boosting nature of security hazards. Generally, associations or the public authority could have zeroed in a more significant part of their network safety liabilities on border security to ensure their urgent shield and framework segments against threats. To this day, the methodology is deficient, as the dangerous advances and change associations can stay aware of it rapidly. Thus, warnings from associations for advanced, more versatile, and proactive ways to handle network safety. Essentially, the National

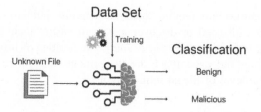

FIGURE 2.3 Cybersecurity processing.

Institute of Standards and Technology gave the rules in danger appraisal structure that suggest a move from persistent constant and checking evaluations. Here, the information-centered way to deal with security instead of the customary model on perimeters of data-focused approaches (Fig. 2.3).

2.5 DL ALGORITHMS FOR CYBERSECURITY

2.5.1 SUPERVISED DEEP LEARNING ALGORITHMS

- FNN: Feedforward Neural Network. This is a fully connected deep neural network. They are a variation of DNN where every neuron is associated with all neurons past layers. FNN doesn't make any supposition on the information and gives an adaptable and universally useful answer for characterization to the detriment of high computational expenses.
- CNN: Convolution Neural Network. This is based on the deep neural convolution feed-forward network. They are a variation of DNN where every neuron gets its info from a subset of neurons of the past layer. This trademark makes CNN powerful at investigating spatial information, yet their exhibition diminishes when applying non-spatial information. CNN is a less cost estimation than feedforward neural networks.
- RNN: Recurrent Neural Network. A variation of DNN whose neurons could forward their yield additionally for plan makes them more complex or for the past layers to prepare than FNN. They dominate as arrangement generators, particularly their new variation, and the long transient memory.

2.5.2 UNSUPERVISED DEEP LEARNING ALGORITHMS

- DBN: Deep Belief Network. They are demonstrated through a phase of Restricted Boltzmann Machines, a structure of neural organizations without a yield layer. And DBN can be effectively utilized for the pre-preparing assignments of the domination in the capacity of highlight extraction. They require a preparation stage with unlabeled data sets.
- SAE: Stacked Autoencoder. They are made by numerous autoencoders, a class of neural organizations where the quantity of info and yield neurons is the equivalent. SAE dominates at pre-preparing assignments also to DBN and accomplishes better outcomes on limited sets.

2.6 CYBERSECURITY USE CASES

We consider the three zones where cyber deep learning algorithms help discover applications such as intrusion identification, malware investigation, and spam analysis. A blueprint of each field is introduced moreover (Fig. 2.4).

2.6.1 INTRUSION DETECTION

The intrusion discovery system (IDS) was built up for recognition of every number of organization attacks inside of the conditions. The IDS distinguishes pernicious organizations exercised by investigating the assembled parcels, lock attack associations, and the alerts to the PC clients from cyberattacks (Chowdhury et al., 2016). Moreover, associates use the firewall as a rudimentary technology for network security systems. The organization's qualities have been evaluated in the host-based intrusion detection (HIDS), which is included in putting the bundles and the screens of the inner framework. Execution of intrusion recognition HIDS accumulates the data by framework calls and application logs, OS review trails, and so forth. Organization-based interruption detection distinguishes the movement in the organization hanging on. The huge intrusion detection algorithms are arranged into two techniques: abuse recognition (signature-based) and inconsistency identification. Mark-based IDS is a strategy that looks at the progression of the bytes or succession with a malignant organization and helps track the framework's detail log, which is caused by bogus caution. Abnormality-based IDS: It would help recognize the oddities or shows genuine and uncommon occasions obvious the framework and amends the irregular traffic design in an organization.

To determine the weakness of these two discovery strategies, hybrid in IDS has been proposed, which joins the intricacy of the oddity and issues analysis framework with the current system. Presently, the self-learning system gets one of the conspicuous techniques. DL is one of the influential ideas (Maleh et al., 2015). Most of the DL arrangements accomplished a high bogus positive rate and high analysis. To incorporate deep learning, the text is changed over genuine esteemed vectors,

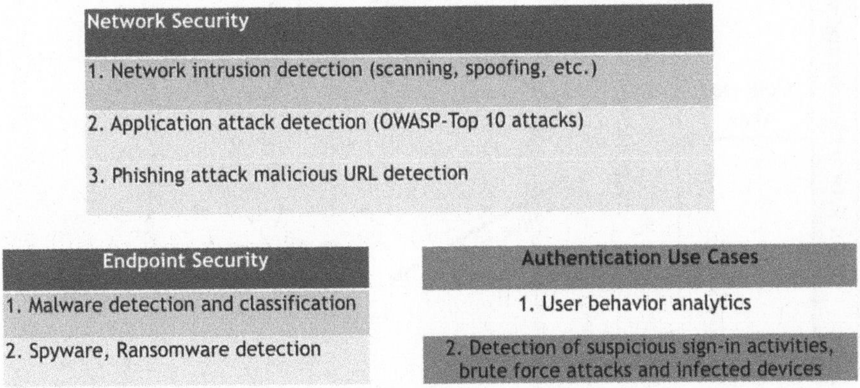

Network Security
1. Network intrusion detection (scanning, spoofing, etc.)
2. Application attack detection (OWASP-Top 10 attacks)
3. Phishing attack malicious URL detection

Endpoint Security	Authentication Use Cases
1. Malware detection and classification	1. User behavior analytics
2. Spyware, Ransomware detection	2. Detection of suspicious sign-in activities, brute force attacks and infected devices

FIGURE 2.4 Use cases of DL in cybersecurity.

various semantic correspondence cycles, and numerous text mining methods. The rise of new smart organization innovations requires improving new techniques in online protection. Ensuring basic foundations from attacks and unapproved access shows cybersecurity is a vital process. This is because many ML methods accompany the deep learning designs among limited scope with low-level components that focus on customary and attack association records. Most strikingly DL accompanies realizing a superior model in AI algorithms. That would help in learning the portrayal methods with a large, progressively hierarchical arrangement. The model for novel deep learning approaches the activity over organizations with a mix of deep learning techniques—this aids in examining the organization traffic over non-symmetric deep intrusion procedures (Fig. 2.5).

The classifiers include convolution neural network (CNN), recurrent neural network (RNN), and long short term memory (LSTM), which perform IDS frameworks only when contrasted with divisional DL processes (Gers et al., 2002). CNN uses an n-gram procedure that is momentarily discussed alongside cross-breed organizations such as CNN, CNN-RNN, CNN-LSTM, and CNN-GRU. These methods help distinguish good and terrible organization ID in organization associations. CNN can acquire elevated level element portrayal from low-level capabilities during extraction measure is neglected. The framework calls demonstrating based methodology with outfit technique is proposed utilizing LSTM calculation for inconsistency-based IDS framework. The intrusion method helps catch the semantic significance of each link and connection over the organization. Outfit techniques center on a bogus alert rate that fits the IDS plan. These are smaller techniques, which helped away from boundaries in a bit of space. This strategy is considered a quick and proficient methodology in consecutive network applications. Use of deep neural networks is utilized for interruption discovery. Further, we have discussed the security issues in self-governing privacy protection.

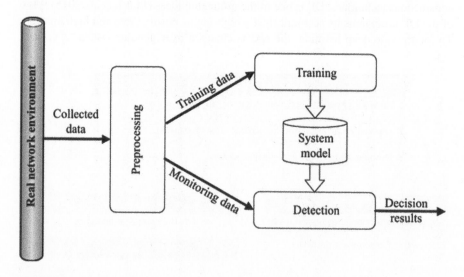

FIGURE 2.5   Intrusion detection.

2.6.2 MALWARE DETECTION

Malware are the programs that upset the data, and records in the framework explain the execution and weakness. At some point, it will prompt absolute collapsing debasement of the framework mechanism. Those are effortlessly gone through various states utilizing illegal programming apparatuses. It can process large amounts of features, making deep learning extremely powerful when dealing with unstructured data. However, deep learning algorithms can be excessive for less convoluted issues because they require entry to a huge bulk of data that needs to be more effective (Vinod et al., 2009). There are a few jobs in which the deep learning method has gotten one of the conspicuous techniques in malware detection investigation (Fig. 2.6).

Double and multi-classifier procedures are utilized for the characterization, giving a better outcome when handled with amended linear unit actuation dropout and capacities over the deep neural networks. The DL approaches are applied with four fundamental layer network configurations and are considered for unobtrusive calculation, including extraction of text strategies like histogram, byte/entropy, string 2D histogram highlights, import features, and PE metadata features all can be utilized. The conversation is made to convey the best solution to forestall overfitting and how the backpropagation strategy is helped for accelerate the overall learning structure in the organization. Recurrent neural networks (RNNs) helped remove the whole data arbitrarily with the projection procedure (Pascanu et al., 2015). The max pooling is consumed for non-direct testing of data and strategic relapse for a definite arrangement of the information. This examined the advanced malware strategy familiarly known as the ransomware issue. It was a sort of crypto viral blackmail that encoded the records and accumulated the data without other information. In deep learning classification, LSTM is applied using API calls by double arrangement grouping the strategy, which assesses the exhibition of old-style ML algorithm techniques and deep neural network organization over malware discovery.

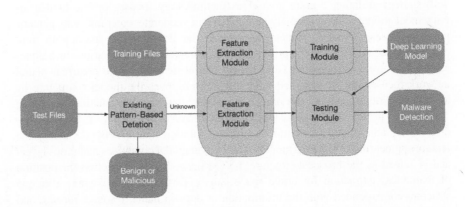

FIGURE 2.6 Malware detection.

2.6.3   ANDROID MALWARE DETECTION

Android gadgets have turned into a well-known one these days among people groups. Malware location turns into a significant test in an android stage. Deep learning alongside NLP accompanies an extraordinary forward leap here. Droid locator is an application of Google that assists in gathering malware information. Here, collected information is developed for dynamic and static processes (McLaughlin et al., 2017; Yuan et al., 2014). The inclusion techniques are extracted and enhanced with a deep belief network. The semantic data extraction from the succession strategy framework utilizes the natural processing development in DL methods. Long-term memory models are developed using various concealed layers to accomplish good results.

Further, the time cost and work process are utilized for grouping by executing diverse structures to accelerate tensor flow operations. In this model, the n-gram enhances the predominant discovery strategy over the android malware. The geography of this network clarifies with design structure to obtain improving results. The adequacy of the API call succession is being considered to play out CNN is being drawn nearer by examining the preparation dimension over the grouping area with advanced signs of negative and true outcomes (Li et al., 2018).

2.6.4   DOMAIN NAME CATEGORIZATION

This is operated using domain name algorithms for the generation process. The malware of domain fluxing have an age space algorithm. Specific malware are encoded for internet protocol addresses to acquire additional correspondence from the worker to the hosts. Here, the investigation DL assortments are used for recognizing malevolent space titles in the enormous scope of enhanced DNS signs inside the LAN process, which utilize deep learning tasks for analyzing domain names with conventional DL calculations. The deep learning techniques are analyzed better than algorithms of conventional networks with additional calculations over ill-disposed surroundings (Vinayakumar et al., 2019). The detailed concentrates on measurable elements over the DGA approach are highlighted by the length of the character space with strategy utilizing n-gram area. This methodology focuses on the hidden arrangement model. The customary method has a moderate outcome with genuine positive values. The DL strategy segregates the dense grade space with non-determined areas. It zeroed the primary-based characters utilizing various techniques such as recurrent, convolution, and hybrid neural networks. The recurrent neural network focuses on the specified model, which improves the model's structure by adding dropouts to conquer the preparation stage along the implantation procedure. To improve prescient exactness CMU model is executed along with recurrent bi-directional. This model is examined with convolution neural networks across the feature engineering of clarified models. The current model comprises numerous layers and is named as the broadest structure. LSTM network links preferred the position of featureless extraction for crude space names. In the proposed work, a unique structure corresponded with the information of domain name, resource locator, and electronic mails to increment the tasks of malicious software discovery range.

2.6.5   ANALYSIS OF PHISHING AND SPAMMING

This work mainly indicates spam emails, which allow unwanted information or data with significant accounts of email IDs to add up. This digitalized electronic spam requires an undefined text message that has shipped to numerous email recipients. Simultaneously, phishing involves cyber acts in digital procedure tricks of individual data, for example, passwords, credit cards, financial balances, etc. These issues are corrected by utilizing deep learning strategies with natural language handling (NLP). The addressed phishing strategies over mail utilize unequal data sets. Fundamentally, different methods such as term frequency—inverse frequency and bag of words with matrix factorization are used for the detection process.

Furthermore, random forest (RF), strategic regression, K-means, and Naive-Bayes are utilized. This accompanies a high metric execution. In the neural organization approach, content extraction assists in getting vector design. A relative report is enhanced based on extricated data sets for utilizing AI methods where decision trees and various DL methods are achieved. The NLP includes extraction strategies using techniques like character inserting and word implanting. CNN frequently obtains various words and characters for insertion procedures. The CNN utilizes all word characters by inserting superior outcomes. The LSTM approach detains all the data sets and is considered a progressive email design by getting into words of sentences (Athiwaratkun & Stokes, 2017). The bidirectional long-term memory is obtained for two instances. One is used for weight registering over privacy and another is phishing of likelihood information along the organization analysis process. The DL neural network utilizes all kinds of characterization in phishing out uniform resource locators. This comprises a certain standard layer organization with extremely geographical features. Vindictive danger over URLs is being examined by character succession. Installing software is utilized by deep neutrals of recurrent and convolution networks with concentrated page development based on specific contacts such as vindictive URLs and quicker page reactions. CNN is influential for picture spam identification and phishing URL recognition contrasted with text portrayal. As of late, linked errands help in email phishing with recognition of messages over data meeting components.

2.6.6   TRAFFIC INVESTIGATION

Here, the volume of solidity affects the web dealing that is being expanded stepwise. Distinguishing the information moved through the organization is considered a significant issue in the rush hour traffic investigation (Sadqi & Maleh, 2022). Here, the conventional technique utilizing AI neural organization and deep learning strategies result in element learning and obscure convention recognizable proofs. While network security consists of firewalls and intrusion recognition framework and interruption framework items center on checking vertical traffic that crosses the edge of an organization with network traffic investigation that arrangements interchanges around attacks. Nowadays, various methods arise with dangerous advancements. This rapidly swaps the awareness of the particular association. Thus, network safety is more versatile and proactive in dealing with cybersecurity outcomes.

This methodology is a better transformation in the non-robotization strategy in the conventional technique. Deep packet structure naturally highlights the network traffic where DL methods are enhanced. This assists in handling complex undertaking problems such as collective testing, numerous deals, etc. The proposed feature engineering focuses on deep learning secure shell convention. This RNN network assists with arranging and modeling the passage by displaying the time arrangement and highlights to recognize measurable traffic stream data (Cho et al., 2014). Attackers are never-ending, adjusting their strategies to evade identification and frequently influence genuine accreditations with believed instruments previously conveyed in a computation, making it hard for associations to distinguish basic security hazards proactively. Cyber traffic items have arisen because of persevering advancement and offering associations a sensible way ahead for combating innovative aggressors. The rise of current organizational innovations requires the improvement techniques for online protection. The basic foundations of attacks are occupied based on the unapproved entry, and this shows cybersecurity is an essential process.

2.6.7 BINARY EXPLORATION

The binary analysis helps hold safety investigation instruments that investigate various codes of binary and identifies all weaknesses of vulnerability cases which conveys open source programming software. Standard research comprehends and scrutinizes certain examples like code discovery with susceptible patterns. Presently, automated computer investigation techniques are joined among DL methods with limited patterns. Here, they have focused on various issues and looked into the operations that tend to be addressed by utilizing networks. The RNN network performs countless tests on machine code scraps (snippets). These parts are analyzed based on the information using a representation of cyber crimes. This generates more significant formation levels for designing binary structures. The current framework assists in obtaining the capacity phase marks in dismantled code that utilizes neural network organization. This stage of operations provides the finest solution to many issues in image recognition, speech recognition, and natural language processing. In the process of deep learning, computation power is more important. It depends on our layers; if the layer is convenient, then a possible amount of GPU and CPU is needed. Otherwise, it's hard to get the result after a day or month or maybe a year. The capability to process large amounts of features makes deep learning extremely powerful when dealing with unstructured data. The argument retrieval module on RNN is executed by analyzing the strategies like saliency planning and sterilization. This framework helps grapping call protocol and phrases with elevated-level precision boundaries to identify parameters accuracy. In the outlined deep learning strategy, codes are combined with the help of software investigation with a product shortcome. TextCNN is broken down by instructions and words of vectors with higher accuracy value towards the data obtained.

2.7 DL METHODS FOR CYBERATTACK DETECTION

Cybersecurity network protection is known for data innovation security. Network safety is significant for military purposes, government use with monetary, corporate workers, and associations to analyze groups of processes and gather them to determine store data on computers and gadgets. The inspired cyberattackers are incredible. The categorization of cyberattack identification strategies is built and dependent on plans created by the pre-owned techniques. In this work, cyberattack strategies utilize types such as convolution neural networks, deep belief networks, auto encoders, restricted Boltzmann machines, and combination learners (Fig. 2.7).

2.7.1 CNN Methods

CNN includes computation of convolution and profundity structure, an agent, and ordinarily utilized procedures in deep learning areas (Athiwaratkun & Stokes, 2017). In particular, CNN obtains multilayer insight variation configuration, which requires negligible preprocessing. The basic design of CNN comprises information and hidden layers with numerous concealed layers which incorporate convolution, pooling, and full association layers. This review sums up the significance of network protection over deep learning procedures. DL procedure has been utilized by specialists lately. CNN obtains less preprocessing, independent of highlight configuration containing earlier information with primary focal points. The attacks are the fundamental difficulties in front of the new online protection arrangements making territory. Convolution neural networks have been applied to arrange security fields with much progressive advancement.

2.7.2 RNN Methods

Since the results of DNN and CNN consider the impact of the current contribution without thinking about data from the past and future time, they could accomplish

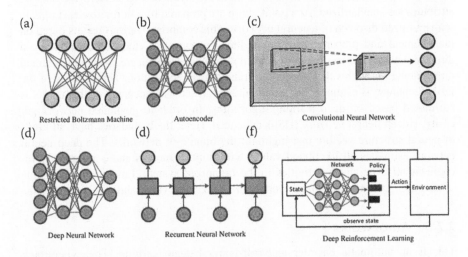

FIGURE 2.7 Structure of DL methods in cyberattacks.

critical execution on order or acknowledge undertakings without time-differing attributes. Including time-subordinate data, RNN is proposed as an uncommon classification of neural network structures, which is planned with "memory" capacity to keep up with past events. The truth is this design structure is based on the human perception that depends on past memory experiences. RNN is great at managing time-arrangement data. Simultaneously, there are still a few issues in the construction plan of RNN, like gradient vanishing or gradient explosion, which drives the inability to recall or show long-term reliance. Consequently, specialists create LSTM and GRU with entryway structures that support memory cells. This effectively keeps long-lasting relationships without fading by going through prior data stream segments.

2.7.3   RBM Methods

RBM is an imaginary network of neurons composed of two layers: the visible layer and the hidden layer. The visible layer addresses the gathered data, but the hidden layer attempts to take in highlights from the visible layer expecting to handle a likelihood grouping of data. The network consists of a limited neuron in a layer with associations to the neurons in the other layer. The links between the layers are symmetric and bidirectional, which permits data to move in both directions. RBM is an energy-based model that utilizes a layer of hidden factors to display probabilistic dissemination over noticeable factors. The visible units comprise the first layer and compare to the perception segments that are one obvious unit for each element of an input design. The hidden model conditions the segments of perceptions and highlights the features of observed dependencies.

2.7.4   DBN Methods

This cyberattack technique is dependent on many layers of DBNs. Here, the data set attributes are standardized. At a point, these are prepared by a normalized set of data with a utilized dispatch of a neural network. This comprises various results based on management and prepares with highlighted outcomes of stack information on a directed network. Accordingly, unlabeled dimensions of data are changed with ideal dimensional highlights that depend on fraud attack recognition. The viability of the DBN technique is evaluated on the required data set. The accuracy of this model is correlated based on deep learning algorithms. In order to guarantee network security, a deep neural network IDS is enhanced. Here, the boundaries have all kinds of neural structure vectors that highlight the bundle of networks. The deep neural network estimates all likelihood values with built-in models and consequently recognizes all cyberattack activities in the organized system. Lastly, this technique obtains the accuracy of trained models in attacks and vulnerability.

2.7.5   Autoencoder

This is an automatic encoder and self-learned deep learning. The cyberattack method is discovered and proposed based on autoencoders. Further, the unsupervised DL enhances and utilizes inadequate autoencoders. At that point, the learned highlights are taken into a regression model of deep learning to characterize the information into general attacks. The malware identification techniques for autoencoders are interfaced with the detection process. For tackling various issues, the autoencoder method and RNN technique are utilized. This helps take out all portrayals of malware from user interfaces and demands to analyze data sets.

2.8 CYBERSECURITY THREATS AND ATTACKS

2.8.1 MALWARE

Malware refers to malicious software involving ransomware, spyware, virus, and worms. This helps in breaching the network from vulnerability with specific users (Rieck et al., 2008). When they click on it, it brings back a dangerous link or email, automatically installing high-risk software. The system malware does the following inside:

- The key component blocks access to the network (ransomware).
- Additional installation of malware or virus software.
- The hand-driven data covertly obtain information (spyware).
- Specific components are disrupted.
- Render the inoperable system.

2.8.2 PHISHING

A phishing attack is a method of transferring fraudulent trade information (Li et al., 2018). This data is retrieved from a trustworthy site or destination. These are normally held on emails. This aims to analyze all the privacy data over credit cards with login information to run the software (malware) on basic machines. This is a specific type of digital cyberattack where users should secure their systems.

2.8.3 MITM

Man-in-the-middle (MitM) is an attack that is also known as an eavesdropping attack. Network protection hazards represent the absolute most genuine monetary and public security difficulties. This happens only on two-party exchanges, which link attackers for snatching data. Here, the attackers disturb the channel traffic and store all data. There are two sections of MitM attacks:

- Unreliable public Wi-Fi: Attackers are submerged with the help of user gadget organization. Unknowingly, all the data of users are transferred to the attackers.
- Once the malware has penetrated a gadget: An attacker can update software and process programming to handle every victim's data or information.

2.8.4   SQL INJECTION

SQL is a structured query language that infuses the monitoring of embedded attackers with malicious codes towards the server of users. This typically offers energy to undetermined data of the user's servers. An attacker completes all the injection processes of SQL just by organizing the malicious software using specific codes inside the weak sites over search engines.

2.8.5   ZERO-DAY EXPLOIT

The weakness vulnerability obtains a zero-day exploit and is declared before a result is executed. Attackers manage to focus on fraudulent activity with a system software exploitation. The zero-day vulnerability is a harmful recognition that obtained prior knowledge.

2.8.6   TUNNELING OF DNS

The DNS tunneling assists in separating the convention traffic ports using non-DNS. This transfers the protocol of HTTP to DNS traffic. The real simulations of tunneling are done using DNS. Various malicious cases obtained DNS and administration of VPN. This mask gets traffic outbound for enhancing the data of DNS with linked web groups. The demands of DNS are handled by exfiltrating data undetermined by cyberattack foundations for malicious use. Similarly, this is obtained in the attackers' infrastructure to the system compromisers.

2.9   CONCLUSION

The DL techniques gradually obtained numerous applications and were embraced for the protection of cyber crimes. These are used for accessing the algorithms that accomplish sufficient outcomes. We determine these strategies for three related cybersecurity issues: intrusion recognition, malware investigation, and spam identification. At first, we propose a unique identification of classes in DL methods and represent the issues occurring concurrently. In this phase, the impact of issues is high-ended, and it is controlled using DL cybersecurity. Our outcomes show the current DL procedures are influenced by a few weaknesses of network safety vulnerability. All methodologies are powerless against cyberattacks that require ceaseless re-preparing and cautious boundary tuning that can't be automated. Additionally, a similar classifier is applied to distinguish various dangerous attacks. Here, the threat attacks are unsatisfactorily high with low detection results. This helps in utilizing diverse DL classifiers for identifying explicit cyberattacks and threats. Deep learning is still in the beginning phase and no end can be drawn. Critical upgrades might be normal, particularly considering the new and promising advancement in adversarial learning. The DL methods can uphold the security administrator tasks and automatically computerize the advantages and disadvantages of cybersecurity. The self-sufficient abilities of DL algorithms should not be overestimated by human management. This facilitates supervision with talented attackers to invade, take information, and even damage a venture. Deep learning is a noticeable algorithm utilized in a few digital protection territories for cybersecurity processes. Including many traditional strategies and ML methods, deep learning algorithms are reviewed as a powerful method to tackle issues. From this investigation, the majority of the deep learning techniques bring the best accuracy, which will be useful in building an ongoing application for examining cyberattacks and malicious tasks over an organization.

REFERENCES

Adamou Djergou, A., Maleh, Y., & Mounir, S. (2022). Machine learning techniques for intrusion detection in SDN: A survey. In Y. Maleh, M. Alazab, N. Gherabi, L. Tawalbeh, & A. A. Abd El-Latif (Eds.), *Advances in information, communication and cybersecurity* (pp. 460–473). Springer International Publishing.

Alazab, M., & Tang, M. (Eds.). (2019). *Deep learning applications for cyber security.* Springer 10.1007/978-3-030-13057-2

Athiwaratkun, B., & Stokes, J. W. (2017). Malware classification with LSTM and GRU language models and a character-level CNN. *2017 IEEE International Conference on Acoustics, Speech and Signal Processing (ICASSP)*, 2482–2486. 10.1109/ICASSP.201 7.7952603

Bhalekar, P. D., & Shaikh, M. Z. (2019). Machine learning: Survey, types and challenges. *International Research Journal of Engineering and Technology (IRJET)*, *6*(3), 8131–8136.

Cho, K., Van Merriënboer, B., Gulcehre, C., Bahdanau, D., Bougares, F., Schwenk, H., & Bengio, Y. (2014). Learning phrase representations using RNN encoder-decoder for statistical machine translation. *ArXiv Preprint ArXiv:1406.1078.*

Chowdhury, M. N., Ferens, K., & Ferens, M. (2016). Network intrusion detection using machine learning. *In Proceedings of the International Conference on Security and Management (SAM), Page 30. The Steering Committee of The World Congress in Computer Science, Computer Engineering and Applied Computing (WorldComp).*

Gers, F. A., Schraudolph, N. N., & Schmidhuber, J. (2002). Learning precise timing with LSTM recurrent networks. *Journal of Machine Learning Research*, 9100, 115–143.

Gollmann, D., & Krotofil, M. (2016). Cyber-physical systems security. In *The new codebreakers: Essays dedicated to David Kahn on the occasion of his 85th birthday* (pp. 195–204). Springer Berlin Heidelberg. 10.1007/978-3-662-49301-4_14

Kolosnjaji, B., Zarras, A., Webster, G., & Eckert, C. (2016). Deep learning for classification of malware system call sequences. In B. H. Kang, & Q. Bai (Eds.), *Australasian joint conference on artificial intelligence* (pp. 137–149). Springer International Publishing.

LeCun, Y., Bengio, Y., & Hinton, G. (2015). Deep learning. *Nature, 521*(7553), 436.

Li, C., Wu, Y., Yuan, X., Sun, Z., Wang, W., Li, X., & Gong, L. (2018). Detection and defense of DDoS attack–based on deep learning in OpenFlow-based SDN. *International Journal of Communication Systems, 31*(5), e3497. 10.1002/dac.3497

Li, J., Sun, L., Yan, Q., Li, Z., Srisa-An, W., & Ye, H. (2018). Significant permission identification for machine learning based android malware detection. *IEEE Transactions on Industrial Informatics*, 3216–3225.

Maleh, Y., Ezzati, A., Qasmaoui, Y., & Mbida, M. (2015). A global hybrid intrusion detection system for wireless sensor networks. *Procedia Computer Science, 52*, 1047–1052. 10.1016/j.procs.2015.05.108

Maleh, Y., Shojaafar, M., Darwish, A., & Haqiq, A. (Eds.). (2019). *Cybersecurity and privacy in cyber-physical systems.* CRC Press. https://www.crcpress.com/Cybersecurity-and-Privacy-in-Cyber-Physical-Systems/Maleh/p/book/9781138346673

Maleh, Y., Sahid, A., & Belaissaoui, M. (2021). Optimized machine learning techniques for IoT 6LoWPAN cyber attacks detection. In A. Abraham, Y. Ohsawa, N. Gandhi, M. A. Jabbar, A. Haqiq, S. McLoone, & B. Issac (Eds.), *Proceedings of the 12th international conference on soft computing and pattern recognition (SoCPaR 2020)* (pp. 669–677). Springer International Publishing.

McLaughlin, N., del Rincon, J., Kang, B., Yerima, S., Miller, P., Sezer, S., Safaei, Y., Trickel, E., Zhao, Z., Doupé, A., & Joon Ahn, G. (2017). Deep Android Malware Detection. *Proceedings of the Seventh ACM on Conference on Data and Application Security and Privacy*, 301–308. 10.1145/3029806.3029823

Pascanu, R., Stokes, J. W., Sanossian, H., Marinescu, M., & Thomas, A. (2015). Malware classification with recurrent networks. *2015 IEEE International conference on acoustics, speech and signal processing (ICASSP)*, 1916–1920. 10.1109/ICASSP.2015.7178304

Rieck, K., Holz, T., Willems, C., Düssel, P., & Laskov, P. (2008). Learning and classification of malware behavior. In D. Zamboni (Ed.), *In International conference on detection of intrusions and malware, and vulnerability assessment* (pp. 108–125). Springer Berlin Heidelberg.

Sadqi, Y., & Maleh, Y. (2022). A systematic review and taxonomy of web applications threats. *Information Security Journal: A Global Perspective, 31*(1), 1–27. 10.1080/19393555.2020.1853855

Sutskever, I. (2013). *Training recurrent neural networks.* Toronto, Ontario, Canada: University of Toronto.

Vinayakumar, R., Soman, K. P., Poornachandran, P., Akarsh, S., & Elhoseny, M. (2019). Improved DGA domain names detection and categorization using deep learning architectures with classical machine learning algorithms. In A. E. Hassanien & M. Elhoseny (Eds.), *Cybersecurity and secure information systems: Challenges and solutions in smart environments* (pp. 161–192). Springer International Publishing. 10.1007/978-3-030-16837-7_8

Vinod, P., Jaipur, R., Laxmi, V., & Gaur, M. (2009). Survey on malware detection methods. *Proceedings of the 3rd Hackers' Workshop on Computer and Internet Security (IIT-KHACK'09)*, 74–79.

Yuan, Z., Lyu, Y., Wang, Z., & Xue, Y. (2014). Droid-Sec: Deep learning in android malware detection. *Proceedings of the 2014 ACM conference on SIGCOMM* (pp. 371–372).

Zhu, B., Joseph, A., & Sastry, S. (2011). A taxonomy of cyber attacks on SCADA systems. *In 2011 IEEE International Conferences on Internet of Things, and Cyber, Physical and Social Computing*, (pp. 380–388). IEEE.

3 Deep Learning Techniques for Malware Classification

Mustapha Belaissaoui
ENCG, University Hassan 1er, Morocco

Yassine Maleh and Soufyane Mounir
Sultan Moulay Slimane University, Morocco

CONTENTS

3.1 INTRODUCTION

Recently, malware has evolved significantly and has become a significant threat to home users, businesses, and governments. Despite the wide use and availability of various anti-malware tools such as anti-virus, intrusion detection systems, firewalls, etc., malware authors can easily escape these precautions by using concealment techniques (Chumachenko & Technology, 2017a).

With the rapid development of the Internet, malware has become one of the major cyber threats today. Any software that performs malicious actions, including stealing information, spying, etc., can be called malware. Kaspersky Labs (2017) defines malware as "a computer program designed to infect a legitimate user's computer and inflict damage in multiple ways."

As the diversity of malware increases, antivirus scanners cannot meet protection needs, resulting in millions of hosts being attacked. According to a malware statistics report, Symantec affirms that more than 357 million new malware variants were observed in 2016 ("Internet Security Threat Report," 2017). Juniper Research (2016) predicts that the cost of data breaches will rise to $2.1 trillion globally by 2019.

In addition, there is a decrease in the skill required for malware development, due to the high availability of attack tools on the Internet today. The high availability of anti-detection techniques and the ability to purchase malware on the black market allows anyone to become an attacker, regardless of skill level. Current studies show that more and more attacks are launched by script-kiddies or are automated (Aliyev, 2010).

Therefore, protecting computer systems against malware is one of the most critical cybersecurity tasks for individual users and businesses, because even a single attack can compromise essential data and cause sufficient losses (Maleh & Ezzati, 2016). Frequent attacks and massive losses dictate the need for accurate and timely detection methods. Current static and dynamic methods do not allow accurate and effective detection, especially regarding zero-day attacks. For this reason, techniques and methods based on machine learning can be used (Chumachenko & Technology, 2017b).

When classifying malicious code families, it is important to identify the unique characteristics of malicious codes, but it is also important to select the classification algorithms used as classifiers correctly. One of the most actively studied fields in classification or recognition techniques is the deep neural network (DNN) related research called depth neural network, which is made by increasing the number of hidden layers of neural networks. In particular, deep neural network-based models have shown excellent performance in image and speech recognition, and there are moves to use them in other areas as well. Malicious code analysis is one such area. Indeed, various malicious code classification models using deep neural networks have been proposed. Many research studies combine classification schemes using recurrent neural networks (NRNs) (Pascanu et al., 2013) and conventional neural networks in the field of image recognition and processing, but just a few in the field of malware and intrusions detection and classification (Chen, 2015).

This paper aims to explore the problem of malware classification, and to propose a new approach combining convolutional neural network (CNN) and long short-term memory recurrent neural network (LSTM). The proposed model has been evaluated on the data provided by Microsoft for the BIG Cup 2015 (Big Data Innovators Gathering).

This paper presents the related work in the next section. Section 3.3 detailed a description of the proposed methodology. Section 3.4 describes the experiments using the proposed model. Section 3.5 presents conclusions and future research directions.

3.2 RELATED WORKS

Two methods of binary analysis are mainly used in the literature: (1) dynamic and (2) static. A dynamic analysis of a binary executes it one or more times at least partially to observe its behavior. The environment in which the binary is executed is controlled to guarantee its containment. In contrast, a static analysis aims to infer the behavior of the binary without executing it. Techniques are available to simulate the program's control flow (e.g., symbolic execution). But these cannot guarantee that all jumps are correctly interpreted or resolved. There are, therefore, advantages and disadvantages inherent in both methods. They are complementary. The joint use of the two techniques is called hybrid analysis.

Several methods have been proposed for applying deep learning to malware detection and malware classification. For example, Saxe et al. (Saxe et al., 2013) presented a malware detection method using a deep neural network (DNN) on a histogram of byte sequences and metadata extracted from headers. Huang et al. (Huang & Stokes, 2016) used the bag-of-words feature consisting of API call n-gram as an input of multi-task DNN, which simultaneously predicts whether a given sample is malware not and to which family it belongs. Other methods targeting Android apps are also proposed [20, 32, 34, 35] (Hou et al., 2016; Li et al., 2018; Yuan et al., 2014; Yuan et al., 2016). MacLaughlin et al. [20] presented a detection method that applies one-dimensional CNN to Java virtual machine instruction sequences.

Kolsnaji et al. (Kolosnjaji et al., 2016) combined a convolutional neural network with long-term memory cells (LSTMs). The authors achieved a recall rate of 89.4%, but do not address the binary problem classification of identifying malware from benign software to detect malware families with deep neural networks, including recurring networks, to classify malware into families using API call sequences. Pascanu et al. [13] conducted experiments to determine whether files were malicious or benign using RNNN and Echo State Networks. Tobiyama et al. (Tobiyama et al., 2016) proposed a malware detection method based on process behavior in potentially infected terminals. The authors found that Echo State Networks performed better with an accuracy of about 95% (5% error rate), but did not attempt to predict malicious behavior from the initial execution. Rhode et al. (Rhode et al., 2017) explored the possibility of predicting whether an executable is executable or not malicious based on a short snapshot of behavioral data. Athiwaratkun et al. (Athiwaratkun & Stokes, 2017) proposed a new one-step malware classifier based on a character-level convolutional neural network (CNN). A method proposed by Gibert Llauradó (Gibert, 2016) is also closely related to our proposed method. This work applies a CNN for malware classification. The author experimented with three different architectures by adding an extra block (a block consists of a convolutional layer followed by a max-pooling layer) each time to its base model. However, their model is still very shallow. Meng et al. (Meng et al., 2017) proposed MCSMGS, a malware classification model based on static malware genetic sequences, which combines static malware genes with convolution neural network. Drew et al. (Drew et al., 2017) performed malware classification on the Microsoft malware data set using a modern gene sequence classification tool and achieved a 97.42% classification accuracy.

This chapter proposes combining conventional neural network (CNN) and LSTM for classifying malware activity.

3.3 METHODOLOGY

3.3.1 Malware Data Set

The Microsoft malware classification challenge data set, which was used as the learning and verification data for the proposed artificial intelligence deep learning–based malware detection system, was presented at the Kaggle machine learning challenge, a machine learning–based data analysis contest hosted by Microsoft in 2015 (Ronen et al., n.d.). Microsoft released a huge data set (almost half a terabyte when uncompressed) consisting of 21,741 malware samples. This data set is divided into two parts: 10,868 samples for training and the other 10,873 samples for testing. Each malware sample had an ID, a 20-character hash value uniquely identifying the sample and a class, an integer representing one of the nine malware family names to which the malware belongs: (1) Ramnit, (2) Lollipop, (3) Kelihos_ver3, (4) Vundo, (5) Simda, (6) Tracur, (7) Kelihos_ver1, (8) Obfuscator.ACY, (9) Gatak. The distribution of classes present in the training data is not uniform and the number of instances of some families significantly outnumbers the instances of other families. Table 3.1 shows the different malware families.

For each observation, we were provided with a file containing the hexadecimal representation of the file's binary content and a file containing metadata information extracted from the binary content, such as function calls, strings, the sequence of instructions and registers used, etc, that was generated using the IDA disassembler tool. Two files represent each malware sample, *.bytes* file, that includes the raw hexadecimal representation of the file's binary content with the executable headers deleted and *.asm* file containing the disassembled code extracted by the IDA disassembler tool. Our experiments only use the *.bytes* files to generate the malware grayscale images. A snapshot of these bytes files are shown in Fig. 3.1(a) and (b).

TABLE 3.1

Malware Families in the Data Set

Family Name	# Train Samples	Type
Ramnit	1541	Worm
Lollipop	2478	Adware
Kelihos_ver3	2942	Backdoor
Vundo	475	Trojan
Simda	42	Backdoor
Tracur	751	TrojanDownloader
Kelihos_ver1	398	Backdoor
Obfuscator.ACY	1228	Any kind of obfuscated malware
Gatak	1013	Backdoor

(a)   (b)

```
00401010 BB 42 00 BB C6 5E C2 04 00 CC CC CC CC CC CC CC       .text:00401174        ;
00401020 C7 01 08 BB 42 00 E9 26 1C 00 00 CC CC CC CC CC       .text:00401177 CC CC CC CC CC CC CC CC          align 10h
00401030 56 BB F1 C7 06 08 BB 42 00 E8 13 1C 00 00 F6 44       .text:00401180 6A 04                push        4
00401040 24 68 01 74 89 56 E8 6C 1E 00 00 83 C4 04 8B C6       .text:00401182 68 00 10 00 00          push        1000h
00401050 5E C2 04 00 CC CC CC CC CC CC CC CC CC CC CC CC       .text:00401187 68 68 BE 1C 00          push        1CBE68h
00401060 8B 44 24 00 8A 08 8B 54 24 04 8B 6A C3 CC CC CC       .text:0040118C 6A 00                push        0
00401070 8B 44 24 04 8D 50 01 8A 08 40 84 C9 75 F9 2B C2       .text:0040118E FF 15 9C 63 52 00        call        ds:GetCurrentProcess
00401080 C3 CC CC CC CC CC CC CC CC CC CC CC CC CC CC CC       .text:00401194 50                push        eax
00401090 8B 44 24 10 8B 4C 24 0C 8B 54 24 00 56 8B 74 24       .text:00401195 FF 15 C8 63 52 00        call        ds:VirtualAllocEx
004010A0 08 50 51 52 56 E8 1E 1E 00 00 83 C4 10 00 C6 5E       .text:0040119B 8B 4C 24 04          mov         ecx, [esp+4]
004010B0 C3 CC CC CC CC CC CC CC CC CC CC CC CC CC CC CC       .text:0040119F 6A 00                push        0
004010C0 8B 44 24 10 8B 4C 24 0C 8B 54 24 00 56 8B 74 24       .text:004011A1 6A 40                push        40h
004010D0 08 50 51 52 56 E8 65 1E 00 00 83 C4 10 8B C6 5E       .text:004011A3 68 68 BE 1C 00          push        1CBE68h
004010E0 C3 CC CC CC CC CC CC CC CC CC CC CC CC CC CC CC       .text:004011A8 50                push        eax
004010F0 33 C0 C2 10 00 CC CC CC CC CC CC CC CC CC CC CC       .text:004011A9 89 01                mov         [ecx], eax
00401100 B0 08 00 00 00 C2 04 00 CC CC CC CC CC CC CC CC       .text:004011AB FF 15 C4 63 52 00        call        ds:VirtualProtect
```

FIGURE 3.1   (a) Snapshot of one-byte file; (b) snapshot of one assembly code file.

3.3.2 DATA PRE-PROCESSING

This work is inspired by the work of Nataraj (Nataraj et al., 2011), which is based on the observation that images of different samples of malware from the same family appear to be similar while images of samples of malware from a different family are distinct. In addition, if the old malware is reused to create new malware binaries, the resulting binaries would be visually very similar. In their work, they calculated image-based characteristics to characterize malware.

To calculate the texture characteristics, they used GIST (Oliva & Torralba, 2001). The resulting characteristic vectors were used to form a classifier of the nearest neighbor with a Euclidean distance. A given malicious binary file can be read as a vector of unsigned 8-bit integers and organized into a 2D array (Nataraj et al., 2011). This table can then be viewed as a grayscale image in the 0.255 range (Fig. 3.2).

Malware authors usually change a small part of the previously available code to produce new malware (Nataraj et al., 2015). If we represent malware as an image, then these small changes can be easily tracked. Inspired by this and previous work (Nataraj et al., 2011), we visualize malware binary files as grayscale images.

Firstly, a given malware binary file is read in a vector of 8-bit unsigned integers. Secondly, the binary value of each component of this vector is converted to its equivalent decimal value (e.g., the decimal value for [00000000] in binary is [0] and for [11111111] is [255]), which is then saved in a new decimal vector representative of the malware sample. Finally, the resulting decimal vector is reshaped to a 2D matrix and visualized as a grayscale image. Selecting the width and height of the 2D matrix (i.e., the spatial resolution of the image) mainly depends on the malware

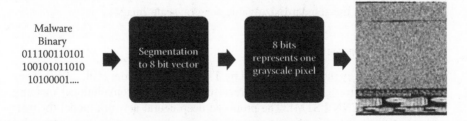

Malware
Binary
011100110101
100101011010
10100001....

Segmentation
to 8 bit vector

8 bits
represents one
grayscale pixel

FIGURE 3.2   Visualizing malware as a gray scale image.

(a)

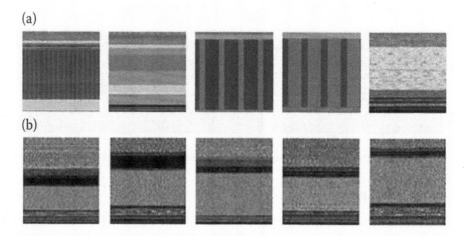

(b)

FIGURE 3.3   (a) Lollipop samples; (b) rammit samples.

binary file size. We use the spatial resolution provided by Nataraj et al. (Nataraj et al., 2011) reshaping the decimal vectors. Malware variants belonging to the same family usually have similar textures (i.e., visual appearance) (Fig. 3.3).

The main benefit of visualizing malware as an image is that the different binary sections can be easily differentiated. In addition, as malware authors only change a small part of the code to produce new variants, images are used to detect small changes while retaining the global structure. Consequently, malware variants belonging to the same family appear to be very similar to images while also being distinct from images of other families. We first pre-process the grayscale image to fulfill CNN's input data requirements. The CNN takes the input image data with the same sizes, when it performs a task like image classification. As a general rule, the image data should have the same length and width (the length/width ratio is 1:1). This is for the convenience of later convolution surgery. Since the executive files have different file sizes, different grayscale image sizes also significantly differ. A large grayscale image can reach 1.04 MB (2048 × 1036 pixels), while a small image is only 120 KB (512 × 472 pixels). It is, therefore necessary to standardize all gray-level images. We use a bilinear interpolation algorithm, an image scaling for standardization. It uses the four closest pixel values in the original image to determine a virtual pixel of the target image, which results in a better effect than the target image. We finally chose 64 × 64 as the standard size value for grayscale images.

3.3.3   THE PROPOSED MODEL

We were inspired by the work proposed by Tsironi et al. (Tsironi et al., 2017). They analyzed gesture recognition using a recurrent short-term convolutional memory neural network (CNN-LSTM). The proposed deep neural network model for malware classification and analysis has the following design architecture. The input to our network is a malware image and the output is set of scores for different

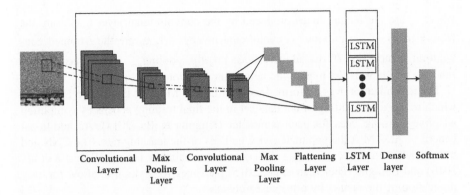

Convolutional | Max | Convolutional | Max | Flattening | LSTM | Dense | Softmax
Layer | Pooling | Layer | Pooling | Layer | Layer | layer
| Layer | | Layer

FIGURE 3.4 The proposed CNN LSTM model.

malware classes. The proposed model involves two convolutional layers, each layer subsequently implementing convolution and max-pooling operations. The flattened output of the last convolutional layer is given to the input nodes of a hidden recurrent LSTM neural network, which is finally connected to a dense layer with a softmax output layer. The CNN and LSTM layers are trained in conjunction with the BackPropagation algorithm based on subsequence. The activation of each output layer unit corresponds to a specific malware class. The one squashing function integrates the convolution layer and the max-pooling layer. Another convolutional and max-pooling layer follows this first level. To interact with the LSTM layer, the CNN layers must be distributed over time. We have expanded our model to distributed time versions of Convolution2D, MaxPooling2D, and Flatten to support the LSTM layer. We experimented with many different network architectures, different numbers and combinations of layers and different filter and pooling parameters. We found that the CNN-LSTM in Fig. 3.4 gave the best performance. Furthermore, we use Dropout (Hinton, 2014) to prevent overfitting and a softmax layer to output the label probabilities.

After the pre-processing step, we have 10,868 labeled samples in our data set. As this is a small number, we use five-step cross-validation to obtain a more robust precision measurement. The data set is mixed and divided into five equal parts, each with roughly the same class distribution as the main data set. During training, we also applied drop layers after each convolutional layer and in the dense layer to avoid over-adjustment and co-dependence between the different filters within the convolutional layer.

The convolution layer and the max-pooling layer are integrated with one squashing function through which the output of a max-pooling layer is transferred in combination with an additive bias:

$$x_j^l = \tanh\left(pooling_{max}\left(\sum_i^{X_j^{l-1}} * k_{ij}\right) + b_j^l\right)$$

where x_j^l are the feature maps produced by the convolutional layer l, x_j^{l-1} are the feature maps of the previous convolutional layer $l-1$, k_{ij} are the i trained convolution kernels and b_j^l the additive bias. Finally, pooling$_{max}$ is the max-pooling function and tanh is the hyperbolic activation function.

The minimization was performed using Adaptive Moment Estimation (ADAM), which reduced over-fitting of the data set in the final training epochs by computing adaptive learning rates for each parameter (Kingma & Ba, 2014). An additional benefit of ADAM is the parameter wise updates of the learning rate. The CNN and training were implemented using the commonly available Theano (Bergstra et al., 2010) and Lasagne (Dieleman et al., 2015) packages for Python to allow for easy replication of the results by other researchers.

We apply LSTM as a network traffic event follows the time series patterns and the current network connection record can be classified based on the past traffic connection records. To capture time series models through time steps of newly formed features from the max-pooling operation in CNN, we feed them to the LSTM layer. The newly built feature map vector is transmitted to an LSTM layer. New feature vectors that are computed from long short-term memory (CNN-LSTM) is an improved method of recurrent neural networks (RNNs) developed to alleviate the vanishing and exploding gradient issue (Hochreiter & Schmidhuber, 1997). In contrast to the conventional simple RNN units, LSTM introduces memory blocks. A memory block contains a memory cell and a set of gates. This appears more effective in capturing long-range dependencies. A recurrent hidden layer function at a time step can be generally defined as follows.

$$
\begin{aligned}
i_t &= \sigma(x^t W_{xi} + h_{t-1} W_{hi} + c_{t-1} W_{ci} + b_i), \\
f_t &= \sigma(x^t W_{xf} + h_{t-1} W_{hf} + c_{t-1} W_{cf} + b_i), \\
o_t &= \sigma(x^t W_{xo} + h_{t-1} W_{ho} + c_{t-1} W_{co} + b_o), \\
c_t &= f_t \odot + c_{t-1} + i_t \odot \tanh(x^t W_{xc} + h_{t-1} + b_c), \\
h_t &= o_t \odot + \tanh(c_t),
\end{aligned}
$$

where x^t is the input to the LSTM block, i_t, f_t, o_t, c_t, h_t are the input gate, the forget gate, the output gate, the cell state, and the LSTM block's output, respectively, at the current time step t. W_{xi}, W_{xf}, and W_{xo} represent the weights between the input layer and the input grid, the forget grid and the output grid. W_{hi}, W_{hf}, and W_{ho} represent, respectively, the weights between the hidden recurrent layer and the forget gate, the input/output gate of the memory block,. W_{ci}, W_{cf}, and W_{co} are, respectively, the weights between the cell state and the input gate, the forget gate and the output gate, and finally, b_i, b_i, and b_o are, respectively, the additive biases of the input gate, the forget gate, and the output gate. The activation functions comprise a sigmoid function. $\sigma(\cdot)$, the hyperbolic activation function tanh(.), and the element-wise multiplication $\odot$.

To avoid overfitting, we use L2 regularization to constrain the convolutional layers' weights and dropout in the dense and LSTM layers. Without regularization measures, representations learned by a neural network may not generalize well. For regularization, we try to use dropout as well as regularization l2 on weight and bias terms in the network in our search space. Dropout (Hinton, 2014) randomly omits a predefined percentage of knots at each training time, which commonly limits overfitting. L2 regularization allows a limited number of weights to become large values.

3.4 EXPERIMENTS AND RESULTS

In this section, we discuss the malware data sets, experiments, and the evaluation scheme.

3.4.1 EXPERIMENTAL SETUP

We conduct experiments using the Microsoft malware data set. In 2015, Microsoft hosted a Kaggle competition for malware classification (Ronen et al., n.d.). In this challenge, Microsoft released a huge data set (almost half a terabyte when uncompressed) consisting of 21,741 malware samples. This data set is divided into two parts: 10,868 samples for training and the other 10,873 samples for testing.

The data set provided by Kaggle for training was divided into two:

- The training set of size $(N - N/10) = 9781$
- The validation set of size $M = N/10 = 1086$

where N is the total size of the data set, $N = 10868$ and $M = 1086$. The validation set was used to search the networks' parameters and know when to stop training. In particular, we stopped training the network if the validation loss increased in 10 iterations.

All the experiments are conducted on a deep learning virtual machine on Windows Azure environment, with 64-bit Ubuntu 18.04 Intel(R) Core i7–4790K CPU @ 4.00GHz ⇥ 8 with 64GB RAM and an NVIDIA Titan X GPU with 12GB memory. To run experiments on GPU, CUDA driver and CUDA Toolkit are needed for Nvidia's GPU–programming toolchain. Keras (Chollet, 2015) is used as a library to build the CNN-LSTM model. In the fivefold cross-validation procedure, we train each model for 100 epochs on our Nvidia 1080 Ti GPU; the model weights are modified by the Adam optimization method (Kingma & Ba, 2014) to minimize the average log-loss criteria.

To evaluate the performance of the proposed model, we report the performance of different methods in terms of accuracy, which refers to the percentage of malware samples labeled correctly.

3.4.2 RESULTS

Our proposed network CNN-LSTM is trained for 100 epochs with a batch size (a set of training data forwarded to the model at once) of 16 when training on the Microsoft malware data set. CNN-LSTM achieved the best performance with a classification accuracy of 98.73% on the validation data of the Microsoft malware data set. Our method outperforms several baseline methods by a significant margin

TABLE 3.2

Performance of different methods on validation test

Model	Accuracy
Meng	98%
Nataraj	97.18%
Rjeck	88%
Han	75%
Drew	97.42%
Garcia	95.62
Kolosnjaji	85,6
CNN-LSTM (ours)	**98,73**

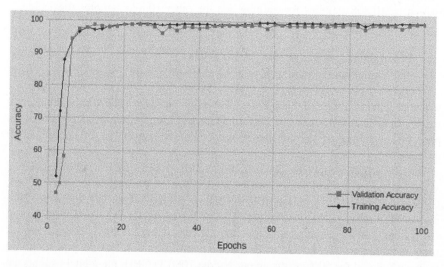

FIGURE 3.5   Training and validation accuracy of CNN-LSTM model.

on both data sets, as shown in Table 3.2. The next figure shows the accuracy and loss of the training and validation data achieved by the CNN-LSTM final model presented in Fig. 3.5 and Fig. 3.6 until they reached 100 epochs. The final CNN-LSTM model achieves an average log loss of 0.0698 on the validation data.

3.4.3 Testing

Usually, Kaggle provides a test set without label in their competitions and the Microsoft Malware Classification Challenge. Therefore, to evaluate our model using the test set, we submit a file with the predicted probabilities for each class to Kaggle. Additionally, submissions in Kaggle are evaluated with two scores, the

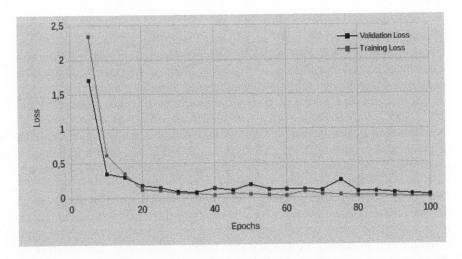

FIGURE 3.6 Loss on training and validation of CNN-LSTM model.

public score and the private score where the first one is calculated on approximately 30% of the test data and the second one is calculated on the other 70%. This submission is evaluated using the multi-class logarithmic loss. The logarithmic loss metric is defined as:

$$logloss = -\frac{1}{N} \sum_{i=1}^{N} \sum_{j=1}^{M} y_{i,j} \log(p_{i,j})$$

where N is the number of malware samples, M is the number of malware classes, $y_{i,j}$ is 1 if the prediction is correct and 0 otherwise, and $p_{i,j}$ is the predicted probability (Ronen et al., n.d.). Upon submitting the predictions of this model for the test malware files to Kaggle, we receive two average log-loss scores: a public score of 0.0691 calculated from 30% of the test data set and a private score of 0.0743 calculated from 70% of the test data set. These results align with the log-loss we obtained on the validation data, which means our final model generalizes well on new data.

3.4.4 Comparison Results

We tested the proposed CNN-LSTM against other deep learning models used for malware classification: Nataraj (Nataraj et al., 2011), Meng (Meng et al., 2017), Garcia (Garcia et al., 2016), Rieck (Rieck et al., 2008), Meng (Meng et al., 2017), kolosnjaji (Kolosnjaji et al., 2016), and Gibert (Gibert, 2016). A brief introduction to each model is provided below. Nataraj's classification model classified malicious codes by visualizing malicious code similar to the proposed model. Gabor filter is used to extract feature points of malicious code images. The extracted feature points are kNN (k-nearest neighbors) algorithm and classified malicious code types. Meng (Meng et al., 2017) proposed a malware classification model that combines static malware genes with deep genes learning methods. The model extracts the gene from the malware sequences with both hardware and informational attributes. Then it makes a distributed representation for each malware gene to represent intrinsic correlation and similarity. Finally, the Static Malware Gene Sequences-Convolution Neural Network is used to build the neural network to analyze the malware gene and perform malware classification. Rieck's (Rieck et al., 2008) classification scheme classified malicious code types into SVMs by monitoring malicious code's behavior pattern and executing malicious code in sandbox environment. Han et al. (Han et al., 2013) proposed a technique to classify malicious codes by comparing malicious codes with various APIs such as hash value, AV test result value, and Packer as well as API used in malicious code. Drew et al. (Drew et al., 2017) performed malware classification on the Microsoft Malware data set using modern gene sequence classification tool. Garcia (Garcia et al., 2016) proposed converting a malware binary into an image and using random forest to classify various malware families. Kolosnjaji (Kolosnjaji et al., 2016) designed a neural network based on convolutional and recurrent network layers to obtain the best characteristics for classifying system call sequences. The performance indicators are based on each paper's most frequently used accuracy. Table 3.2 compares the proposed classification technique with previous research results.

Compared to the existing methods and experiment results, we find that our jointed architecture of a CNN and LSTM model performs better than the CNN and RNN models alone in malware classification. We take advantage of both the CNN and the LSTM models, thus getting higher classification accuracy than the existing models. CNN extracts the local features of input and LSTM process sequence input while learning the long-term dependencies and getting malware feature representation.

3.5   CONCLUSION AND FUTURE WORK

Malware is increasingly posing a severe security threat to computer systems. It is essential to analyze malware behavior and categorize samples so that robust programs to prevent malware attacks can be developed. Towards this endeavor, we presented a new deep neural network architecture based on CNN and LSTM for malware classification and analysis. We first convert malware samples to grayscale images to train a CNN for classification. Experimental results on Microsoft malware classification data sets demonstrate that our proposed model achieves better than state-of-the-art performance. We showed the effectiveness of the proposed CNN-LSTM model through extensive experiments. Our deep learning model achieves an accuracy of 98.73% in the cross-validation procedure. The model takes little time to classify the malware class of a binary file, making it very convenient to use in practice.

We will continue to modify and test our deep learning model by applying more complex deep learning architectures to achieve better performance for future work. Moreover, testing our deep learning approach on larger data sets with more malware classes achieves a higher accuracy rate.

REFERENCES

Aliyev, V. (2010). *Using honeypots to study skill level of attackers based on the exploited vulnerabilities in the network.* Chalmers University of Technology.

Athiwaratkun, B., & Stokes, J. W. (2017). Malware classification with LSTM and GRU language models and a character-level CNN. *2017 IEEE International Conference on Acoustics, Speech and Signal Processing (ICASSP),* 2482–2486. 10.1109/ICASSP. 2017.7952603

Bergstra, J., Breuleux, O., Bastien, F. F., Lamblin, P., Pascanu, R., Desjardins, G., Turian, J., Warde-Farley, D., & Bengio, Y. (2010). Theano: A CPU and GPU math compiler in Python. *Proceedings of the Python for Scientific Computing Conference (SciPy), Scipy,* 1–7.

Chen, Y. (2015). *Convolutional neural network for sentence classification by.* (Master's thesis, University of Waterloo). Chicago. https://uwspace.uwaterloo.ca/bitstream/handle/10012/9592/Chen_Yahui.pdf

Chollet, F. (2015). Keras: Deep learning library for theano and tensorflow. Https://Keras.Io/k, *7, 8.*

Chumachenko, K., & Technology, I. (2017a). Machine learning for malware detection and classification. *Bachelor's Thesis Information Technology.*

Chumachenko, K., & Technology, I. (2017b). Machine learning for malware detection and classification. *Bachelor's Thesis Information Technology.*

Dieleman, S., Schlüter, J., Raffel, C., Olson, E., Sønderby, S. K., Nouri, D., ... & De Fauw, J. (2015). *Lasagne: first release.* Zenodo: Geneva, Switzerland, 3, 74.

Drew, J., Hahsler, M., & Moore, T. (2017). Polymorphic malware detection using sequence classification methods and ensembles. *EURASIP Journal on Information Security, 2017*(1), 1–12.

Garcia, F. C. C., Muga, I. I., & Felix, P. (2016). Random forest for malware classification. *ArXiv Preprint ArXiv:1609.07770.*

Gibert, D. (2016). *Convolutional neural networks for malware classification.* Master Thesis, University Rovira i Virgili, Tarragona, Spain. https://www.covert.io/research-papers/deep-learning-security/Convolutional%20Neural%20Networks%20for%20Malware%20Classification.pdf

Han, B. J., Choi, Y. H., & Bae, B. C. (2013). Generating malware DNA to classify the similar malwares. *Journal of the Korea Institute of Information Security and Cryptology, 23*(4), 679–694.

Hinton, G. (2014). Dropout: A simple way to prevent neural networks from overfitting. *Journal of Machine Learning Research, 15,* 1929–1958.

Hochreiter, S., & Schmidhuber, J. (1997). Long short-term memory. *Neural Computation, 9*(8), 1735–1780.

Hou, S., Saas, A., Chen, L., & Ye, Y. (2016). Deep4MalDroid: A deep learning framework for android malware detection based on linux kernel system call graphs. *2016 IEEE/WIC/ACM International Conference on Web Intelligence Workshops (WIW),* 104–111. 10.1109/WIW.2016.040

Huang, W., & Stokes, J. W. (2016). MtNet: A multi-task neural network for dynamic malware classification. *International Conference on Detection of Intrusions and Malware, and Vulnerability Assessment,* 399–418.

Internet Security Threat Report. (2017). Retrieved from Https://Www.Symantec.Com/Content/Dam/Symantec/Docs/Reports/Istr-22-2017-En.Pdf

Kingma, D. P., & Ba, J. (2014). Adam: A method for stochastic optimization. *ArXiv Preprint ArXiv:1412.6980.*

Kolosnjaji, B., Zarras, A., Webster, G., & Eckert, C. (2016). Deep learning for classification of malware system call sequences. In B. H. Kang, & Q. Bai (Eds.), *Australasian joint conference on artificial intelligence* (pp. 137–149). Springer International Publishing.

Li, J., Sun, L., Yan, Q., Li, Z., Srisa-An, W., & Ye, H. (2018). Significant permission identification for machine learning based android malware detection. *IEEE Transactions on Industrial Informatics, 14*(7), 3216–3225.

Maleh, Y., & Ezzati, A. (2016). Towards an efficient datagram transport layer security for constrained applications in internet of things. *International Review on Computers and Software, 11*(7), 611–621. 10.15866/irecos.v11i7.9438

Meng, X., Shan, Z., Liu, F., Zhao, B., Han, J., Wang, H., & Wang, J. (2017). MCSMGS: Malware classification model based on deep learning. *2017 International Conference on Cyber-Enabled Distributed Computing and Knowledge Discovery (CyberC),* 272–275. 10.1109/CyberC.2017.21

Nataraj, L., Karthikeyan, S., Jacob, G., & Manjunath, B. S. (2011). Malware images: Visualization and automatic classification. *Proceedings of the 8th International Symposium on Visualization for Cyber Security,* 4:1–4:7. 10.1145/2016904.2016908

Nataraj, L., Karthikeyan, S., & Manjunath, B. S. (2015). SATTVA: SpArsiTy inspired classificaTion of malware VAriants. *In Proceedings of the 3rd ACM Workshop on Information Hiding and Multimedia Security* (pp. 135–140). ACM.

Oliva, A., & Torralba, A. (2001). Modeling the shape of the scene: A holistic representation of the spatial envelope. *International Journal of Computer Vision, 42*(3), 145–175. 10.1023/A:1011139631724

Pascanu, R., Tour, D., Mikolov, T., & Tour, D. (2013). On the difficulty of training recurrent neural networks. *International Conference on Machine Learning, 2,* 1310–1318.

Rhode, M., Burnap, P., & Jones, K. (2017). Early-stage malware prediction using recurrent neural networks. *ArXiv Preprint ArXiv:1708.03513,* 1–28.

Rieck, K., Holz, T., Willems, C., Düssel, P., & Laskov, P. (2008). Learning and classification of malware behavior. In D. Zamboni (Ed.), *In International conference on detection of intrusions and malware, and vulnerability assessment* (pp. 108–125). Springer Berlin Heidelberg.

Ronen, R., Radu, M., Feuerstein, C., & Yom-Tov, E. (2018). *Microsoft malware classification challenge.* 1–7. arXiv preprint arXiv:*1802.10135*. 10.1145/2857705.2857713

Tobiyama, S., Yamaguchi, Y., Shimada, H., Ikuse, T., & Yagi, T. (2016). Malware detection with deep neural network using process behavior. *2016 IEEE 40th Annual Computer Software and Applications Conference (COMPSAC), 2,* 577–582. 10.1109/COMPSAC.2016.151

Tsironi, E., Barros, P., Weber, C., & Wermter, S. (2017). An analysis of convolutional long short-term memory recurrent neural networks for gesture recognition. *Neurocomputing, 268,* 76–86. 10.1016/j.neucom.2016.12.088

Yakura, H., Shinozaki, S., Nishimura, R., Oyama, Y., & Sakuma, J. (2018). *Malware analysis of imaged binary samples by convolutional neural network with attention mechanism.* Proceedings of the Eighth ACM Conference on Data and Application Security and Privacy (pp. 127–134).

Yuan, Z., Lu, Y., & Xue, Y. (2016). DroidDetector: Android malware characterization and detection using deep learning. *Tsinghua Science and Technology, 21*(1), 114–123.

Yuan, Z., Lyu, Y., Wang, Z., & Xue, Y. (2014). Droid-Sec: Deep learning in android malware detection. *Proceedings of the 2014 ACM Conference on SIGCOMM* (pp. 371–372).

Section II

Computational Intelligence for Cybersecurity Applications

Section II

Computational Intelligence for
Cybersecurity Applications

4 Machine Learning and Blockchain for Security Management in Banking System

Oshin Sharma and Nidhi Pandey
Department of Computer Science & Technology,
SRM University, Delhi-NCR, Ghaziabad, UP, India

CONTENTS

DOI: 10.1201/9781003319917-6

4.1   INTRODUCTION

Artificial intelligence has become a trendy field. Its main objective is to reduce human efforts for performing any task in any field, such as: medicine, retail, banking, education, finance, marketing, research, and many others. Artificial intelligence involves machines being trained to think and perform like humans (Donepudi, 2017). However, we live in a world of big data where data is growing exponentially; therefore, the field of data science has emerged to process this huge data. Data science also uses machine learning to find patterns and training machines to understand those patterns from their experience. Machine learning and data science work together for many applications: spam filtering, banking and finance, social media, prediction systems, and recommendation systems (Injadat et al., 2021). None of the authors has comprehensively reviewed machine learning and blockchain in this area. Thus, this study focuses on the data generated in the banking sector and how machine learning and data science under the umbrella of artificial intelligence help the banking sector. Machine learning algorithms are built on clients' behavior on the Internet during transactions and are capable enough to detect transactional frauds after analyzing billions and millions of data. Fraud detection is one of the thriving applications of machine learning in the banking sector. Machines are trained, validated, and tested over the historical transactional data set, and later on, the testing phase can easily classify fraud and non-fraud transactions in real time.

Earlier studies about financial crime show that 33% of financial crime was reported in the United Kingdom and United States in April 2020 during the COVID pandemic (Abu-Salih et al., 2021). This could provide the global shifts towards a digital world where financial services need to be monitored using new technologies to reduce digital crimes and their possibilities (Yang et al., 2021). To deal with financial crimes and fraud transactions, many researchers have proposed different algorithms and expert systems that we have discussed in Section 4.2. Blockchain is one of the upcoming innovative technologies that could be helpful in secure and safe financial services that do not include a trusted middleman during any transaction processing. This study discusses recent work done in financial crimes and money laundering cases. The evolution of blockchain and various ongoing types of research concerning financial crimes have been discussed in Section 4.3. Section 4.4 discusses different machine learning models for secure and safe Internet banking and online transaction, along with the benefits of ML in the banking and finance sector. Furthermore, the proposed model for a secure banking system has been proposed and discussed in Section 4.5. Section 4.6 provides future research directions and open issues that could be further considered as research objectives or implemented in secure banking systems, and finally, Section 4.7 concludes the entire article.

4.2 BACKGROUND AND RELATED WORKS

In recent years, blockchain has gained huge attention, and many measures have been implemented for fraudulent detection (Khan & Salah, 2018). A vast amount of transactions are being made daily and there are chances of cyberattacks on those transactions. The blockchain has come to the rescue by providing security measures to block and ensure safe transactions. Earlier, fraud detection was very time-consuming and led to a huge loss for the companies, as they had to rely on a third party for the whole scrutiny process (Dhieb et al., 2020). With the integration of blockchain and machine learning algorithms, studies have proved that they have saved more time over fraud detection and risk management.

The authors (Viji et al., 2021) aim to identify the abnormal activity at ATM booth surveillance using artificial intelligence techniques. The HMDB-51 and CAVIAR data sets are used for training using SVM and K-means clustering algorithms. The training of unlabeled raw data sets uses the K-means clustering algorithm to make clusters and determine suspicious or abnormal activity patterns. After the pattern recognition, the binary classification is made using the SVM classification algorithm to determine the normal or abnormal activity. The proposed hybrid model GOA (Grasshopper Optimizer Algorithm) by combining the best features of GOA and Ant Lion Optimization Algorithm (ALO) is introduced, which further results in better classification metric values.

Another work (Dhieb et al., 2020) developed a SISBAR model for an insurance firm that detects fraudulent claims made by an unauthorized user. The XGBoost and VFDT (very fast decision tree) algorithms were used for the batch and incremental learning strategies that help better detect and classify different types of anomaly detection in insurance firms. XGBoost has also proved its efficiency in detecting future claims amount and future behavior of the customer. The implementation of blockchain simulation framework Hyperledger fabric is developed using the Hyperledger composer module to provide the security. Their proposed model, SISBAR, has improved the performance in decreasing the claim refund losses (Table 4.1).

TABLE 4.1
Proposed Systems in Recent Literature

Author	Approach Used	Proposed System	Findings
(Alimolaei, 2015)	ROC curve	Fuzzy expert system	94% accuracy was obtained in detecting suspicious user behavior.
(Deng et al., 2019)	GBDT-DE	Integrated insider trading identification model	1. Accuracy and efficiency have improved 2. Four indicators were demonstrated and are relatively important in identification of insider activity; they are: ERCSM, ROA, CR5, and TAT.

(Continued)

TABLE 4.1 (Continued)
Proposed Systems in Recent Literature

Author	Approach Used	Proposed System	Findings
(Dhieb et al., 2020)	XGBoost and VFDT (very fast decision tree) algorithms	Smart insurance system based on blockchain and artificial intelligence (SISBAR)	Hyperledger fabric composer module was developed to emulate the blockchain network using REST APIs.
(Boughaci & Alkhawaldeh, 2020)	K-means clustering	A hybrid system that comprises machine learning and blockchain technologies	K-means clustering to classify transactions in Bitcoin.
(Rouhollahi, 2021)	Logical AND were used over the results of supervised and unsupervised models	Hybrid pipeline system that includes both supervised and unsupervised applications	Producing better Precision and F1 score results by applying Logical AND operator.
(Viji et al., 2021)	K-means clustering and SVM classifier	Hybrid GOA (combining the best features of GOA and ALO)	The proposed anamoly detection model outperforms better classification metric values.
(Cui et al., 2021)	Stochastic Gradient Descent	Ranking Metric Embedding Based Multi-Contextual behavior Profiling Model (ReMEMBeR)	Performs better in detection large bunch of fraudulent transactions.
(Sanober et al., 2021)	A stacked-based novel approach for feature selection	Deep learning framework for fraudulent detection using SPARK	Autoencoder is used to classify the fraudulent anomaly detection.

4.3   BLOCKCHAIN AND ITS BENEFITS IN BANKING AND FINANCE

Blockchain technology is a promising platform for dealing with security aspects of today's digital era. It is a decentralized system where the trusted third party is missing from the network, and the level of trust is established with the communicating nodes within the network (Maleh et al., 2021). The evolution of blockchain technology started with the concept of cryptocurrencies. Still, later on, the implementation of this concept in various applications such as health care, banking, finance, and the supply chain market has gained a lot of insights. The main features of blockchain technology are confidentiality, availability, and integrity of data without any third party. In technical terms, we can call it a distributed ledger maintained in a logical peer-to-peer network, and no one can get insights into what is happening between data and machines (Liu et al., 2020). Thus, blockchain is providing a trusted environment among people in different applications.

Blockchain allows the data to be stored in shared and public databases in immutable blocks or linked blocks. Each block contains data in transactions and the hash function, which refers to the previous block. Each block has its unique number and hash, generated with SHA-256 & SHA-512 cryptographic hash algorithms. The architectural components of blockchain are peer-to-peer networks, blocks, transactions within the ledger, validation process, and proof of work.

4.3.1 PEER-TO-PEER NETWORK (P2P)

This network work on IP protocol supports distributed architecture of computing. It is a combination of different nodes linked to each other rather than a single server and centralizes the whole network. P2P provides a high level of security due to the lack of one-point failure or attack. A blockchain P2P network is of two types: private and public networks. The public network is also a permission-less network where any individual can join the network. In contrast, a private network is a permission-based network that needs the verification of every individual before joining the network.

4.3.2 BLOCKS

Blocks are the types of data structures that contain a set of transactions that can be distributed to all the nodes in the network. Blocks have information about transactions such as: block version, timestamp, previous block hash, and cryptographic number nonce (Maleh et al., 2020). Blocks can be compared to a printed receipt of a single transaction completed by an ATM machine, and on the other hand, blockchain can be compared to all the records or transactions done by all the users. There are three types of blocks in a blockchain. The first block of every blockchain is known as the Genesis block and provides the synchronization of nodes within the network. Second, the valid blocks contain a block's sequence of validated transactions. Everyone needs to solve a cryptographic puzzle or get the network's permission to become a valid block in the blockchain. Finally, the blocks created by miners but not accepted by the network due to time lag are known as orphan blocks.

4.3.3 TRANSACTIONS WITHIN A LEDGER

Transactions are the smallest building block for blockchain technology (El-Latif et al., 2022). They contain the sender, recipient's address, and data. The sender sends the data after adding digital signatures on the hash and public key of the recipient and then the transaction is announced publicly over the network. The transaction needs to be authorized and approved before adding into the blockchain. Every node will process and verify the transaction, and most nodes must agree that a transaction is valid. Every transaction must be timestamped.

4.3.4   PROOF-OF-WORK (POW)

Proof-of-work involves solving a mathematical cryptographic puzzle and then getting its rewards. Blockchain technology involves miners competing in the network to make transactions successful by creating a new valid block. As soon as the miner starts a valid block, he gets the rewards. As miners have to go through a lot of trials, guesses, and errors before a valid block is generated, therefore the entire process gets its name: "proof-of-work." Fig. 4.1 shows how blockchain works between two entities where Alein wants to send 100 BTC to Brown, and they are requesting the transaction to be mined. Once Alein starts the transaction, all the active users in the network will receive the request to verify the transaction. Transactions will be mined using some hash function, and all the participating nodes verify the transaction. After verification, the transaction will be forwarded to the memory pool of the blockchain, which contains several verified transactions. Further, the new block is added to the existing blockchain and the transaction is mined with a subsequent hash function. Finally, the transaction is complete and Alein has added 100 BTC to Brown's account.

4.3.5   BLOCKCHAIN TOWARDS THE BANKING SYSTEM

The banking sector deals with the highest level of money exchange among all the transactions and has become one of the popular areas for fraudsters. These fraudsters are becoming more intelligent and flexible these days, so the banks should also be agile and flexible in identifying and preventing frauds. India reported an increase of 83,638 banking frauds of 1.38 Lakhs in 2021 (businesstoday, 2022). Therefore, fraud detection is crucial to fight cyberattacks, money laundering, and credit card transactions. The banking system can fully use fraud detection tools to protect its customers from cyber theft and provide them with good and secure quality services.

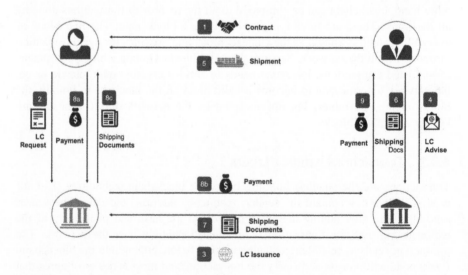

FIGURE 4.1   Letter of credit transaction flow.

Moreover, the banking system should become accustomed to these current digital technologies as quickly as possible; hence, the banking industry is taking the lead in adopting blockchain (Maleh et al., 2022). As discussed above, a blockchain is a distributed ledger for maintaining the transaction records between two entities. These entities can share this ledger across the network without any third party or authority. Following are a few benefits of blockchain technology in the banking system, especially letter of credit transaction flow.

Blockchain has cut down the requirement of third-party verification and that's why transactions are processing faster.

- Cutting down the third party from the entire transaction process of buying and selling assets such as commodities and stocks also reduces the asset exchange fees. It saves millions of dollars in worldwide trading.
- Trade finance is another area that is revolutionizing using blockchain technology by reducing the manual paperwork, such as credits, invoices, and bills, and making information digital.
- The entire network can access this digital information. Thus, blockchain provides many benefits for the whole banking system.
- The concept of smart contracts allows different entities to process the transactions with automated constraints, which further maintains the authenticity of data.
- Blockchain provides decentralized and distributed secure solutions for the banking sector, making it impracticable for fraudsters to temper, corrupt, or steal the data.

Thus, blockchain is one of the stepping stones to making the banking system as secure as possible.

4.4 MACHINE LEARNING–BASED SECURE TRANSACTION PROCESSING SYSTEMS

Machine learning comes under artificial intelligence, which deals with pattern recognition and classification. A thing that makes machine learning unique is that a number of models are being trained on various data sets and can produce results when they are exposed to the new raw data. The crime rate of money laundering is increasing daily in the financial industry, and the prior detection of unusual behavior or suspicious activity in the transaction is very important. An intelligent and powerful tool is required to quickly detect the activity as a shutter so the client can take some preventive measures. Machine learning comes into view whenever better pattern detection or good classification is required. With machine learning models, the false positive prediction is being reduced and transaction monitoring on alert is being investigated. It has been estimated that 98% of detections are false positives; only 1–2% are real threats (Liu et al., 2020). The huge amount of transactional data being uploaded daily makes it difficult to detect the nature or pattern of the transaction. To make the detection fast, machine learning

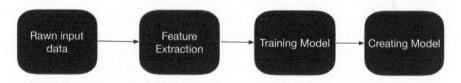

FIGURE 4.2   Machine learning model.

models are the big savior. Fig. 4.2 depicts the machine learning model and the flow of various processes during the model's training.

4.4.1   INPUT RAW DATA

A huge amount of raw data is available for fraudulent prediction. Supervised and unsupervised learning algorithms are used better to predict good and bad transactions (Yassine MALEH, 2020).

4.4.2   FEATURE EXTRACTION

Feature extraction helps for the dimensionality reduction; thus, we are already dealing with the unnecessary features that are not required for the classification, as the important features that are required could be:

- All transaction details of the customer (time, location, amount)
- Customer's credentials (email, mobile number)
- Mode of payment
- Preferred bank/location, etc.

4.4.3   TRAINING ALGORITHM

An intelligent algorithm should be made that will be able to classify fraudulent and non-fraudulent transactions. The training should be done based on the above-extracted features. The training algorithms can be any supervised and unsupervised learning techniques.

4.4.4   CREATING A MODEL

After the algorithm's training is over, the model should be ready for the prediction. There are many models that are used in classification.

4.4.5   SUPPORT VECTOR MACHINE (SVM)

Support vector machine (SVM) is a supervised learning algorithm that can be used for classification and regression purposes. The classification is done with the help of a hyperplane in two dimensions, i.e., for two classes. There are two types of classification used: linearly separable, where a hyperplane can separate all the positive and negative points linearly (with a straight line) and non-linearly separable, where a linear hyperplane is challenging to find that separates all the points linearly.

4.4.6 DECISION TREES

A decision tree is a supervised machine learning algorithm for classification purposes. It is used for the rule-based classification modeling method. It is a tree-based model where nodes define attributes, branches represent outcomes, and leaf nodes hold the class label. The formation of decision nodes is based on entropy and information gain, which helps to remove the irrelevant features during tree formation. The decision tree helps to determine the possibility of any event like the occurrence of fraud detection at an early stage.

4.4.7 RANDOM FOREST

Random forest is a combination of multiple decision trees that helps to improve the performance of predicting the result more accurately. It is an ensemble technique that combines various models for learning the model. It helps to deal with the errors generated in a single tree (Bhalekar, P. D., & Shaikh, 2019), which increases overall performance. They often overfit and deal with missing and unbalanced data; their runtime is very fast and provides an explainable score to the users.

4.4.8 XGBOOST

Extreme gradient boosting (XGBoost) is an ensemble technique that combines various models for better results. It runs on many iterations to improve the poor fit training data to good fit training data. It is a gradient boosting algorithm of decision trees that focuses on performance and speed. It makes the best use of cache optimization.

4.4.9 NEURAL NETWORK

Neural network or artificial neural network (ANN) is a subset of machine learning that learns from real data and mimics the decisions of humans. It is used for pattern recognition, and they are the best applicable algorithm for any kind of recognition. They are extremely fast in decision making and tend to adapt to changes in behavior and accurately detect the pattern.

4.5 INTEGRATION OF ML AND BLOCKCHAIN

Machine learning and blockchain can complement each other as blockchain provides the highest level of security, and machine learning can improve blockchain performance. In other words, machine learning is an intelligent technique to detect malicious transactions over the non-trusted network. Machine learning will automate tasks or decision making by reducing human intervention. The combination of

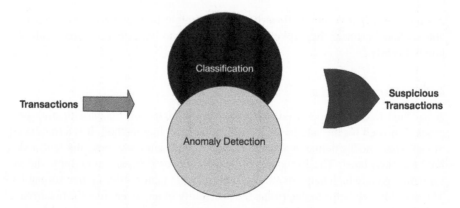

FIGURE 4.3 ML models for classifying suspicious transactions.

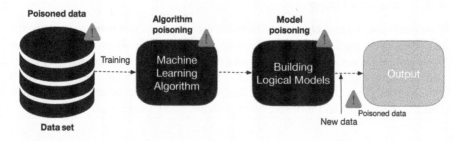

FIGURE 4.4 Target areas for attacks in the ML modeling process.

these two technologies is beneficial for protecting financial data by declining fraudulent transactions in advance. Many researchers have proposed different models considering ML and blockchain as the best combination for a secure environment. Fig. 4.3 shows the use of machine learning models for classifying suspicious transactions.

However, machine learning models have provided benefits in every sector, from health care to finance. Still, it has also made the entire machine learning process more vulnerable to attacks. Data sets used by machine learning algorithms could be poisoned data that can be manipulated easily. Machine learning algorithms and models could also be poisoned to reduce this technology's efficiency. Fig. 4.4 shows different target areas for attacks during the machine learning process. Blockchain can play a critical role in securing the entire machine learning process.

4.5.1 Application Areas: Integration of ML and Blockchain

4.5.1.1 Recommendation System

Recommendation systems works on personalized information, and the concept of blockchain technology runs these recommendation systems without any centralized authority. Smart cards are the building block for blockchain, which creates items, ratings, and scores; all of these assets are tamper proof. Most decentralized recommendation systems provide privacy, integrity, public availability of rating, audit ability, incentives, and reputation (Casino & Patsakis, 2020; Lisi et al., 2021; Wang et al., 2019).

- *Smart cities:* Smart cities have introduced the concept of connected vehicles, which collect and distribute data to the entire network. Thus, when the term *data* comes into the frame, its security aspects also need to be discussed. Therefore, a blockchain-based batch authentication protocol has been designed for smart cities (Bhushan et al., 2020). Data collected by the vehicles is verified in the form of transactions. Once the transaction is created in the blockchain, it is mined with the appropriate blockchain algorithm. Hyperledger sawtooth is one of the proposed models for using blockchain in smart cities (Bagga et al., 2021).
- *Health care:* The healthcare industry considers its data secure and safe and does not want to share it with any third party. Here also, blockchain can be integrated with machine learning through smart cards. Smart cards impose access control rules on the data access methods. (Alqaralleh et al. 2021) proposed a GO-FFO model for secure medical image data set and includes the following steps: data collection, secure transaction, value encryption, and data classification. The main issues resolved by their approach were data security and privacy.
- *Secure banking:* Machine learning and blockchain contribute toward the detection of suspicious transactions in advance. As blockchain helps in financial transactions while opening an account, funds transfer, and payment methods, machine learning is incorporating their features by collecting information about users, their credit history, GPS, linked Aadhar card, handset details, and many others. Moreover, machine learning can classify the fraud users available in the network by analyzing their earlier behavior. Classification and anomaly detection is the best combination for recognizing suspicious transactions. Banking transactions create massive amounts of data with several features such as transaction ID, amount, account type, transaction branch, source bank, destination bank, transaction date and time, and so on. Thus, it is essential to protect this data using some recent technologies. N. Dhieb et al. (Dhieb et al., 2020) proposed an ML-blockchain-based secure model for an insurance company that reduces human intervention, secures transactions, and alerts for suspicious transactions. The XGBoost machine learning algorithm has been used to predict client's risk, fraudulent transactions, and future behavior. Fig. 4.5 shows the ML-blockchain-based model for securing an insurance company's blockchain network where data containing customer information is constantly fed to a machine learning model to improve the accuracy of the blockchain network.

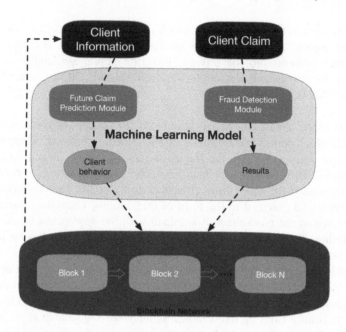

FIGURE 4.5 Machine learning model for blockchain network of an insurance company.

TABLE 4.2

Challenges and Benefits of Integrating Machine Learning and Blockchain

Blockchain Models	Smart Contracts	Distributed Network
Challenges in implementing ML	Secure execution of implementing ML	Heterogeneous data access
Process	Automatic execution of ML models through smart contracts	Implementation of access control rules through authentication protocol
Benefits	• Privacy • Model poisoning protection • Trust	• Trust • Data poisoning protection • Trust

Although the integration of ML and blockchain provides the highest level of security, many challenges should be considered while implementing them together. Table 4.2 provides the challenges and benefits of their integration.

4.6 THE PROPOSED FRAMEWORK

Blockchain is a decentralized network for peer-to-peer communication for secure transactions. As we discussed above, blockchain provides secure communication without the participation of any third party. Therefore, blockchain gives a secure

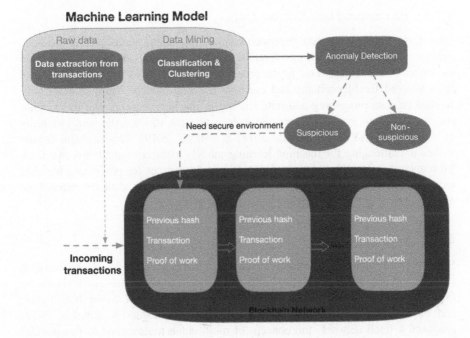

FIGURE 4.6 Proposed ML-blockchain framework for secure transactions.

network for funds transfer between two users. Fig. 4.6 provides the overall architecture of the proposed ML-Blockchain model for secure banking transactions.

We discussed the benefits of machine learning and blockchain and their integration into the banking sector in Sections 4.3–4.5. Machine learning provides automation of tasks and decision making where trained models will extract the raw data from high-volume transactions. Support vector machines (SVMs) and decision trees have been used here to solve classification problems or classify suspicious and non-suspicious transactions. Classification and decision trees provide the best combination for solving classification and regression problems. The machine will be trained for anomaly detection or to identify the suspicious and non-suspicious users by predicting their future behaviors depending on their past behaviors. Then, suspicious transactions are fed to the blockchain network to make them more secure. Thus, the proposed model helps to reduce fraudulent transactions over the network and make the banking transactions secure.

4.7 FUTURE RESEARCH DIRECTIONS

Integration of blockchain and machine learning is an emerging area of research for communication and networking systems with many challenges and open issues that need to be explored further. This section discusses a few open challenges and future research directions about the performance of blockchain and machine learning in secure banking transactions.

4.7.1 PROCESSING HIGH-VOLUME DATA

Processing high-volume data generated from various applications such as medical, cybersecurity, Internet of Things, fraud detections, and many others is very useful in the current era or future. Due to the processing capabilities of big data, it has also been adopted for blockchains and machine learning models. Many authors have worked on data processing and data sharing in machine learning and blockchain-secure healthcare systems where blockchain ensures the security and reliability of shared data (AVRP & Baruah, 2018; Zhu et al., 2019). This research further makes it challenging for machine learning models to explore unlabeled raw data. Moreover, data labeling, storing, and computing resources for processing big data require powerful processors and thus, the adoption of big data for blockchain and machine learning is a challenging area for research.

4.7.2 SCALABILITY ISSUES

Scalability of blockchain networks causes bottleneck situations in networking systems and requires lots of effort from researchers and academicians. It should be fast and scalable to process and store high-volume data in IoT-based, health care, and blockchain-based banking networks. In 2019, Rakshit (A. Rakshit, 2019) proposed a fetch network, the concept of multi-chain transactions to run parallel transactions. Transactions are dispersed among different groups, which further operate the transaction using different processing resources to maintain and make the network faster. Thus, the miner who sits in the blockchain network will solve the puzzle by processing the transactions in parallel rather than solving hashing problems. Machine learning also plays an important role in training the model to select appropriate resource lanes for transactions. Training ML models for this scalable blockchain network is very challenging.

4.7.3 RESOURCE MANAGEMENT

Resource management is a very interesting and signification area for future research where researchers should manage the resources efficiently over the network. Resource management includes resource allocation, resource scheduling, and re-source computation. Resource management in blockchain deals with many research issues, such as optimal allocation algorithm should be designed to select the appropriate mining node. Another issue is access control and used to provide guaranteed quality of services to users. Access control can also use ML models to collect accurate estimations of users' requirements and their required services. The implementation of access control in blockchain networks using machine learning model is a challenging task.

4.8 CONCLUSION

This chapter discusses the blockchain, its applications, and the benefits of block-chain in the banking sector. We also discussed the integration of machine learning and blockchain for a secure banking environment that has become a new era of security in communications and networks. We first gave an overview of machine learning and blockchain, basic concepts, and supported literature for blockchain and secure banking. Then we presented different models for integrating blockchain and machine learning, including target areas for attackers in machine learning models. We also introduced ML, a blockchain-based network for an insurance company to provide a secure blockchain environment to their organization. Then, we discussed the benefits and challenges of the integration of ML-blockchain network. We also proposed one blockchain-ML-based framework for secure banking, which we will implement in further research. This chapter gives a brief synopsis to researchers and academicians about the integration of ML blockchain and how to use this integration on a different application.

The integration of ML blockchain is a very broad area for research along with many challenges that need to be addressed. This chapter briefly discusses machine learning, blockchain, and their integration toward secure banking.

REFERENCES

Abu-Salih, B., Al-Tawil, M., Aljarah, I., Faris, H., Wongthongtham, P., Chan, K. Y., & Beheshti, A. (2021). Relational learning analysis of social politics using knowledge graph embedding. *Data Mining and Knowledge Discovery*, 35(4), 1497–1536. 10.1007/s10618-021-00760-w

Alimolaei, S. (2015). An intelligent system for user behavior detection in Internet Banking. In *4th Iranian Joint Congress on Fuzzy and Intelligent Systems (CFIS)*, 1–5. 10.1109/CFIS.2015.7391642

Alqaralleh, B. A. Y., Vaiyapuri, T., Parvathy, V. S., Gupta, D., Khanna, A., & Shankar, K. (2021). Blockchain-assisted secure image transmission and diagnosis model on Internet of Medical Things Environment. *Personal and Ubiquitous Computing*. 10.1007/s00779-021-01543-2

AVRP, S., & Baruah, P. K. (2018). Blended learning-assimilating authentic data into deep learning models. In *IEEE 25th International Conference on High Performance Computing Workshops (HiPCW)*, 75–80. 10.1109/HiPCW.2018.8634015

Bagga, P., Sutrala, A. K., Das, A. K., & Vijayakumar, P. (2021). Blockchain-based batch authentication protocol for Internet of Vehicles. *Journal of Systems Architecture*, 113, 101877. 10.1016/j.sysarc.2020.101877

Bhalekar, P. D., & Shaikh, M. Z. (2019). Machine learning: Survey, types and challenges. *International Research Journal of Engineering and Technology*, 6(3), 8131–8136.

Bhushan, B., Khamparia, A., Sagayam, K. M., Sharma, S. K., Ahad, M. A., & Debnath, N. C. (2020). Blockchain for smart cities: A review of architectures, integration trends and future research directions. *Sustainable Cities and Society*, 61, 102360. 10.1016/j.scs.2020.102360

Boughaci, D., & Alkhawaldeh, A. A. K. (2020). Enhancing the security of financial transactions in Blockchain by using machine learning techniques: Towards a sophisticated security tool for banking and finance. In *1st International Conference of Smart Systems and Emerging Technologies (SMARTTECH)*, 110–115. 10.1109/SMART-TECH49988.2020.00038

businesstoday (2022). *India saw 229 banking frauds per day in FY21, less than 1% amount recovered*. Https://Www.Businesstoday.in/Union-Budget-2022/Banking/Story/India-

Saw-229-Banking-Frauds-per-Day-in-Fy21-Less-than-1-Amount-Recovered-315685-2021-12-15.

Casino, F., & Patsakis, C. (2020). An efficient blockchain-based privacy-preserving collaborative filtering architecture. *IEEE Transactions on Engineering Management*, *67*(4), 1501–1513. 10.1109/TEM.2019.2944279

Cui, J., Yan, C., & Wang, C. (2021). ReMEMBeR: Ranking metric embedding-based multicontextual behavior profiling for online banking fraud detection. *IEEE Transactions on Computational Social Systems*, *8*(3), 643–654. 10.1109/TCSS.2021.3052950

Deng, S., Wang, C., Wang, M., & Sun, Z. (2019). A gradient boosting decision tree approach for insider trading identification: An empirical model evaluation of China stock market. *Applied Soft Computing*, *83*, 105652. 10.1016/j.asoc.2019.105652

Dhieb, N., Ghazzai, H., Besbes, H., & Massoud, Y. (2020). A secure AI-driven architecture for automated insurance systems: Fraud detection and risk measurement. *IEEE Access*, *8*, 58546–58558. 10.1109/ACCESS.2020.2983300

Donepudi, P. K. (2017). AI and machine learning in banking: A systematic literature review. *Asian Journal of Applied Science and Engineering*, *6*(3), 157–162.

El-Latif, A. A. A., Maleh, Y., Petrocchi, M., & Casola, V. (2022). Guest Editorial: Advanced computing and blockchain applications for critical industrial IoT. *IEEE Transactions on Industrial Informatics*, *18*, 8282–8286. 10.1109/TII.2022.3183443

Injadat, M., Moubayed, A., Nassif, A. B., & Shami, A. (2021). Machine learning towards intelligent systems: Applications, challenges, and opportunities. *Artificial Intelligence Review*, *54*(5), 3299–3348. 10.1007/s10462-020-09948-w

Khan, M. A., & Salah, K. (2018). IoT security: Review, blockchain solutions, and open challenges. *Future Generation Computer Systems*, *82*, 395–411. 10.1016/j.future.2017.11.022

Lisi, A., de Salve, A., Mori, P., Ricci, L., & Fabrizi, S. (2021). Rewarding reviews with tokens: An Ethereum-based approach. *Future Generation Computer Systems*, *120*, 36–54. 10.1016/j.future.2021.02.003

Liu, Y., Yu, F. R., Li, X., Ji, H., & Leung, V. C. M. (2020). Blockchain and machine learning for communications and networking systems. *IEEE Communications Surveys & Tutorials*, *22*(2), 1392–1431. 10.1109/COMST.2020.2975911

Maleh, Y., Baddi, Y., Alazab, M., Tawalbeh, L., & Romdhani, I. (2021). *Artificial Intelligence and Blockchain for Future Cybersecurity Applications*. Springer. 10.1007/978-3-030-74575-2

Maleh, Y., Lakkineni, S., Tawalbeh, L., & AbdEl-Latif, A. A. (2022). Blockchain for cyber-physical systems: Challenges and applications. In Y. Maleh, L. Tawalbeh, S. Motahhir, & A. S. Hafid (Eds.), *Advances in Blockchain Technology for Cyber Physical Systems* (pp. 11–59). Springer International Publishing. 10.1007/978-3-030-93646-4_2

Maleh, Y., Shojafar, M., Alazab, M., & Romdhani, I. (2020). *Blockchain for Cybersecurity and Privacy: Architectures, Challenges, and Applications*. CRC press. 10.1201/9780429324932

Rakshit, A., & Kumar, S. (2019). Fraud detection: A review on blockchain. *International Research Journal of Engineering and Technology*, *9*(1), 1040–1050.

Rouhollahi, Z. (2021). *Towards Artificial Intelligence Enabled Financial Crime Detection*. http://arxiv.org/abs/2105.10866

Sanober, S., Alam, I., Pande, S., Arslan, F., Rane, K. P., Singh, B. K., Khamparia, A., & Shabaz, M. (2021). An enhanced secure deep learning algorithm for fraud detection in wireless communication. *Wireless Communications and Mobile Computing*, *2021*, 6079582. 10.1155/2021/6079582

Viji, S., Kannan, R., & Jayalashmi, N. Y. (2021). Intelligent anomaly detection model for ATM booth surveillance using machine learning algorithm: Intelligent ATM surveillance model. In *International Conference on Computing, Communication, and Intelligent Systems (ICCCIS)*, 1007–1012. 10.1109/ICCCIS51004.2021.9397103

Wang, S., Huang, C., Li, J., Yuan, Y., & Wang, F.-Y. (2019). Decentralized construction of knowledge graphs for deep recommender systems based on blockchain-powered smart contracts. *IEEE Access*, 7, 136951–136961. 10.1109/ACCESS.2019.2942338

Yang, J., Tang, Y., & Beheshti, A. (2021). Design methodology for service-based data product sharing and trading. In M. Aiello, A. Bouguettaya, D. A. Tamburri, & W.-J. van den Heuvel (Eds.), *Next-Gen Digital Services. A Retrospective and Roadmap for Service Computing of the Future: Essays Dedicated to Michael Papazoglou on the Occasion of His 65th Birthday and His Retirement* (pp. 221–235). Springer International Publishing. 10.1007/978-3-030-73203-5_17

Yassine M. (2020). Machine learning techniques for IoT intrusions detection in aerospace cyber-physical systems. *Machine Learning and Data Mining in Aerospace Technology*, 836. 10.1007/978-3-030-20212-5_11

Zhu, L., Dong, H., Shen, M., & Gai, K. (2019). An incentive mechanism using shapley value for blockchain-based medical data sharing. In *IEEE 5th International Conference on Big Data Security on Cloud (BigDataSecurity), IEEE International Conference on High Performance and Smart Computing, (HPSC) and IEEE International Conference on Intelligent Data and Security (IDS)*, 113–118. 10.1109/BigDataSecurity-HPSC-IDS.2019.00030

5 Machine Learning Techniques for Fault Tolerance Management

Harinahalli Lokesh Gururaj
Department of Information Technology, Manipal Institute of
Technology Bengaluru, Manipal Academy of Higher
Education, Manipal, India

Francesco Flammini
University of Applied Sciences and Arts of Southern
Switzerland (CH)

*Beekanahalli Harish Swathi, Nandini Nagaraj,
and Sunil Kumar Byalaru Ramesh*
Department of CSE, Vidyavardhaka College of Engineering,
Mysuru, Karnataka

CONTENTS

5.1 INTRODUCTION

Fault tolerance is used in communication systems. In the fastest development of the Internet technologies, a fault-tolerance mechanism is required to provide high opportunity and high accuracy in a system. And it is particularly prominent in distributed network systems. In general, it is important in a large-scale environment. Fault tolerance approaches can be classified into two types, proactive and reactive. Proactive approaches predict errors, faults, and failures and replace the

DOI: 10.1201/9781003319917-7

suspected components. Reactive approaches reduce the effect of faults by taking necessary actions. Some fault treatment policies can also prevent faults from being reactivated. Usually, in a distributed system, users want the system to remain operational despite technical failures, even if some of the participants of these network systems have crashed. With a large number of participants and long running time, the probability that the hosts crash during the execution is inevitable, regardless of the physical reliability of each host. Thus, an effective system must be designed and executed so that the system can seamlessly tolerate a reasonable number of host failures, and the occurrence of a good number of host failures is acceptable. Failure detection and process monitoring are the basic components of most techniques for fault-tolerance (tolerating failures) in distributed network systems. Such as intermediate system to intermediate system (IS-IS), ensemble, transits, and air traffic control systems. Now, how to design failure detectors over local networks is a relatively well-known issue, but it is still far from being a solved problem with large-scale systems. Because a large-scale distributed system has lots of difficulties, which need to be addressed if we simulate them as a wired network environment, such as the potentially very large number of monitored processes, the higher probability of message loss, the ever-changing topology of the system, and the high unpredictability of message delays, all the above prominent factors fail to be addressed by the traditional solutions. Failure detectors should be executed as a typical generic service shared among distributed applications rather than redundant ad hoc network implementations for effective communication in large-scale distributed network systems and their importance.

If such a generic service can be achieved, it is straightforward to apply failure detectors in any application to ensure the fault tolerance requirement. Although many ground-breaking advances have been made in failure detection, such as service remains on a distant horizon. There are two main reasons for fault: node failure and malicious error. Different types of failure, such as hardware failure and software failure, can be found. Fault tolerance is a setup or configuration that prevents a PC or community device from failing in the event of an unexpected hassle or error, to make a laptop or community fault-tolerant calls for that the client or industrial employer business organization to anticipate how a computer or network tool can also fail and take steps that assist save you that kind of failure.

Communication infrastructure called network-on-chip, for routing the data across the chip it needs a link component and modular router, reactive fault tolerance techniques are commonly used, these systems are affected when the error occurs (Wang et al., 2019). Anomaly detection techniques are compared based on their effectiveness in observing the fault tolerance mechanism based on the anomalies. These anomalies are accurately detected before failure occurs while detecting types of anomalies (Jin et al., 2018).

Fault tolerance has improved the accuracy and availability of the system. Three necessary terms are used in fault tolerance, fault, error, and failure, as shown in Fig. 5.1 (Khalil et al., 2020). Fig. 5.1 shows that a system is said to fail when it does not fulfill the requirements. An error is part of the system state that may lead to failure and causes of a fault.

Causes   Result

FIGURE 5.1   Relation diagram of fault, error, and failure.

5.2   RELATED WORK

In this section, we briefly discussed existing methodologies and their contributions. Ke Wang et al. (Wang et al., 2019) proposed basic transmission for multi-core frameworks on the network that are referred to as network-on-chip (NOC), based on a system on chip architecture (SOC). This technology is exposed in various fields such as fault mechanisms and timing errors. This chapter proposed a proactive fault tolerance technique with reinforcement learning to improve noise performance and fault tolerance. They determine the proactive error approach system for effectively finding an error and revising those errors in a router and processing of transportation. Here, the decision tree algorithm is used. This results in improving noise performance while using different fault strategies. One is selected as optimal among various fault tolerance strategies, reducing overall network consumption and latency.

Srinikethan Madapuzi Srinivasan et al. (Srinivasan & Truong-Huu, 2019) proposed three phases of the machine learning procedure. In particular, machine learning–based link fault identification and localization (ML-LFIL) recognizes and restricts connect failure by breaking down the estimations caught from the typical traffic streams, including the total flow rate and packet loss. ML-LFIL works based on three strategies. First, it identifies the disconnection in a node. A second strategy determines the failure of a connection. The third stage helps to reconnect the node. Here three algorithms are utilized. The support vector machine helps isolate the data in two different classes by identifying the ideal isolating hyperplane. Multilayer perceptron (MLP) is the backpropagation algorithm used for training the neural network. Random forest (RF) is a classifier algorithm to construct the decision tree. These algorithms train the learning model based on the mininet platform. The outcome shows that ML-LFIL is superior in distinguishing proof and confinement of connection issues with up to 97% precision.

Srinikethan Madapuzi Srinivasan et al. (Srinivasan et al., 2018) proposed traffic engineering based on a machine learning approach to find the current failure in the link node. Machine learning algorithms adopt passive techniques, and a propagation mechanism is used to evaluate network traffic behavior. Three different machine learning algorithms train the model. Naive-Bayes: it has low complexity during forecasting and training. Logistic regression: here, the hypothesis performs between the input features and output variable in the prediction process. Support vector machine: separates the information and focuses on two classes. Decision tree (DT): it can be classified as non-straight focuses on different direct surface limits. Random forest: it helps recognize the significant highlights from the informational preparation index. These algorithms are helping to train the learning model in the mininet platform with the iperf3 tool.

The results show that a random decision tree algorithm outperforms other algorithms for both topologies with a minimum accuracy in localizing link failures among the examined machine learning algorithms.

Chaochao Feng et al. (Feng et al., 2010) proposed two models, the NOC architecture model, and the fault model. Network-on-chip architecture is based on the Nostrum (Wang et al., 2019). The borderline that separates the network on chip architecture from 2D mesh topology is that it connects the output to the input of the same switch. Model faults can be classified into constant fault or defective links in fault. The input port number is similar to the number of output ports in the deflection switch. Connecting all four ties on it, the switch fault is patterned. As long as the network is not dismantled, the terror area can be in any shape. After modeling, the next step is to apply a reconfigurable fault-tolerant deflection routing algorithm. It contains Q routing, fault-tolerant deflection routing algorithm (FTDR), and hierarchical Q-learning deflection routing algorithm (FTDR-H). The Q-learning strategy is utilized to reform the routing table by the deflection routing algorithm proposed in the paper to evade errors. It is impervious to the form of a lapse zone. FTDR Algorithm and FTDR-H Algorithm overshadows other defecting routing algorithms.

Tram Truong-Huu et al. (Truong-Huu et al., 2019) proposed a machine learning approach based on traffic engineering (TE) for quick and versatile loss recuperation. The backup path is calculated for each primary path, and the best backup path is selected with that maximum goodness value. It is determined based on three attributes: packet loss ratio, round-trip delay, and aggregate flow size apprehended at both source and destination. In this paper, the proposed model is trained by various machine learning methods, such as gradient boosting, linear regression, neural networks, decision tree, random forest, and support vector machine. The outcome of the approach proves that loss recuperation time is decreased.

Vindhya N S et al. (Vindhya & Vidyavathi, 2018) proposed adaptive routing algorithms with machine learning algorithms for predicting the failure in a NOC. The deficiency in NOC infers inaccessible connections in the system. In those two cases, the connection that can go disconnected are permanent faults, referred to as topological faults and temporary faults: data casualty during the transmission. Here they deliberate on fault tolerance based on the adaptive routing algorithm. Overcoming this, machine learning algorithms are used to predict the failure in a NOC. The decision tree of a machine learning algorithm is used. For construction, a decision tree is based on the attribute. They are temperature and link utilization with the relevant data set using the ID3 algorithm. The results show that NOC improves its exhibition and network inertness by 30%, based on the typical benchmark.

Zhilong Wang et al. (Wang et al., 2017) proposed a support vector machine; a double exponential smoothing algorithm is used for detecting errors or failure in an optical network. The main focus is to identify the failure in the optical network. To introduce a decision function from the support vectors in training data monitored by a support vector machine. It is a binary classification algorithm. The actual usage of the algorithm is to find a hyperplane line. In this method, first, the controller selects indicators from collecting the information. The indicators are input optical power, laser bias current, laser temperature offset, usual time, output optical power, and environment temperature. The second is to train the model and the third is to predict the model. The combination of SVM and DES gives a high precision of 85%.

Bashir Mohammed Irfan et al. (Mohammed et al., 2019) proposed fault tolerance redundancy. In the network, identification of node or connection failure infers fault detection. This paper mainly focuses on communication links. The fault is the origin of interconnection malfunction. The ML paradigm uses the existing information to deliver added importance to decision making. It effectively utilizes bandwidth and also increases redundancy characteristics of fault tolerance. Also, the complexity of setting up and planning opposes a deterministic and logical answer for this issue and real-time implementation. From standard defined supervised objects, there is an available data set created by parameter. Packet sniffers such as wire sharks are tools that extract network parameters to identify the most likely errors that occur.

5.2.1 COMPARATIVE ANALYSIS OF EXISTING METHODOLOGIES

In this section, Table 5.1 shows the performance of existing methodologies. We can see the system's accuracy from the results by considering the literature survey. There are some drawbacks and limitations. We mention the algorithms and their performance based on the above literature survey.

TABLE 5.1
Comparative Analysis of Other Methodologies

Number	Algorithms	Limitations	Accuracy
(Wang et al., 2019)	Reinforcement learning	Less accurate result due to fewer number of data sets taken.	75.24%
(Srinivasan & Truong-Huu, 2019)	ML-LFIL Backpropagation Random forest	They used both the training and testing data sets; hence, accuracy is low.	RF – 73%
(Srinivasan et al., 2018)	Support vector machine Random forest Decision tree	The method gives less accuracy.	Overall accuracy ranges from 43%–82%
(Feng et al., 2010)	Reinforcement learning FTDR, FTDR-H	Less accurate because the method is based only on training data sets.	72%
(Truong-Huu et al., 2019)	Decision tree Linear regression Neural networks Random forest Support vector machine	More time consumption with less accuracy	70%
(Vindhya & Vidyavathi, 2018)	Decision tree	Less data sets used.	Overall accuracy ranges from 60%–85%

5.3   SYSTEM ARCHITECTURE

Our proposed system helps identify the fault-tolerant node that fails due to particular faults and is quickly recovered and processed. Here we use machine learning techniques like SVM and KNN algorithms to detect and help recover the nodes. Here, SVM classifies the fault tolerance job or not. Besides, KNN is used to identify the distance of job failure. We energized the fault nodes and helped in further failure avoidance and helped it go to further processing.

Fig. 5.2 shows the design of the fault tolerance mechanism. Whenever the reference signal like a job is identified, the reference signal is moved to the references controller. Then the controller is diagnosed with the help of actuators (processers). Once fault diagnosis is verified, if there are any faults, it will be notified to the fault tolerance mechanism, and again reinitiated. So, this is a sequential process where the actuators will continuously monitor the job setup processing. And once it fails and reschedules the process, it gives the output if it is not rescheduled.

Supervised learning is somewhat common in classification problems because it's often the target that makes the computer learn the classification system we created. Recognizing numbers is a common example of learning to classify (Satheesh et al., 2020). In this chapter, a support vector machine, K-Nearest Neighbor, is used.

As shown in Fig. 5.3, first we have to upload the data set; once the data sets are uploaded, then it has to preprocess, to generate training data sets. Next, we consider those data sets are trained data sets. Then segregation is done for testing data. After this, classification is done based on the input data. By extracting features like the amount of support the application provides based on the SVM and KNN comparison, we discover fault tolerance and then restart the tasks to address them.

5.3.1   SUPPORT VECTOR MACHINE (SVM)

SVM is a supervised learning algorithm that builds a classifier that maximizes the margin of separation between samples in a training set. It can handle very large areas of features because SVM training is implemented in this way. The dimensions of the ranked vectors have no distinct effect on the performance of SVM as is on the performance of the traditional classifier (Pradhan, 2012; Widodo & Yang, 2007).

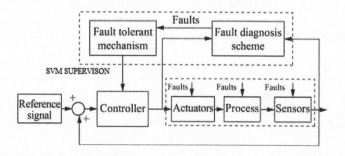

FIGURE 5.2   Architecture diagram.

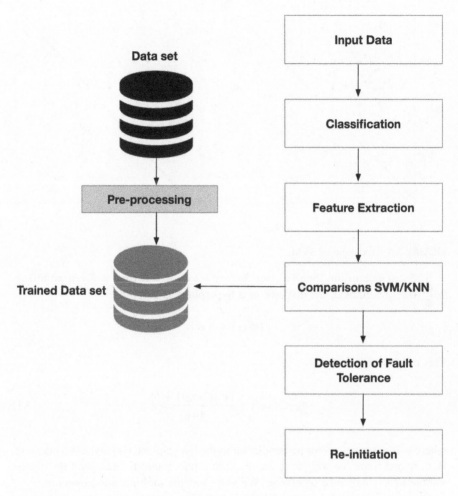

FIGURE 5.3 Steps performed in fault tolerance detection.

This is why it is noted to be particularly effective at high-volume classification problems. This will also benefit breakdowns in classification because the number of features it should have is the basis for fault diagnosis may not be limited. An example of a linear SVM classifier is shown in Fig. 5.4. We specifically focus on the binary classification problem in SVM, the most common case, where a data set has precisely two classes. The primary objective of SVM is to generate a hyperplane function f(x) between data samples in classes y0 (positive samples) and y1 (negative samples). Consider a training set.

Fig. 5.4(a) depicts an example of a linear classifier (solid line) generated using SVM. The samples that define the boundary (support vectors) are encircled. With samples (x1,y1),(x2,y2),(x3,y3), …, (xn,yn) where, $wTx + b \geq 0$ for $di = +1$ and $wTx + b < 0$ for $di = -1$. The objective of SVM is to find an optimal hyperplane.

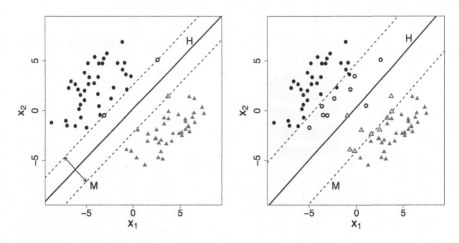

FIGURE 5.4 Example of SVM.

The distance of any line is given by, $ax + by + c = 0$ from a given point say, $(x0, y0)$ is taken as d, the distance of a hyperplane is given as:

$$wT\Phi(x) + b = 0.$$

This can be written as,

$$d_H(\emptyset(x_0)) = \frac{|w^t(\emptyset(x_0)) + b|}{\|w\|_2} \tag{5.1}$$

where w is a normal vector perpendicular to the hyper-plane f(x) and b is a constant. Both w and b are the weighting factors with a maximum distance with the closest sample unless indicated otherwise. We use (·) as the multiplication operator.

Where w is Euclidean norm for the length of w given by,

$$\|w\|_2 =: \sqrt{w_1^2 + w_1^2 + w_1^2 \ldots \ldots \ldots w_n^2} \tag{5.2}$$

Using Lagrangian multipliers, this problem can be formulated as quadratic programming (QP) optimization problem:

$$L(x, a) = f(x) - ag(x),$$

where $\nabla(x, a) = 0$

Partial derivatives wrt x recover the normal parallel constraint.
Partial derivatives λ recovers the g(x,y) = 0.
Generally,

$$L(x, a) = f(x) + \Sigma\_i a\_(i) g\_i(x)$$

Lagrangian formula defined as:

$$\min L_p = \|w\|^2 - \sum_{i=1}^{l} a_i y_i (x_i \cdot w + b) \sum_{i=1}^{i} a_i \tag{5.3}$$

Here, α represents Lagrange multipliers for each sample and L_p indicates the primordial form of the optimization problem.

ALGORITHM 1   SUPPORT VECTOR MACHINE [SVM]

Step 1. Collect the fault tolerance data set features for training.

Step 2. Use all the training samples to train and initialize them to SVM.

Step 3. Find the best fault tolerance feature for each feature and categorize them.

Step 4. Calculate the generalized on each related feature.

Step 5. Order the features and find the top percentage of useful features.

Step 6. Again, retrain the remaining samples in SVM.

Step 7. Binary features classification.

5.3.2   K-Nearest Neighbor (KNN)

K-Nearest Neighbor is a simple but effective method for classification. The main drawbacks regarding KNN include the first one is low efficiency, being a lazy learning method that it bans in many applications such as dynamic web mining for a large repository, and the second one is its dependence on choosing the best value of K (Guo et al., 2003).

ALGORITHM 2   K-NEAREST NEIGHBOR [KNN]

Step 1. Raw Data: In this stage, the historical fault-tolerance data is agitated from Kaggle or Gitup and this historical data is utilized to predict failure nodes.

Step 2. The next step is data pre-processing. The data pre-processing steps are listed below:

    a. Data transformation: Normalization.

    b. Data cleaning: Fill in missing null values.

    c. Data integration: Integration of data files.

After the data set is transformed into a pure data set, the data set is split into training and testing sets to evaluate. Here, the training values are taken as the more recent values. Testing data is kept as 20% of the total data set.

Step 3. The user now inputs the relevant data where it is to find and resolve fault tolerance. If it occurs, it is known as a test data set.

Step 4. Now, we classify the uploaded data set according to the system needs using the KNN algorithm and feature extraction after it is ready for the next step. Initialize the k value, which we take from test data set; from obtained k value, we calculate distance, consider nearest neighbor's, and make the classification (class).

Step 5. Feature Extraction: Only the features to be fed are extracted in this layer. We will choose the feature from the above classification process.

Step 6. Here, the data will be compared with the trained data using KNN and predict the fault tolerance and help the fault nodes to get re-initiated. The data obtained from the classification is mixed i.e., it is not supervised. Then, using KNN, we compare and make clusters to predict and analyze the node failure and help it re-energize.

As shown in Fig. 5.5, we have to initialize the k value as add value, the range between 20%. Then we calculate the distance of every job that appears in the network. Here, classify the jobs based on the distance through the radius. Located actuators are identified, and then we re-initiated the job classification for the server.

We come across the different machine learning algorithms in the existing systems with their performance. Among these, the KNN algorithm gives more accuracy (Zhu Kai Lu et al., 2013). In our project, we consider both KNN and SVM algorithms to analyze the fault tolerance in the network router. And these two algorithms give an accuracy of up to 95%.

5.4   RESULT ANALYSIS

In this section, each figure below represents the result of the proposed methodology. K-Nearest Neighbor and support vector machine are employed to analyze the fault tolerance of network routers. These algorithms effectively predict the failure in a node (Table 5.2).

Fig. 5.6 shows the specific iteration level, time cost, estimation for identifying the job process, and the radius frequency of hybrid data. These features are required for processing each job as average value and the accuracy for reinitiating the jobs. Finally, it defines a time cost investment for the jobs and the accuracy of a re-initialization of jobs.

Fig. 5.7 shows a graphical representation of the radius and distance of every job, which appears in the network and is also based on the job. So, this will help to classify the job, whether it has to reinitiate or not.

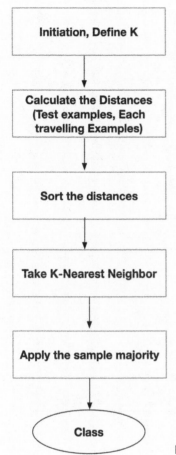

FIGURE 5.5   Processing of KNN algorithm.

TABLE 5.2
Experimental Setup

Item	Entity Used
Platform	Google Colab, Jupyter notebook
Data Generated	Yes, data has been generated at campus networks
Experiment	Iterative tests are conducted based on test and training data set
Pre-processing	Support vector machine (SVM) algorithm was used for data pre-processing

Fig. 5.8 shows the specific iteration level, time cost, estimation, and accuracy for identifying the job. These facial characteristics are necessary for the subject to a series of actions to achieve a result of each reinitiating the task. After some time, it delimits an opportunity cost investment for the task and the precision or correctness of a re-initialization of a task.

```
*** SVM model training finished ***
iter            = 8
time cost       = 0.0440 s
obj             = -0.3568
pData           = 77.7778 %
nData           = 22.2222 %
nSVs            = 3
radio of nSVs   = 6.6667 %
accuracy        = 91.1111 %

*** SVM model test finished ***

time cost       = 0.0040 s
accuracy        = 99.0476 %
```

FIGURE 5.6 Time cost with an accuracy of hybrid kernel.

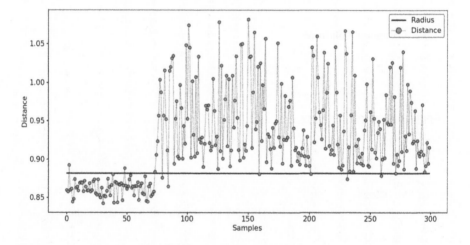

FIGURE 5.7 Radii with distance calculation using SVM for fault tolerance.

Fig. 5.9 indicates the heat map representation, because of the jobs that have been initiated in the scheduling of jobs. Here, slots or nodes are defined for the test data set, training data set, and support vector configured in the network.

Fig. 5.10 specifies the iteration, the time cost, and the accuracy of each node of a single kernel. These elements are required for converting each job as an average value and efficiency for reinitiating the jobs. Finally, it defines a time cost investment for the jobs and the accuracy of a re-initialization of jobs.

Fig. 5.11 shows the graphical representation of the radius and distance of every task presented in the network, establishing the job in a single throughput. So, this will categorize the task, whether it has to reinitiate or not.

Fig. 5.12 shows the area under the curve (AUC) calculation. It gives the calculation through analysis with the false-positive rate (FPR) and true positive rate

```
*** SVM model training finished ***

iter                = 13
time cost           = 0.0312 s
obj                 = -0.7767
pData               = 87.5000 %
nData               = 12.5000 %
nSVs                = 13
radio of nSVs       = 6.5000 %
accuracy            = 97.5000 %



*** SVM model test finished ***

time cost           = 0.0156 s
accuracy            = 96.6667 %


Calculating the grid (0100*0100) scores...

Grid scores completed. Time cost 3.0622 s
```

FIGURE 5.8 Time cost and accuracy linear kernel.

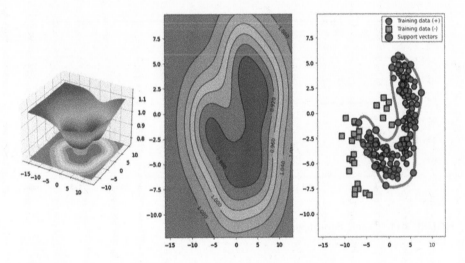

FIGURE 5.9 Fault tolerance of heat map generation using a kernel.

(TPR, also called sensitivity). Here it measures the classifier that can be used to distinguish between the classes that have been generated and the classes that have been terminated during the rescheduling of the jobs.

Fig. 5.13 depicts the graphical illustration of the radius and distance of each mission, which is presented within the network primarily based on the KNN model. The operation of KNN is based totally on the category of the nearest one or a few samples. The output of the KNN is the elegance label to the new sample, which is anticipated primarily based on one or extra nearest samples. The KNN effects may additionally deviate as it simplest underlines is the closest sample.

```
*** SVM model training finished
iter                  = 9
time cost             = 0.0469 s
obj                   = -0.7960
pData                 = 100.0000 %
nData                 = 0.0000 %
nSVs                  = 34
radio of nSVs         = 34.0000 %
accuracy              = 99.0000 %

*** SVM model test finished ***

time cost             = 0.0000 s
accuracy              = 96.3542 %
```

FIGURE 5.10 Time cost and accuracy of the single kernel.

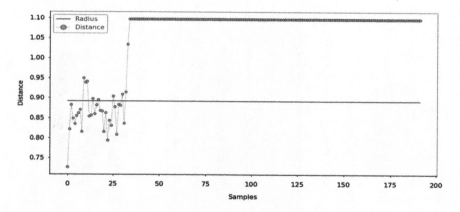

FIGURE 5.11 Single throughput.

Fig. 5.14 gives a graphical illustration of the radius and distance of each mission, which is presented within the network primarily based on the SVM model. The SVM models can solve problems with non-linear decision boundaries. The kernel function operation is required to identify the faulty nodes. The kernel functions commonly used in SVM are polynomial, Gaussian, and Radian bias.

Fig. 5.15 shows the accuracy comparison between SVM and KNN in identifying faulty nodes. SVM and KNN exemplify numerous important exchange-offs in device learning. SVM is less computationally worrying than KNN and is less difficult to interpret. However, it can pick out the most straightforward limited set of patterns. On the other hand, KNN can discover very complex patterns, but its output is tough to interpret. The comparison graph concludes that SVM has achieved swell accuracy compared to KNN.

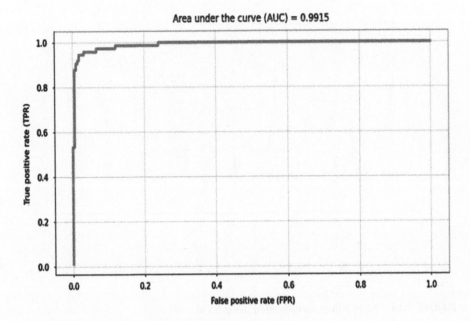

FIGURE 5.12   AUC calculation of nodes.

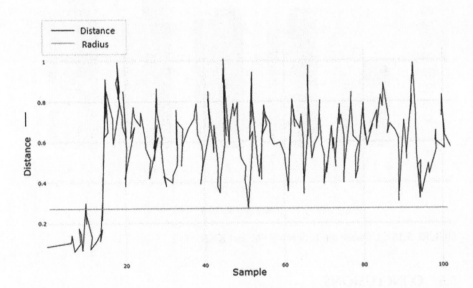

FIGURE 5.13   Node failure identification using KNN.

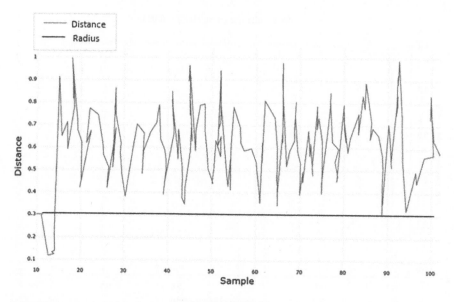

FIGURE 5.14 Node failure identification using SVM.

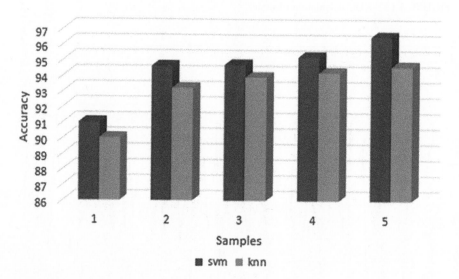

FIGURE 5.15 Comparison between SVM and KNN.

5.5 CONCLUSIONS

The proposed methodology uses SVM and KNN approaches to solve the fault-tolerance problem in jobs scheduled by considering the energy radius and distance. This chapter suggested methods that solve the problem of initiating jobs that are failing at the clusters. We have identified that each layer has its faults and fault-tolerance issues. We first explore the relative node fault failure detection, which is an important issue for supporting dependability in distributed systems, and often is an important performance bottleneck in the event of node failure. Here, we analyze the failure detection by considering the hybrid, kernel, and single node with an area under the curve (AUC) calculation, time cost using the machine learning technique, and process the failed nodes in a better solution in terms of reliability and energy effectively. This means that to achieve fault tolerance, different aspects and features must be targeted, and no single-focused technology will be able to provide the reliability expected in commercial networks. SVM and KNN are effectively used for fault tolerance analysis of network routers using machine learning techniques.

REFERENCES

Abu Alsheikh, M., Lin, S., Niyato, D., & Tan, H.-P. (2014). Machine learning in wireless sensor networks: Algorithms, strategies, and applications. *IEEE Communications Surveys & Tutorials*, *16*(4), 1996–2018.

Alsultanny, Y. A. (2013). Fault tolerance effect on computer networks availability. In IADIS International Conference e-Learning.

Ayodele, T. O. (2010). Types of machine learning algorithms. InTech.

Boutaba, R., Salahuddin, M. A., Limam, N., Ayoubi, S., Estrada-Solan, N. S. F., & Caicedo, O. M. (2018). A comprehensive survey on machine learning for networking: Evolution, applications, and research opportunities. *Journal of Internet Service and Application*, *9*, 16.

Chouikhi, S., Korbi, I. e. E., Ghamri-Doudane, Y., & Saidane, L. A. (2015). A survey on fault tolerance in small and large scale wireless sensor networks. *Computer Communications*, *69*, 22–37.

Dey, A. (2016). Machine learning algorithms: A review. *International Journal of Computer Science and Information Technologies*, *7*(3), 1174–1179.

Feng, C., Lu, Z., Jantsch, A., Li, J., & Zhang, M. (December 4, 2010). A reconfigurable fault-tolerant deflection routing algorithm based on reain forcement learning for network-on-chip (Noc). In NoCArc'10, Atlanta, Georgia, USA.

Feng, Y., Tang, S., & Dai, G. (2011). Fault-tolerant data aggregation scheduling with local information in wireless sensor networks. *Tsinghua Science and Technology*, *16*(5), 451–463.

Guo, G., Wang, H., Bell, D., Bi, Y., & Greer, K. (2003). KNN model-based approach in classification. In R. Meersman, Z. Tari, & D.C. Schmidt (Eds.), *On the Move to Meaningful Internet Systems 2003: CoopIS, DOA, and ODBASE. OTM 2003. Lecture Notes in Computer Science*, vol. 2888. Berlin, Heidelberg: Springer.

Jin, S., Zhang, Z., & Chakrabarty, K. (2018). Towards predictive fault tolerance in a core-router system: Anomaly detection using correlation-based time-series analysis. *IEEE Transactions on Computer-Aided Design of Integrated Circuits and Systems*, *37*(10), 2111–2124.

Karunaratne, S., & Gacanin, H. (2019). An overview of machine learning approaches in wireless mesh networks. *IEEE Communications Magazine*, *57*(4), 102–108.

Khalil, K., Eldash, O., Kumar, A., & Bayoumi, M. (2020). Machine learning-based approach for hardware faults prediction. *IEEE Transactions on Circuits and Systems I: Regular Papers*, *67*(11), 3880–3892.

Khan, S. A., Bölöni, L., & Turgut, D. (2015). Bridge protection algorithms technique for fault tolerance in sensor networks. *Ad Hoc Networks*, *24*(part A), 186–199.

Lee, M.-H., & Choi, Y.-H. (2008). Fault detection of wireless sensor networks. *Computer Communications, 31*(14), 3469–3475.

Mohammed, B., Awan, I., Ugail, H., & Younas, M. (2019). Failure prediction using machine learning in a virtualized HPC system and application. *Cluster Computing, 22,* 471–485.

Mohapatra, H., & Rath, A. K. (2020). Fault-tolerant mechanism for wireless sensor network. *IET Wireless Sensor Systems, 10*(1), 23–30.

Pradhan, A. (2012). Support vector machine—A survey. *International Journal of Emerging Technology and Advanced Engineering, 2*(8), 82–85.

Qiao, A., Aragam, B., Zhang, B., Xing, E. P. (2019). Fault tolerance in iterative-convergent machine learning. In Proceedings of the 36th International Conference on Machine Learning, California, PMLR97, 5220–5230.

Radetzki, M., Feng, C., Zhao, X., & Jantsch, A. (2013). Methods for fault tolerance in networks-on-chip. *ACM Computer Survey, 46*(1), 1–38.

Satheesh, N., Rathnamma, M. V., Rajeshkumar, G., Vidya Sagar, P., Dadheech, P., Dogiwal, S. R., Velayutham, P., & Sengan, S. (2020). Flow-based anomaly intrusion detection using machine learning model with software defined networking for OpenFlow network. *Micro Processors and Microsystems, 79,* 103285.

Sharma, D., & Chandra, P. (29 October 2017). Software fault prediction using machine-learning techniques. *Smart Computing and Informatics, 78,* 541–549.

Srinivasan, S. M., & Truong-Huu, T. (2019). Machine learning-based link fault identification and localization in complex networks. *IEEE Internet of Things Journal, 6*(4), 6556–6566.

Srinivasan, S. M., Truong-Huu, T., & Gurusamy, M. (Augst 6–8, 2018). TE-based machine learning techniques for link fault localization in complex networks. In IEEE 6th International Conference on Future Internet of Things and Cloud, Barcelona, Spain.

Truong-Huu, T., Prathap, P., Mohan, P. M., & Gurusamy, M. (11 July 2019). Fast and adaptive failure recovery using machine learning in software defined networks. In IEEE International Conference on Communications Workshops.

Vindhya, N. S., & Vidyavathi, B. M. (December 14–15, 2018). Network on chip: A review of fault tolerant adaptive routing algorithm. In 3rd International Conference on Electrical, Electronics, Communication, Computer Technologies and Optimization Techniques.

Wang, K., Louri, A., Karanth, A., & Bunescu, R. (March 25–29, 2019). High-performance, energy-efficient, fault-tolerant network-on-chip design using reinforcement learning. In Design, Automation & Test in Europe Conference & Exhibition, Florence, Italy.

Wang, M., Cui, Y., Wang, X., Xiao, S., & Jiang, J. (2018). Machine learning for networking: Workflow, advances, and opportunities. *IEEE Network, 32*(2), 92–99.

Wang, T.-Y., Han, Y. S., Varshney, P. K., & Chen, P.-N. (2005). Distributed fault-tolerant classification in wireless sensor networks. *IEEE Journal on Selected Areas in Communications, 23*(4), 724–734.

Wang, Z., Zhang, M., Wang, D., Song, C., Liu, M., Li, J., Lou, L., & Liu, Z. (2017). Failure prediction using machine learning and time series in optical network. *Optics Express, 25*(16), 18553–18565.

Widodo, A., & Yang, B.-S. (2007). Support vector machine in machine condition monitoring and fault diagnosis. *Mechanical Systems and Signal Processing, 21*(6), 2560–2574.

Zhu Kai Lu, G., Li, X., & Lu, K. (25 May 2013). A fault-tolerant K-means algorithm based on storage-class memory. In IEEE 4th International Conference on Software Engineering and Service Science (ICSESS).

6 An Efficient Approach for Image Detection and Recognition Using Artificial Intelligence in Cyber-Physical Systems

Musarrat Saberin Nipun, Rejwan Bin Sulaiman, and Amer Kareem
University of Bedfordshire, United Kingdom

CONTENTS

DOI: 10.1201/9781003319917-8

6.1   INTRODUCTION

In this 21st century, face detection and recognition have become an important and exciting area of research for students and experts. This is because of its worth in real life and the rapidly growing demands of information and technology for a comfortable and secure lifestyle. Every day scientists are discovering new technologies to ensure the highest comfort of human life and security in every purpose. Face detection and recognition have become more popular recently because of the invention of active algorithms, a big database of facial images, and the performance measurements algorithm of face recognition methods (Phillips et al., 2000). Security systems are more dependent on face recognition software because compared to normal security systems, biometrical expertise always provides a higher level of security (Ballad et al., 2011).

Though there are many different options for biometric security like fingerprints and retina scans, all these face recognition is accepted by all individuals due to their deferential and non-invasive identification and validation (D. R. Patel, 2008). For example, in fingerprint recognition, a person can hurt his finger and cannot be able to access it where required. In the worst case, a terrorist can cut the finger and use it for access where fingerprint recognition is needed. For this reason, the face is the most trusted security system for individuals.

Many experts used different techniques and algorithms for the face recognition system to ensure the improvement and efficiency of the system. Implementing some languages is not very satisfactory, like java, as the processing speed was slow and had some complex issues. This project uses python as a programming language, and the standard API OpenCV library is utilized. This paper will detect and recognize movie actor images as its main goal is to apply the different algorithms for face detection and recognition, and then show the results achieved from them and then analyze the different results. Finally, it will provide a conclusion about which algorithm serves better. In other words, this work can be considered a research-based project, providing information on different implementation techniques and comparisons.

Researchers are trying to solve methodological barriers that limit AI's real-time application. Various research has been done in different domains such as information efficiency (Bin Sulaiman et al., 2022), biometric identification (Vitaly Schetinin et al., 2018), diabetes prediction (Hassan et al., 2021), customer assistant chatbot (Rejwan Bin Sulaiman, 2022), pneumonia detection (Amer Kareem et al., 2022), and credit card fraud detection (Rejwan B.S., 2022). Despite these limitations, researchers are working to gain the ML power to detect images in real-time videos.

6.1.1 PROJECT BACKGROUND

When choosing the topic for a project I analyze different ideas and finally come up with the most interesting and emerging idea that would certainly be a great resource for the researcher who works in artificial intelligence. At first, we studied some more research papers and watched tutorials to learn more about the face detection and recognition project. While researching, we could not find any specific paper where all the face detection and recognition techniques are explained elaborately with examples and provides the implementation information. Moreover, a comparison of all the techniques and their results is not available in one paper. Though, it takes more time to research the topic; finally, we planned for a project which would be more resourceful as this will represent every basic concept of face detection and recognition project and will also provide comparative analysis within the methods. This paper aims to build an application-based project which also provides useful research data, so that, in the future, those who are willing to work with this kind of project, can have a clear concept by reading this paper.

We prepared our project proposal based on the face detection and recognition project to complete our goal. We take the movie actor images to make the research and implementation more interesting. Though we are implementing the system, this project can be said to be a research project as well, as we are showing all the techniques and their efficiency analysis for face recognition.

Another reason for choosing this topic is its popularity of this subject. For example, these face recognition systems are used for security purposes. Still, besides this, social networks, like Facebook, also provide this face recognition service when we upload or tag photos. So, nowadays, face recognition system is popularly being used in many sectors, and research about this will add extra value in terms of knowledge about artificial intelligence.

6.1.2 PROJECT AIM, SCOPE, AND OBJECTIVES

This proposed system will detect and recognize movie actors' faces from images.

One renowned and the publicly available movie has been selected for this implementation. Here, we selected the superhero movie *X-men* for experimenting with our project work. We used the images of the two main actors in that movie for face recognition. One is Hugh Jackman, who played the role of Wolverine, and another one is James McAvoy, who was the "professor" in that movie. From that movie, some images are publicly available in the cloud without any copyright issue, and we chose only those images to be used for our project. These two actors' images are being used to train the system for face recognition and as a test image to ensure that the algorithm recognizes the faces properly. A few more features are included in this project, including face detection from live video streaming.

The challenge of this project includes finding out the algorithm's lack when the system fails to show the expected result. It can happen if the video/image is not properly clear or there is a change in lighting. Another challenge is to find out how the system handled this failure. Comparing the algorithm's highest accuracy rate is also a big challenge.

Though face recognition is a very demanding research topic, there are still a lot of scopes to research on this subject and find a more efficient implementation method. This project will be helpful to those who have an interest in face recognition but are a beginner in this field. As this paper uses OpenCV, the most popular and efficient API for face detection and recognition, and implements the algorithm using one of the demanding programming languages, Python, it will help beginner students planning to make their career in deep learning/machine learning. Moreover, this paper not only shows the concepts and techniques of face recognition, but also provides the idea of implementation and clear comparison analysis to decide which algorithm is needed to be used in which situation. Besides this, this system will show the implementation using movie actors' faces, motivating the young learners about face recognition. The complete system can be used as a security system component where face detection and recognition are needed, such as in any shopping mall, retail shops, ATM booths, cars, banks, and even in homes with CCTV activated. So, daily face recognition system will increase, and an easy and efficient system will always be in demand.

6.2 LITERATURE REVIEW

When starting a project, one crucial requirement is gathering knowledge about other works on the same or similar subject. It helps to find out the difficulties and drawbacks of previous work, which need to be improved in future research. It also provides information about what technologies are currently available to implement the system and a brief idea of which one is more efficient and can be improved. The literature review is the broader meaning of deep analysis, finding logical proof, planning robust solutions, and reaching an efficient conclusion.

The face recognition process has a very rich background history. Much research has been done in the past few years on the need for an efficient face recognition system. The research goal was to introduce a more accurate face recognition system with less time and test and analyze the proposed system; also, to compare various face recognition algorithms previously tested by expertise.

The platform of face recognition algorithm was pioneered by Service and Kirby (lata, Y.V. et al., 2009), who followed the Eigenfaces approach for a face recognition system. (Ali, E.S. et al., 2021). Sirovich and Kirby implemented software that can identify a subject's head, compared the characteristics with other known faces it already had in its database, and then recognized it.

Another face recognition algorithm was invented, using independent component analysis done by Bartlet, Movellan and Sejnowski (Bazama, A. et al., 2021). Two types of algorithm methods have been in consideration for face recognition. One is PCA, which means principal component analysis, and another is ICA, independent component analysis. PCA is based on the idea of pixels, where important data of an image is stored in pairwise relationships (Bhattacharya, A., 2021). On the other hand, ICA is focused on the logic that some important data can contain high-order statistics. Finally, researchers Maryam Mollaee and Mohammad Hossein Moattar proposed an improved ICA model showing better facial recognition system accuracy (Sujay, S.N. et al., 2019).

The previous Eigenface method had a problem that it could not identify a face in different illumination conditions. To solve this problem, in 1996, using Linear Discriminant Analysis, a new method was developed for dimensional reduction, which is called Fisherface (Kirana, K.C. et al., 2018). A face detection algorithm was proposed by Viola and Jones using HAAR Cascade and AdaBoost (Smashing Magazine, 2019).

6.2.1 FACE RECOGNITION FROM A MOVIE ACTOR'S IMAGE

Most recently, other research has been done by Remigiusz Baran and Filip Rudzinski in 2016 (Ballad et al., 2011), similar to this one, that also recognized faces from the movie actor's image or video. Though the research plot is the same, this research took a different approach while implementing the system. That was based on a content discovery and delivery platform known as the IMCOP system (Baran & Zeja, 2015). IMCOP is an SOA-driven platform where the intelligent utilities that are needed for the face recognition system are implanted as REST (Representational State Transfer) web services, which is called IMCOP's Metadata Enhancement Service (MES). Every single MES service is processing a different task.

6.3 RESEARCH METHODOLOGY

A few methods are being used for face detection and face recognition. In this project, as we are using OpenCV, and we will implement all the renowned techniques for face detection and recognition, and from the achieved result, we will compare the accuracy of the techniques. The face detection and recognition methodologies are discussed in separate sections in this report.

6.3.1 RESEARCH METHODOLOGY FOR FACE DETECTION

Face detection has achieved more popularity due to its invention of real-time applications. Still, there is a lot of research going on in face detection, to make the algorithm more efficient and accurate. Face detection is not at all an easy task because it always includes faces and it is hard to detect all the variances of a face appeared; for example, pose variation, like a smile, no-smile, with hair, no hair, with a beard, no beard, etc. To handle these things, the choice of tools is always important, so we are using OpenCV here. OpenCV is a computer vision and machine learning software library mainly aimed at real-time computer vision and is open for all to use (Opencv.org, 2019). This library has more than 2500 algorithms, including machine learning tools for classification and clustering, image processing and vision algorithm, basic algorithms and drawing functions, and GUI and I/O functions for images and videos (Opencv.org, 2019). OpenCV library has some built-in pre-trained classifiers for detecting faces, eyes, and smiles, etc. Specifically, for face detection, OpenCV has two pre-trained classifiers:

1. HAAR C
2. LBP Cascade classifier

We will use them in our project and the details of these classifiers are discussed in this report.

6.4 HAAR CASCADE CLASSIFIER

Paul Viola and Michael Jones invented this algorithm. In this algorithm, a function is trained with different images. This function is called a cascade function. Images can be positive and negative. Images that include a face are called positive images and without a face are called negative images. This approach is mainly based on machine learning.

This algorithm has two stages, as follows:

1. **Selecting HAAR feature:** Assume that we have an input image. A large number of HAAR features are needed to get the facial features. That starts by extracting HAAR features from each image. To estimate a single feature one by one, each window has set on top of the image. This feature takes the sum of the pixels under the black part of the window and does the same for the white part. Then subtract the summation value gained from the white part of the window from the summation value gained from the black part of the window. By doing this subtraction, this feature gets a single value. After that, to calculate enough features, each window is set on all feasible locations of the image depending on the size.

2. **Creating an Integral Image:** This method creates an integral image to make the algorithm fast. Before this, excessive computation occurred while performing operations on all pixels. This integral image minimizes the computation rate only by four pixels. The region surrounding the eyes is darker than the region of the nose and cheeks. The first stage of features concentrates on this attribute. In the second stage, the features are based on the attribute that the bridge of the nose is lighter than the eyes.

6.4.1 EIGENFACES FACE RECOGNIZER

The Eigenfaces facial recognition method uses the principal component analysis technique, which marks a notable difference with the more classical methods, called geometric or local methods, which are based on the particularities of the analyzed face, and whose flaws lie in its lack of precision, as well as its sensitivity to information that is not relevant. The method used here is qualified as global, since the whole face is then analyzed. The main technique of this method is to extract the component which causes the most variation in an image. This component is called the principal component. Therefore, another name for this technique is principal component analysis. This is also called a holistic approach, and the prediction is based on the entire training set. If the images are from two different classes, this method could not provide any specific solution for these images. Here, a class means a person. This is a machine learning technique where grayscale pictures are used for training the recognizer.

When we look at any face, our brain automatically determines that all the parts of a face are not important to remember. It extracts the most unique and relevant data that it will use to recognize the face in the future. This algorithm also considers the same process. These recognizers first looked at the person's every training image and focused on that part of the face with maximum change. Then, it extracts the important and useful features from the face and reads the distinct features like eyes, nose, mouth, etc. It gathers information about the variance of the face and rejects that part of the face that is not important to memorize. For example, it focuses from eyes to nose or nose to mouth as there is a significant change. When it reads multiple faces, it memorizes these distinct features to recognize the face in the future and differentiate it from others. In this way, it not only memorizes the important data face but also, as it rejects the unimportant contents, it helps to save memory. The important components are called principal components, shown in the figure below. The principal component analysis (PCA) algorithm trains itself by extracting these components shown in the picture. This algorithm keeps a separate record of principal components for each face, which means it knows which principal components belong to which face.

In this algorithm, it is essential to have some lights in every image; also, the eyes need to be matched in every image. Another important thing to remember is that every image's number of pixels should be the same and in grayscale. For example, we can assume that a n × n pixels image where each row is joined to make a vector. As a result, it makes a $1 \times n^2$ matrix. Here, all the images that will be used for the training data set are stored in a single matrix, leading to a column matrix equivalent to the number of images. Then, to get an average human face, the matrix is standardized. Unique features of each face have been calculated by subtracting the average face from the image vector created for each image. Each of the columns in the resulting matrix represents the difference between each face from the average face. After this step, it is needed to compute the covariance matrix from the result matrix. From the training data, to find out the eigenvectors using principal component analysis, eigen analysis has been performed. In the result matrix where the covariance matrix has been found diagonal, it has the highest variance, which is considered the first eigenvector. Then, the second eigenvector's next highest variance is the second eigenvector, which is 90 degrees to the first one. Then, the next highest variation will be the third one. This process is going to be the same as this for further vectors. Here, each column is assumed to be an image and matches the face, and these faces are called eigenfaces. It takes an image as input to recognize a face and then resizes it to match the same dimension of the eigenface it already retrieved. When this algorithm gets a new image to feed, it repeats the same process on the image. It compares the components with the list of the components it already stored while training and search the best match with the given components and returns the recognition result.

This principal component analysis causes problems with large numbers. Another important fact of this algorithm is that it also considers light and shadow as important components when recognizing a face. Even the same face cannot be recognized if it is analyzed under diverse lighting conditions. This algorithm undermix the values while calculating the distribution and fails to be classified efficiently, which causes a problem while matching the features.

6.4.2   Fisherfaces Face Recognizer

The next algorithm is the Fisherfaces recognizer, a developed version of the previous one.

We discussed the process of eigenface face recognizer earlier, but it also has some deficiencies. For example, in eigenfaces, if the image has some slight changes, such as changes in lighting or shadow, it overlooks the other images. Still, this slight change is also an unimportant feature to consider. In the end, maybe it creates some features from the outside source, which is not important to consider, and for this, it may be unable to determine actual facial features.

Fisherfaces (Belhumeur et al., 1997) algorithm is similar to the eigenfaces algorithm. Still, it has some slightly different techniques than the eigenfaces method, which made it more developed. This algorithm also uses a holistic approach. It also uses the principal component analysis technique, but it changes that technique a bit as it takes into consideration classes. As it is described earlier, eigenfaces cannot differentiate two pictures from different classes during the training session. Still, Fisherfaces uses a method to differentiate two pictures from different classes. For this, it uses the Linear Discriminant Analysis method. The goal of using this method is to minimize the variation within a class by comparing the variation between the classes. To do this, it uses a total average of faces and takes the average per class.

Eigenfaces algorithm extracts important features that present all the persons' faces. Here, the Fisherfaces algorithm only extracts the features, which will help to differentiate one person from all others. This way, it brings out the differentiation features of a person from others and the features are not dominant on other features. Like the eigenface algorithm, Fisherfaces has some disadvantages too. Any slight changes in images from any outside source could create confusion within the features, which will hamper the accuracy rate. The outside source can be the change of light and shadow, as described earlier.

6.4.3   Local Binary Pattern Histograms (LBPH) Face Recognizer

The last algorithm we are going to discuss in this section is the local binary pattern.

The goal of this algorithm is to work with 3×3 pixel blocks. The difference between this one and the others we have already discussed is that this one is not a holistic approach though it requires grayscale images for training.

Previously, we discussed that both the features are unable to present a proper accuracy rate in face recognition due to the effect of light and shadow, and in real-life scenarios, it is impossible to confirm perfect light conditions in every image. To overcome this lacking, the LBPH face recognizer algorithm improved its functions.

LBPH does not look at the whole image. Rather, it searches for the local features of an image. Like the LBPH face detection techniques here, this algorithm compares each pixel with its neighboring pixel and searches the local construction of an image. It shifts an image by taking a 3×3 window. It compares the pixel of the center of that image to its neighboring image while shifting each local part of an image. The neighboring pixels with values lower than the center value are marked 1, otherwise 0. Then, the algorithms read that binary values maintain the clockwise order under a 3 × 3 window and make a binary pattern like 11100011, the local feature in some areas of the image. Then, the same process iterates in the whole image, and the algorithm gets a list of local binary patterns.

After that, the histogram part comes, which completes the algorithm for the face recognizer. After getting the list of local binary patterns, it is needed to convert them into a decimal number, shown in the above picture. Then, we can make a histogram with these decimal values.

Finally, in the training data, we will find one histogram for every face image, which means if we have 100 images for training data at the end, the LBPH face recognizer will find 100 histograms for each face and save them for face recognition in future. An important feature of this algorithm is that it can also track which histogram belongs to whom.

Finally, when we do the test data face recognition, this algorithm makes a new histogram for that test image. Then it compares that histogram with all the other histogram it already has from its training data set and find the best-matched histogram. It returns the person label associated with that histogram.

We will see this by implementing all the algorithms and comparing their results in the next sections.

6.5 SYSTEM IMPLEMENTATION

While finalizing the project ideas, we researched various software and languages used for face detection and recognition so that we could choose the best one for our project. Some more software like a visual studio and programming languages like C#, Java, etc., are popular for coding face detection and recognition. Still, after analyzing, we found out that OpenCV is providing the biggest library for face detection and recognition, making this process easier. To implement the library gifted by OpenCV, we realized that the programming language Python is the best to use, as it implements the techniques more easily and is also user-friendly. No hardware tools were needed in this project implementation, but a few more dependencies were added to implement the project, making the process simple. Before starting the coding part, first, we installed the above software. Though Matplotlib was optional to install, we installed it to see the results in an organized manner. On the other hand, while implementing a face recognition system, to make the computing easier, we used the NumPy array to feed data as input to the OpenCV function as it contains a powerful implementation of N-dimensional arrays.

The coding part starts with importing the required modules.

6.5.1 HAAR CASCADE CLASSIFIER

At first, we created a folder in the project's name, "face detection and recognition." Inside this, we create another folder named "OpenCV files," where we stored the OpenCV XML classifiers, which we'll be going to use for face detection and recognition. At the beginning of our Python coding, first we loaded the HAAR cascade XML classifier. There is a recognized class in OpenCV, which is cv2.CascadeClassifier. This class takes the HAAR training image and then loads it.

Using the OpenCV classifier, when trying to load any image, it loads the image into BGR color as OpenCV does many of the operations in grayscale. Then it shows the gray image. First, we implemented the face detection algorithm for the HAAR cascade classifier.

The loaded cascade classifier is being used to detect the faces. This classifier has a built-in function within it which is called the "detectMultiScale" function. Here, to find the faces in the image, we use detectMultiScale functions. This is a general function that is being used to detect an object. Here, we use this function to detect faces in a test image, and it has some parameters which we pass through the function. The parameters include:

- Image: This function is called for detecting the face, so the first parameter is the color scale for the image, e.g., gray.
- scaleFactor: The scale factor parameter is being used to determine the distance of faces, as some of the faces can be near to the camera, which will appear larger, and the faces in the back can be shown as smaller. The scale factor reimburses for this.
- minNeighbors: To detect an object, this detectMultiScale function uses a moving window, and it determines all the objects into an image until it finds the face. This parameter defines the other objects.

There can be other parameters for this detectMultiscale function that can be used at any time based on the need for expected result.

So, using this detectMultiScale function, we can find faces in the image, and this function also represents the positions of the face in the image. After finding the face positions using the OpenCV built-in rectangle function, a rectangle has been drawn onto the original colored image. Finally, the algorithm returns the image to verify if the detection is correct and find the real face in the image. Then, we use matplotlib to convert the gray image into its original BGR color.

Though this detectMultiScale function is very helpful to detect a face, to make this reusable to all the faces in an image, we use one more function, called "detect_faces." It also takes three input parameters: loaded CascadeClassifier, the test image, and the scale factor. Inside the function, we made a copy of the original image and converted it to the grayscale so that all the operations of the face detectors could be done on that copy grayscale image. Then, we called the detectMultiScale built-in function from the cascade classifier to provide the list of detected faces as previously discussed. We repeat the full process, as described earlier, just as we did it inside this detect_faces function, so the function can be reusable. We detect all the faces from a group image using this function with the help of the HAAR cascade classifier.

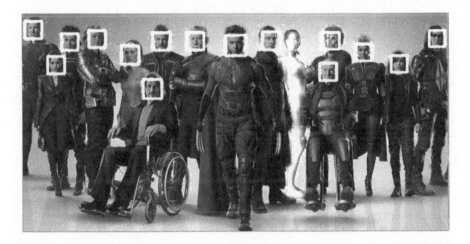

6.5.2 LBP Cascade Classifier

As we are using OpenCV, the coding is much easier than ever. To run the algorithm for the LBP cascade classifier, we simply replace the HAAR cascade classifier XML file with the LBP cascade classifier file, and loading this classifier also detects the faces. For implementation, we did not make any change in coding.

As the discussion about face detection implantation from the image is complete, we move on to the next part of face detection, which includes detection from live video streaming.

6.6 TRAINING DATA PREPARATION

The training data preparation exactly follows four steps. They are discussed below in points.

- Inside the training_data folder, we create subfolders s1 and s2 for each actor, where we put their images in their dedicated folder. While training the data, one step is to read the folder names.
- The subfolder names follow the format s1 and s2, where s is the subject and 1 or 2 is an integer representing the label. This label number clarifies which label is dedicated to which subject. For example, s1 means the subject in this folder has label one, and s2 means the subject in this folder has label 2. In this step, we extract the integers, which we will use in the next step.
- From the subject folder, read all the images and detect the face from each of the images.
- Add each face to the faces vector with the corresponding person label, extracted in the previous step.

We used the LBP cascade classifier in the coding part to detect the face. After that, for preparing the training data, we defined a function named "prepare_training_data". This function takes the path as a parameter where we store the training_data subjects. This function follows those four steps of data preparation stated below.

In step 1, to read the names of all folders stored with training data, we defined a method named "os.listdr" that takes the path as a parameter. Then, we defined the labels and face vectors.

In step 2, the algorithm extracts the label information from each subject folder name, because the folder name provides the label information of each subject.

In step 3, the algorithm reads the name of all images of the current subject and moves those images one by one. Then, using OpenCV's built-in "imshow" and "waitkey" method, the algorithm showed the current image, which is being moved and temporary halt the code flow for 100 ms interval. Then, the algorithm implements the face detection code on the current picture to detect the face from the image.

In step 4, the algorithm adds the detected face and label with its respective vectors.

6.7   TRAINING THE FACE RECOGNIZER

After the training data preparation, the next step is to train the face recognizer. In the research methodology section, we already discussed the face recognition methods provided by OpenCV. Here, we are going to use LBPHFaceRecognizer. The most interesting part is that the coding will remain the same; we will just change the recognizer and see the results.

The algorithm already prepares the train data and now initialize the face recognizer with "face_recognizer = cv2.face.createLBPHFaceRecognizer()" this code. Now, the next part is to train the recognizer. For this, we use a method called "train," where we pass the faces-vector and labels-vector as parameters. Here, before passing the label vector, we convert the value into NumPy array as OpenCV expects the value to a shape of an array.

6.8   PREDICTING FACES

The final part is to predict the faces as the training data is already prepared, and the recognizer is ready and trained. This is the crucial part where we will be able to find out if the algorithm used is recognizing the trained faces or not. For this, two test images are selected from the movie actor faces, which we already give training to the recognizer. After detecting the face from the test image and then using our train recognizer method, we pass those faces to see if it can predict the face. For this, we created one function, which we named "predict," where we called the method for face recognizer to test the recognizer on the given test images. Then, we called two utility OpenCV built-in functions inside the predict funtion, one is "draw_rectangle" to draw rectangle box around the face and another is "draw_text" to write the name of the actor near the rectangle box. Finally, after defining the "predict" function successfully, we called the function on the test images. We showed whether the face recognizer accurately can predict the face of the test images or not.

6.9   TEST RESULT ANALYSIS

After completing the system implementation, the next necessary part is to evaluate all the test results we have achieved using all of the face detection and recognition techniques. From the evaluation of the test results, we will be able to find out which technique is faster and which provides more accuracy. Depending on that, we can select the best technique while considering which situation we are using the algorithm.

6.9.1   FACE DETECTION SPEED AND ACCURACY TEST

As we know, OpenCV provides two classifiers for face detection. We use both of them in the same algorithm to see which is faster. To find out the calculating speed, we use a group image. After that, we write a code to detect the time delay. First, we load both the classifier and the test image. Then, we used one of the library functions provided by Python, which is time(), to keep track of time. Before we start detecting faces on that test image, we take the input for start time t1, then call the function for face detection, and finally, define the end time t2.

Then we calculate the difference between start and end time, which we initialize as dt1. The result of dt1 is the time the classifier takes to complete the detection.

We used the same image and same code to test both classifiers. The HAAR cascade classifier finds all the faces within 0.07 sec., and the accuracy rate is also 100%. In the image, there was one of the faces wearing a mask. Still, it is being detected by the algorithm. That is because all of the faces here are frontal and close to the camera. If a face is far from the camera or wearing a mask, it is sometimes difficult to find that face, which is discussed later in this report. We found that the face detection time for LBP is lower than the HAAR cascade classifier, which is only 0.03 seconds, but it detects 5 faces. So, the accuracy is not as high as the HAAR cascade classifier. We found that 5 out of 7 faces have been detected, proving the accuracy rate of almost 72%, but it is 0.04 sec faster than the HAAR cascade classifier.

6.9.2   CHALLENGES INVOLVED WITH ACCURACY RATE

Above we showed that, in the case of accuracy, the HAAR cascade classifier is more reliable than LBP classifier, which is true. Still, in some cases it is hard to find all the actual faces from the test image because of the slight changes in images. It can happen if one of the faces is far from the camera or has a lighting issue. In this experiment, within 16 faces, 15 faces have successfully detected by the HAAR cascade classifier. The classifier cannot detect the face which is wearing a musk. This is because the pattern is different from other faces as it is wearing a mask, and the face is far from the camera. Moreover, look at the face with deep concentration. You can be able to see that, the left side of the face is darker from the right side of the face, which makes it difficult for the HAAR cascade classifier to detect the face as it cannot be able to compare the distance between the eyes, nose, etc. and also cannot be able to determine the principal component of that face.

Though the algorithm could not find all the faces but still its accuracy rate for faces with principal component is admirable and the accuracy rate is almost 94% using the HAAR cascade classifier.

We used the same image for detection using the same algorithm for the LBPH cascade classifier. In this experiment, there were seven images, and all seven detected. Two false positive faces, representing that using the LBPH cascade classifier, the accuracy rate is almost 44%, which means less than 50%. The false positive result may happen because of the change of the lights and shadow in the image.

So, it can be said that getting a 100% accurate result is not always possible, but to get the possible accurate result, a HAAR cascade classifier can be used. However, it takes a bit more time than the LBPH cascade classifier.

6.9.3 FACE RECOGNITION TESTING

Now, we move on to testing our face recognizers. As the previous section shows, we use an LBPH face recognizer to recognize the faces. We found that our used algorithm, prepare the training data successfully. Then it counts the number of trained face and trained labels for those faces, which is 6. Then it starts predicting the image and when the algorithm successfully recognizes the faces it shows "prediction complete" and return the images with faces that are successfully recognized. Their names are also written on top of the face box. So, it is easy to recognize the faces using the LBPH recognizer.

Then, we used the same algorithm to test the other two, eigenfaces recognizer and fisherfaces recognizer by changing that one-line recognizer initialization code in our algorithm. The algorithm works successfully up to detecting the training face and their labels, but the recognizer failed to train itself. The error is showing that to use the eigenface method, all the train images must have to be equal size. Here, we used images which are different in size from one another. Also, it defines the expected size is within 27,889 pixels, whereas our training image's pixel size was 6724 pixels. So, what we can see from that test result is, in eigenfaces method it is important to maintain the image size and pixels to conquer the accurate recognition result. We tried the same with the Fisherface, recognizer, showing the same test result as eigenfaces. So, the most convenient way to recognize a face is to LBPH face recognizer as this recognizer did not give us any size or pixel limit for the images and easily trained the recognizer with the given image, also successfully recognize the faces. However, converting each training and test image into same size and within 27,889 pixels, the accurate result is achieved with the LBPH face recognizer. OpenCv also has a built-in function, which is cv.resize(), to resize any image to expected size. We used this function to achieve the correct result.

After finding and analyzing the test results, in the next section we will show the comparison within the face detection and recognition techniques and decide which technique is more efficient.

6.10   EFFICIENCY COMPARISON

6.10.1   COMPARISON WITHIN THE FACE DETECTION CLASSIFIER

In this paper, we showed two classifiers for face detection. We used both for face detection and showed the test result in the previous section. From the literature review, system implementation, and test result analysis, we found some advantages and disadvantages of both classifiers, which are shown in Table 6.1.

6.10.2   COMPARISON WITHIN THE FACE RECOGNITION ALGORITHM

We discussed three of the face recognizer algorithms in this paper. We found out the algorithm's efficiency while implementing them, analyzing their test results, and also from the literature review we have researched before starting our implementation. Below is a difference between principal component analysis used by eigenfaces and linear discriminate analysis used by Fisherfaces (Table 6.2).

These are some important differences shown in the table, but the analysis we found while implementing is described in detail below.

TABLE 6.1

Comparison Between HAAR Cascade Classifier and LBP Classifier

Classifier Algorithm	Advantages	Disadvantages
HAAR Cascade Classifier	1. High face detection accuracy 2. Amount of false positives is less	1. Comparably complex computation 2. Slow performance 3. Less accuracy rate if the faces are black 4. Hard to find faces in different lighting conditions 5. Not very much robust to occlusion 6. HAAR does all the computation in floats, which is very difficult for an embedded system
Local Binary Pattern Cascade Classifier	1. Simple computation system 2. Fast performance 3. Takes less time while training the faces 4. Can detect local illumination changes 5. Robust to occlusion than HAAR 6. LBP does all the calculations in integer which is useful for an embedded system.	1. Less face detection accuracy rate 2. Amount of false negative, is high

TABLE 6.2

Comparison Between PCA and LDA

Principal Component Analysis Eigenface

1. This analysis observes the greatest variance.
2. It maximizes the variation.
3. Differentiation between feature classes are not accurate
4. Take more space and time
5. Suitable for representing set of data
6. The first component of PCA is shown in image (Dinalankara, Lahiru. 2017)

Linear Discriminate Analysis-Fisherfaces

1. It observes an interesting dimension to maximize the differences between the mean of the normalized classes. [21]
2. It minimizes the variation and maximizes the mean distance between different classes.
3. Differentiation between features are better than PCA
4. Takes less space and fast
5. Suitable for classification
6. The first component of LDA is shown in image (Dinalankara, Lahiru. 2017)

From this implementation, it has been found that the training data set should be bigger to get the accurate face recognition in case of the eigenface recognition algorithm. It cannot predict faces when there is less training data, increasing the number of training data, and made the wrong recognition accurate, though it did not help to recognize more subject. Not only this, but also this algorithm has some limitations that we already discussed in our result analysis section, that including test images, all the training images should be the same size and the pixel value is also defined by this algorithm.

In the Fisherfaces algorithm, we found the same result as the eigenface algorithm in our implementation and the limitations with image size and pixel were the same as the eigenfaces algorithm. However, from some literature review, we found out that the Fisherfaces algorithm behaves quite differently with the change in the number of training images. Sometimes it recognizes the correct picture with 20 training images and with increases in the number of training images, the result is the same or worse.

The best algorithm for recognition was LBP from our implementation, as it recognized the trained faces from the test image within the shortest time and was also accurate. Moreover, there were no dependencies for size limit, like the eigenface and Fisherfaces algorithms. We used any picture size, and though each was not the same size, it still worked fine. The literature review also found that this algorithm is broadly used to recognize the face because of the accuracy rate.

6.11 CONCLUSION

This article discusses a project for face identification and recognition utilizing photos of movie actors, essentially a research-based endeavor. This article introduces the basic concept of face detection and identification and then implements it using only the classifiers provided by OpenCV. It analyzed the findings of similar initiatives and then demonstrated the fundamental concepts of face detection and recognition in part on the research technique. Through extensive research and execution, it has been shown that the HAAR cascade classifier is the most effective for face detection. Face detection in live video streaming was likewise satisfactory with this classifier, even when the subject's head moved concurrently. Though we used three recognizers for face recognition and obtained successful results, when all variables are considered, the Local Binary Pattern paired with the HAAR cascade is the best solution for face recognition discovered in this experimental project that can be implemented as a complete system. Additionally, it will be a cost-effective system that may be used for automatic attendance tracking, and security systems in autos and ATMs, among other applications.

This article provides an overview of the whole face detection and identification system for a beginner. Still, advanced implementation can be accomplished by combining a few other approaches with this information. In the future, there is a scope to use this face detection and identification approach to research wound detection and recognition, finalizing the necessary therapy for that wound, which will significantly impact the healthcare system.

REFERENCES

Ali, E. S., Hasan, M. K., Hassan, R., Saeed, R. A., Hassan, M. B., Islam, S., Nafi, N.S., & Bevinakoppa, S. (2021). Machine learning technologies for secure vehicular communication in internet of vehicles: Recent advances and applications. *Security and Communication Networks, 2021.*

Ballad, B., Ballad, T., & Banks, E. (2011). *Access Control, Authentication, and Public Key Infrastructure.* Sudbury, MA: Jones & Bartlett Learning.

Baran, R. & Zeja, A. (2015). The IMCOP system for data enrichment and content discovery and delivery. In *International Conference on Computational Science and Computational Intelligence* (pp. 143–146). 10.1109/CSCI.2015.137

Bazama, A., Mansur, F., & Alsharef, N. (2021). Security system by face recognition. *AlQalam Journal of Medical and Applied Sciences, 4*(2), 58–67.

Belhumeur, P., Hespanha, J., & Kriegman, D. (1997). Eigenfaces vs. fisherfaces: Recognition using class specific linear projection. *IEEE Transactions on Pattern Analysis and Machine Intelligence, 19*(7), 711–720.

Bhattacharya, A. (2021). Face recognition system. In Mitchell, S., Blake, M., Cunningham, D., & Gopalan, S. (2008). A SOADriven content discovery and retrieval platform. In *10th IEEE Conference on E-Commerce Technology and the 5th IEEE Conference on Enterprise Computing* (pp. 424–427). 10.1109/CECandEEE.2008.145

Bin Sulaiman, R., Schetinin, V., & Paul, S. (2022). *Review of Machine Learning Approach on Credit Card Fraud Detection.* Human-Centric Intelligent Systems, Springer Nature.

Dinalankara, L. (2017). Face detection & face recognition using open computer vision classifies. *Face Detection & Face Recognition Using Open Computer Vision Classifies, 1*(1), 6–8.

Hassan, M. M., Billah, M. A. M., Rahman, M. M., Zaman, S., Shakil, M. M. H., & Angon, J. H. (2021, July). Early predictive analytics in healthcare for diabetes prediction using machine learning approach. In *12th International Conference on Computing Communication and Networking Technologies* (ICCCNT) (pp. 01–05). IEEE.

Hassan, M. M., Peya, Z. J., Mollick, S., Billah, M. A. M., Shakil, M. M. H., & Dulla, A. U. (2021, July). Diabetes prediction in healthcare at early stage using machine learning approach. In *12th International Conference on Computing Communication and Networking Technologies* (ICCCNT) (pp. 01–05). IEEE.

He, D.-C., & Wang, L. (1990). Texture unit, texture spectrum, and texture analysis. *IEEE Transactions on Geoscience and Remote Sensing, 28*(4), 509–512.

Kareem, A., Liu, H., & Sant, P. (2022). Review on pneumonia image detection: A machine learning approach. *Human-Centric Intelligent Systems,* 1–13.

Kirana, K. C., Wibawanto, S., & Herwanto, H. W. (2018, October). Emotion recognition using fisher face-based viola-jones algorithm. In *5th International Conference on Electrical Engineering, Computer Science and Informatics* (EECSI) (pp. 173–177). IEEE.

Lata, Y. V., Tungathurthi, C. K. B., Rao, H. R. M., Govardhan, A., & Reddy, L. P. (2009). Facial recognition using eigenfaces by PCA. *International Journal of Recent Trends in Engineering, 1*(1), 587.

Opencv.org (2019). *About.* [online] Available at: https://opencv.org/about/ [Accessed 2 Sep. 2019].

Patel, D. R. (2008). *Information Security: Theory and Practice. In: Prentice-Hall Information Security: Theory and Practice* (pp. 9–10). United States: Prentice-Hall.

Phillips, P., Moon, H., Rizvi, S., & Rauss, P. (2000). The FERET evaluation methodology for face-recognition algorithms. *IEEE Transactions on Pattern Analysis and Machine Intelligence, 22*(10), 1090–1104.

ProjectManager Team. (2017). *What is Gantt chart*. Available: https://www.projectmanager. com/gantt-chart [Last accessed 3 Sep. 2019].

Schetinin, V., Jakaite, L., Nyah, N., Novakovic, D., & Krzanowski, W. (2018). Feature extraction with GMDH-type neural networks for EEG-based person identification. *International Journal of Neural Systems*, 28, 1750064. 10.1142/ S0129065717500642

Smashing Magazin. (2019). *Understanding and using REST APIs — Smashing Magazine*. [online] Available at: https://www.smashingmagazine.com/2018/01/understanding-using-rest-api/ [Accessed 6 Sep. 2019].

Sujay, S. N., & Reddy, H. M. (2019). Extended local binary pattern features based face recognition using multilevel SVM classifier. *International Journal of Recent Technology and Engineering*, 8(3), 4123–4128.

Sulaiman, R. B. (2022). AI based Chatbot: An approach of utilizing on customer service assistance. 10.13140/RG.2.2.24571.05921. arXiv preprint arXiv:2207.10573.

Sulaiman, R. B., & Schetinin, V. (2022). Deep neural-network prediction for study of informational efficiency. In K. Arai (Ed.), *Intelligent Systems and Applications. IntelliSys 2021. Lecture Notes in Networks and Systems* (vol. 295). Cham: Springer. 10.1007/ 978-3-030-82196-8_34

Section III

Blockchain and Computational Intelligence for Cybersecurity Applications

Section III

Blockchain and Computational Intelligence for Cybersecurity Applications

7 Artificial Intelligence Incorporated in Business Analytics and Blockchain to Enhance Security

Mamata Rath, Subhranshu Sekhar Tripathy, and Niva Tripathy
Department of Computer Science and Engineering DRIEMS (Autonomous) Cuttack, Odisha, India

Chhabi Rani Panigrahi and Bibudhendu Pati
Department of Computer Science, Rama Devi Women's University Bhubanewar, India

CONTENTS

7.1 INTRODUCTION

Artificial intelligence in data analytics and blockchain-related business issues has discovered achievement as of late because of an exponential increment in purchaser information and promptly accessible computational power. Imagining and translating this information to help essential business leadership with counseling organizations is testing, and there is a degree for progression. The precise time spent on a venture (cost) supports the profitability of these associations. The flow research

DOI: 10.1201/9781003319917-10

aims to build a report with a visual examination showing results from these methods to give intuitive choice help (Maleh et al., 2022).

Blockchain is an open, decentralized ledger that logs transactions between two parties without needing third-party authentication. It has hype because business professionals and programmers realized that this would significantly reduce the cost of transactions in the future. The real hype behind blockchain started when business opportunists saw the potential in investing in these and analyzing its impact on financial institutions. About blockchain, Satoshi Nakamoto first coined "Bitcoin." This enabled the distribution of digital information without the fear of duplication. Blockchain has been used in health care, transportation, public surveys, contract management, supply chains, and insurance. According to *Forbes*, about 15% of all financial transactions have integrated blockchain technology. The current mechanics of blockchain operate on two concepts called proof of work and proof of stake. Mr. Vitalik Buterin gets the credit for developing a public blockchain called Ethereum, where the algorithm does data mining to create a new block. The proof-of-work concept in blockchain operates on the mechanics where a user initiates a transaction and packages it into a blockchain. Data miners verify the transaction by solving a complicated mathematical problem. The first one to solve the mathematical problem wins a reward and that transaction is successful.

A good paradigm of how an AI can be a disruptive technological paragon via blockchain comes straight from deep learning. Blockchain as a highly secure storage medium presents a technological quantum leap in maintaining data integrity. Furthermore, blockchain's immutability constructs a productive environment for creating high-quality, permanent, growing data sets for deep learning (Maleh et al., 2022). The combination of AI and blockchain could impact fields like the Internet of Things (IoT), identity, financial markets, civil governance, smart cities, small communities, supply chains, personalized medicine, and other fields, thereby delivering benefits to many people.

The data for these activities is gathered from a counseling business' customer relationship management (CRM) database. So far, simple factual models and machine learning choice trees have been tested. Exploration will continue with arbitrary woods, neural systems and support vector machine (SVM) models. A model UI and perception of the outcomes have likewise been introduced here. In this examination, the review about the advancement of man-made reasoning to increased age is displayed. Over the most recent 20 years, the phrasing of man-made reasoning, otherwise called AI, has been picking up believability from the regular populace in light of its developing nearness and utility in our everyday exercises by taking care of issues. In this paper, we characterize and outline the historical backdrop of the AI to give a superior understanding of the present and eventual fate of the equivalent. Machine learning and deep learning are important scientific advanced strategies that speak to genuine innovative/information conditions of the AI.

To understand what blockchains are we first need to understand their relationship with Bitcoins. To put it simply, Its a quote by Sally Davies, FT Technologies Reporter. The most significant innovation for which everyone in this world expects a revolution in technology, as it can tackle issues from space exploration to countering psychological repression, and notwithstanding making craftsmanship, the potential of artificial intelligence is becoming progressively obvious.

On October 31, 2008, Satoshi Nakamoto unconfined the Bitcoin White Paper, outlining a merely peer-to-peer electronic cash/digital asset transmitted system. This is the first popular blockchain implementation attributed to birthing today's blockchain industry. Since then, additional blockchains have been popularized, including Ethereum, various Hyperledger project solutions, and numerous others, including "blockchain-like" solutions such as GuardTime's KSI products.

7.1.1 MOTIVATION

The motivation for this exploration-based chapter is to substance out the real utilization of involving AI in data analytics and blockchain being utilized in the different industries today and to show significant patterns and future use cases for technologists who need to get a layout of future vision that is needed for how man-made consciousness may be encouraged and comprehend the intelligence associated with gadgets in the coming time. This article has been composed given the research purpose of experts or officials, scientists, students, and researchers.

7.1.2 CHAPTER ORGANIZATION

The organization of this research chapter has been done in the following way. The next section offers a detailed literature review of many contributions by eminent research analysts. Section 7.3 provides the prominence of artificial intelligence in data analytics. Section 7.4 illustrates the core topic of assortment of AI with blockchain technology. Section 7.5 is observation and analysis of the research. The last section offers a brief conclusion of the research work.

7.2 LITERATURE STUDY

Artificial intelligence has progressed tremendously within the last two decades by contributing to almost all sectors of society, including business sectors. Due to the scarcity of fundamentally sound professional people in all respects in recent times business system is facing noteworthy confront. Simulated intelligence has been discussed by scientific authors and took a shot at including artificial intelligence in data science and business applications. Nowadays, e-commerce-based business applications in retail shops, production units, banking sectors, healthcare units, and home appliances everywhere, safe and secure e-transactions are possible due to secure algorithms implemented by very powerful artificial intelligence techniques. Expert systems use machine learning–based artificial neural networks and deep learning networks to handle pattern recognition and cybersecurity threats efficiently in maximum case studies. Further, there is a lot of contribution of AI to blockchain technology, which makes business activities more secure, efficient, and flexible. This section provides a literature review of the current article.

H. B. Patel and Gandhi (2018) describe different application fields of big data and artificial intelligence. Diversified fields of AI include machine learning, expert systems, NLP, robotics, and speech processing and machine vision. Many experts in the artificial intelligence field, explorers, and many foundations center around the fact that the concern of AI is that it is a black box and individuals don't feel good when they don't see how the logic is carried out.

With regards to Industry 4.0, the principle approach to understanding savvy production is to manufacture a keen industrial facility incorporated with cutting-edge innovations, for example, the Internet of Things (IoT), distributed computing, and man-made consciousness (AI). With the plan to stress the job and capability of distributed computing and AI in improving the keen production lines' exhibitions, for example, framework adaptability, proficiency, and knowledge, research extensively outlined and clarified the AI application in a cloud-assisted smart factory (CaSF). J. M. Keller (2014) presented a vertically incorporated four-level CaSF design. Likewise, the key AI advancements engaged with the CaSF are ordered and depicted by the intelligent connections in the engineering chain of command. At last, the principle issues and specialized difficulties of AI innovations in the CaSF frameworks are presented, and some conceivable arrangements are likewise given. The use of AI in savvy production lines has quickened the execution of business 4.0 to a specific degree.

Finding a suitable PHRASE permits the recovery of records containing a precise expression, which assumes a significant job in many AI applications for cloud-based IoT, for example, clever medicinal information investigation. So as to shield delicate data from being spilled by specialist co-ops, archives (e.g., facility records) are typically scrambled by information proprietors before being re-appropriated to the cloud. This, nonetheless, makes the pursuit activity an incredibly testing errand. Existing accessible encryption plans for multi-watchword look activities neglect to perform state seek, as they are unfit to decide the area relationship of different catchphrases in a questioned expression over encoded information on the cloud server side. N. Bari et al. (2014) present P3, a productive security-saving expression scan conspire for canny encoded information handling in cloud-based IoT. This plan misuses the homomorphism encryption and bilinear guide to decide the area relationship of different questioned watchwords over scrambled information. It likewise uses a probabilistic trapdoor age calculation to secure clients' inquiry designs. Careful security investigation shows the security ensured accomplished by P3. They actualize a model and lead broad tests on genuine world data sets. X. He et al. (2018) proposes a novel data-driven situation awareness approach for future grids using large, random matrices for big data modeling for business development.

Attack discovery issues in the brilliant system acted like authentic learning issues for different attack circumstances in which the estimations are found in a bunch of online settings. In this strategy, machine learning figurings are used to portray either secure or attacked estimations. An attack identification framework is given to mishandle any available prior data about the system and surmount goals rising out of the small structure of the issue in the proposed procedure. Without a doubt, cluster and electronic learning computations (coordinated and semi-directed) are used with a decision and feature level mix to display the attack discovery issue. The associations among quantifiable and geometric properties of attack vectors used in the attack circumstances and learning estimations are bankrupt down to perceive impalpable attacks using authentic learning systems. The proposed computations by M. Ozay et al. (2016) are examined on various IEEE test systems. Preliminary examinations show that machine learning computations can recognize attacks with displays higher than attack discovery figurings that use state vector estimation methodologies in the proposed attack recognition structure.

7.3   APPLICATION OF ARTIFICIAL INTELLIGENCE IN BUSINESS ANALYTICS

The decision of some difficulties with artificial intelligence lies in the advancement of the up-and-coming age of computing foundation, for example, quantum computing, which saddles subatomic wonders, for example, ensnarement, to do tasks on information unquestionably more rapidly than the present computers. We need to make sense of the programming models. Because the programming models for quantum are unique in relation to those we use currently, there must be a rehash that will require some serious energy." There are basic scientific components in the domain of AI that are associated with every system that implements intelligence-based logic into the AI system.

Fig. 7.1 shows the application of AI in different fields for data security, personal security, financial trading, and many more business-related sectors. A visual investigation arrangement tends to be the predominant issue in the operational decision management (ODM) region. In ODM, which has its underlying foundations in artificial intelligence (expert systems) and management science, it is progressively imperative to adjust business choices to business objectives. In our work, we consider choice models (executable models of the business space) as ontologies that portray the business area, and generation decides which business rationale of choices to be made over this cosmology. Executing a choice model creates a gathering of choices to set aside a few minutes for individual cases. In the first phase, knowledge of the choice rationale is given, and the aggregated realities

FIGURE 7.1   Application of AI in different fields.

without anyone else's input are displayed here. Table 7.1 displays details of artificial intelligence and its role in data analytics. To perform a detailed study and review of related applications, the details of technical approaches and subject matters used by many contributors are presented in Table 7.1.

TABLE 7.1

Artificial Intelligence and Its Applications in Business Analytics

Authors	Year	Data Analytics–Based Research Theme	Business Analytics–Based Applications
N. Bari, R. Vichr, K. Kowsari, S. Berkovich	2014	23-bit metaknowledge template toward big data knowledge discovery and management	Big data, classification algorithms, data mining, vectors, motion pictures, knowledge discovery, correlation
A. D. Popescu, V. Ercegovac, A. Balmin, M. Branco, A. Ailamaki	2012	Same queries, different data: Prediction of performance	Predictive models, data models, analytical models, computational modeling, estimation, context
S. K. Gupta, D. Phung, S. Venkatesh	2012	A nonparametric Bayesian Poisson gamma model for count data	Data models, analytical models, Bayesian methods, dictionaries, face, load modeling, indexes
H. B. Patel, S. Gandhi	2018	A review on big data analytics in health care using machine learning approaches	Big data, medical services, data mining, tools, linear regression, logistics, conferences
R. Alfred	2016	The rise of machine learning for big data analytics	Business intelligence, supervised learning
J. M. Keller, A. R. Buck, A. Zare, M. Popescu	2014	A human geospatial predictive analytics framework with application to finding medically underserved areas	Training, biomedical imaging, artificial neural networks, geography, vectors, sociology, statistics
L. Cazzanti, A. Davoli, L. M. Millefiori	2016	Automated port traffic statistics: From raw data to visualization	Ports (computers), artificial intelligence, pipelines, big data, databases, visual analytics, stakeholders
X. He, L. Chu, R. C. Qiu, Q. Ai, Z. Ling	2018	A novel data-driven situation awareness approach for future grids using large random matrices for Big Data modeling	Big data, eigenvalues and eigenfunctions, power system stability, topology, anomaly detection
A. Epishkina, S. Zapechnikov	2016	A syllabus on data mining and machine learning with applications to cybersecurity	Data mining, computer security, data analysis, big data, information security, correlation

TABLE 7.1 (Continued)
Artificial Intelligence and Its Applications in Business Analytics

Authors	Year	Data Analytics–Based Research Theme	Business Analytics–Based Applications
P. I. Cowling, S. Devlin, E. J. Powley, D. Whitehouse, J. Rollason	2015	Player preference and style in a leading mobile card game	Games, artificial intelligence, production facilities, Google, Monte Carlo methods, data collection, land mobile radio
J. Rogers, D. Simmons, M. Shah, C. Rowland, Y. Shang	2019	Deep learning at your fingertips	Data analysis, emotion recognition, deep learning, real-time systems, data collection, tools, servers
J. Krause, A. Dasgupta, J. Swartz, Y. Aphinyanaphongs, E. Bertini	2017	A workflow for visual diagnostics of binary classifiers using instance-level explanations	Analytical models, predictive models, machine learning, collaboration, visual analytics
B. K. Tannahill et al.	2013	Modeling of a system of systems via data analytics, a case for big data in SoS	Mathematical model, neural networks, principal component analysis, training, training data, analytical models
T. Nguyen, V. Nguyen, T. Nguyen, S. Venkatesh, M. Kumar, D. Phung	2016	Learning multifaceted latent activities from heterogeneous mobile data	Bluetooth, IEEE 802.11 standard, Bayes methods, computational modeling, mobile communication
B. Broeksema, T. Baudel, A. Telea, P. Crisafulli	2013	Decision exploration lab: A visual analytics solution for decision management	Decision making, statistical analysis, data visualization, analytical models, visual analytics
D. R. Harris, A. D. Baus, T. J. Harper, T. D. Jarrett, C. R. Pollard, J. C. Talbert	2016	Using i2b2 to bootstrap rural health analytics and learning networks	Data models, standards, medical services, collaborative work, sociology, statistics, vocabulary
Y. Yetis, R. G. Sara, B. A. Erol, H. Kaplan, A. Akuzum, M. Jamshidi	2016	Application of big data analytics via cloud computing	Cloud computing, big data, data analysis, programming, urban areas, servers
S. Monteiro, B. Vijaya	2017	Ontology population from complex sentences document	Ontologies, sociology, statistics, natural language processing, data analysis, redundancy, OWL
A. Cook, P. Wu, K. Mengersen	2015	Machine learning and visual analytics for consulting business decision support	Business, user interfaces, predictive models, profitability, visual analytics, neural networks, support vector machines

(Continued)

TABLE 7.1 (Continued)

Artificial Intelligence and Its Applications in Business Analytics

Authors	Year	Data Analytics–Based Research Theme	Business Analytics–Based Applications
S. Sobolevsky, E. Massaro, I. Bojic, J. M. Arias, C. Ratti	2017	Predicting regional economic indices using big data of individual bank card transactions	Business, economic indicators, urban areas, predictive models, education, microeconomics
A. Gupta, S. Jagadish	2017	Machine learning–oriented gesture-controlled device for the speech and motion impaired	Speech, sociology, statistics, algorithm design and analysis, microcontrollers, machine learning algorithms
Y. Tian, S. Tatikonda, B. Reinwald	2012	Scalable and numerically stable descriptive statistics in system ML	Accuracy, numerical stability, standards, higher order statistics, approximation algorithms, equations, correlation
M. S. Simi, K. S. Nayaki	2017	Data analytics in medical data: A review	Data analysis, predictive models, medical diagnostic imaging, classification algorithms, decision trees, artificial neural networks, prediction algorithms
T. Nguyen, D. Phung, S. Gupta, S. Venkatesh	2013	Extraction of latent patterns and contexts from honest social signals using hierarchical Dirichlet processes	Data models, hidden Markov models, context, data mining, Bayes methods, accelerometers, bluetooth
D. D. Nauck, D. Ruta, M. Spott, B. Azvine	2006	A tool for intelligent customer analytics	Bayesian methods, machine learning, network servers, management training, algorithm design, and analysis

7.4   BLOCKCHAIN TECHNOLOGY AND THE USE OF AI

This section presents a high-level introduction to blockchain technology. However, Satoshi Nakamoto (pseudonym) and his/creation, Bitcoin, popularized blockchain technology. (There are currently arguments that Bitcoin was not the first blockchain.) Today there are various flavors of blockchain. Here we plan to generalize blockchain with samples in some of those flavors. Additional research, prototyping, and due diligence should be exercised before making any long-term decisions. Lastly, it is the opinion of the author that no single blockchain solution will fulfill all needs. As many of the blockchain technologies are paradigm specific, one should educate themselves on when and how to implement a blockchain solution.

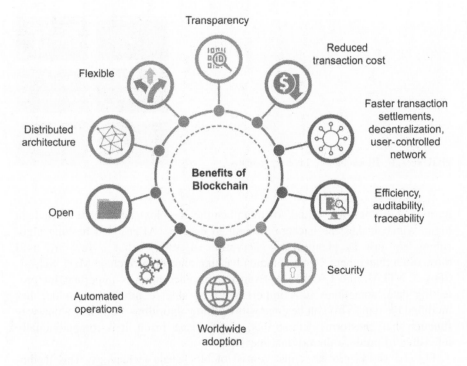

FIGURE 7.2 Blockchain features.

Perhaps more importantly, when NOT to implement a solution. Blockchain can be described as the collection of records linked with each other, strongly resistant to alteration, and protected using cryptography.

Fig. 7.2 shows the features of blockchain. The worldwide economy's most demanding and universal patterns develop the need for undertakings to cooperate successfully and proficiently. These community-oriented business situations rely upon ongoing procedures in portable settings where the cooperation between accomplices is led. To help the arranging and control these portable business procedures is mind-boggling. A cell phone upheld design is exhibited as a structure to empower process management in portable situations.

7.5 TRANSACTIONS IN BLOCKCHAIN

Transactions in blockchain take place as follows. The first sender passes the number of Bitcoins he wants to send to the receiver and his and the receiver's unique wallet address through a hashing algorithm. All of these are part of the transaction details. These details are encrypted using encryption algorithms and the sender's private key. This is done to digitally sign the transaction and to indicate that the transaction came from the sender. This transaction is now available in the network.

The message or transaction can be decrypted only by the receiver's private key, which is known to the receiver only. Artificial intelligence–based encoded

FIGURE 7.3   Blockchain technology benefits.

hashing algorithms are written to strengthen the complex and secured blockchain logic, which makes the hackers difficult to decrypt. AI-encoded hashing algorithms are just as plentiful as encryption algorithms, but a few are used more often than others. Some common hashing algorithms include MD5, SHA-1, SHA-2, NTLM, and LANMAN. Even though encryption is important for protecting data, sometimes it is important to be able to prove that no one has modified the data. This can be done with hashing algorithms. A hash is a one-way function that transforms data so that, given a hash result, it is computationally infeasible to produce the original message.

Fig. 7.3 shows processes that consist of blockchain technology. This methodology proposes a portable BPM life cycle comprising five urgent strides to adapt to the multifaceted nature to build a versatile joint effort. Radio frequency identifying device (RFID) is turning into a piece of our day-to-day existence with a wide scope of utilizations, for example, naming items, store network management, and so forth. These brilliant and little gadgets have amazingly compelled assets as far as territory, computational capacities, memory, and power. Simultaneously, security and protection issues stay a significant issue. Consequently, with the huge arrangement of low-asset gadgets, expanding needs to give security and protection to such gadgets, has emerged.

7.6   PROOF OF WORK IN BLOCKCHAIN

Miners validate block by block. Miners need to solve complex mathematical problems. Miners who solve this first add the blocks to the blockchain and are rewarded with 12.5 BTC (Bitcoins). The process of solving a complex mathematical problem is called proof of work. The process of adding a block to the blockchain is called mining.

Asset proficient cryptographic nascent become essential for acknowledging security and productivity in obliged situations and implanted frameworks like RFID labels and sensor hubs. Among those natives, a lightweight square figure assumes a noteworthy job as a structure obstructs security frameworks. Another lightweight square figure named Few was additionally created, which is appropriate for very compelled situations and implanted frameworks. Table 7.2 details the research theme of artificial intelligence and blockchain technology.

TABLE 7.2

Details of Research Theme of Artificial Intelligence and Blockchain Technology

Authors	Year	Theme on Blockchain Research	Associated Concept/Topic Focus/ Challenge Area
D. Das, S. Sarkar	2018	Machine-to-machine learning based framework for ad-hoc IoT ecosystems	Ad-hoc IOT ecosystems, M2M, decentralized version, connect-and-transmit process, centralized compute-storage server, data stream, device malfunctions, live devices, machine-to-machine learning, video recorders, anomaly detection models, storage workstation, blockchain-powered decentralized server, cell phones, camera-microphone, and smartphones.
B. Ray, M. Howdhury, J. Abawajy, M. Jesmin	2015	Secure object tracking protocol for networked RFID systems	Secure object tracking protocol, networked RFID system, radiofrequency identification technology, NRS system security, distributed system, object traceability, object visibility, lawful business operation, physically unclonable function, PUF, Diffie-Hellman algorithm, cryptographic primitive, security protocol description language, SPDL model, automated claim verification tool Scyther.
Chie Dou	1994	A highly parallel architecture for concurrent rule match of AI production systems	Symbolic form, CAM cell array, CAM block, arrays, VLSI implementation, forward-chaining production systems, artificial intelligence.
K. Hui, W. Siu	2007	Extended analysis of motion-compensated frame difference for block-based motion prediction error	Motion-compensated frame difference signal, block-based motion prediction error, hybrid video codecs, first-order Markov model, separable autocorrelation model, motion-compensated codecs, block-based motion compensation.
C. Saksupawatta Nakul, W. Vatanawood	2018	Event-B formalization of basic supply chain patterns	Supply chains, reliability, business process models, supply chain operations, Event-B prover, supply chain patterns, supply chain event patterns, ordinary timed Petri net, and production processes.
G. Pan, Q. Dou, L. Xie	2007	Study on distributing pattern of shared data in CC-NUMA system	Distributing pattern, shared data, CC-NUMA system, cache coherence protocols, and large-scale systems.

(Continued)

TABLE 7.2 (Continued)

Details of Research Theme of Artificial Intelligence and Blockchain Technology

Authors	Year	Theme on Blockchain Research	Associated Concept/Topic Focus/ Challenge Area
A. Zakeri, M. Saberi, O. K. Hussain, E. Chang	2018	An early detection system for proactive management of raw milk quality: An Australian case study	The early detection system, high microbial index, proactive management, raw milk quality, Australian case study, cold dairy supply chain, machine learning, and rule-based approach.
H. Guan, Z. Zhang, T. Tan	2018	Inception donut convolution for top-down semantic segmentation	Network architecture design, spatial context information, adjacent cells, multiscale feature extraction, larger kernel size, inception-block donut convolutional network, top-down semantic segmentation task, object-scales contexts, chain sampling, most off-the-shelf bottom-up based methods.
C. Gao, Haitian Liu, Xiangfen Wang, Jiaoying Huang	2015	Configuration circuit design for the burn-in test of CLB based on the structure	Configuration circuit design, burn-in test, configurable logic block, CLB, field programming gate array, FPGA reliability assessment, military fields, aerospace fields, logic unit, combinational logic, sequential logic, Xilinx Spartan-3, RAM chain mode, shift register mode, SliceL, 4-input XOR chain mode, 4-input NXOR mode.
O. Adam, P. Chikova, A. Hofer	2005	Managing inter-organizational business processes using architecture for M-business scenarios	Inter-organizational business process management, M-business architecture, mobile collaborative business scenario, real-time business process, mobile device-supported architecture, mobile-BPM-life cycle.
C. Kiekintveld, M. P. Wellman	2005	An analysis of the 2004 supply chain management trading agent competition	Supply chain management, agent behavior, strategic interaction, supplier market condition, customer sales market, supply and demand, market behavior, 2004 Trading Agent Competition.
B. Sakiz, E. Kutlugun	2018	Bitcoin price forecast via blockchain technology and artificial intelligence algorithms	Crypto money transfer, blockchain, distributed architecture, Bitcoin forecasting, Bitcoin price forecast, digital currency, blockchain system, artificial intelligence.
K. Qayumi	2015	Multi-agent based intelligence generation from very large data sets	Multi-agent based multiagent-based intelligence generation, very large data sets, blockchain technology, cloud

TABLE 7.2 (Continued)

Details of Research Theme of Artificial Intelligence and Blockchain Technology

Authors	Year	Theme on Blockchain Research	Associated Concept/Topic Focus/ Challenge Area
			computing, decentralized management, distributed management, big data–mining systems, scalable distributed system-based approach.
C. Dou	1993	A highly parallel match architecture for AI production systems using application-specific associative matching processors	Highly parallel match architecture, AI production systems, application-specific associative matching processors, execution time, content-addressable memories, CAM blocks, symbolic form, working memory, and parallel evaluating inter conditions.
Xi-Ren Cao	2003	Constructing performance sensitivities of Markov systems with potential as building blocks	Markov systems, performance sensitivity, performance potentials, perturbation realization factors, Markov chains, performance derivatives, performance differences, performance optimization, discrete event dynamic systems, perturbation analysis, Markov decision processes, and reinforcement learning.
L. Yu, L. Wu	2007	Comments on "A separable low complexity 2D HMM with application to face recognition"	Face recognition, separable low complexity 2D HMM, hidden Markov model.
G. Li, S. Xing, H. Xue	2009	Improved chain-block algorithm to RVM on large-scale problems	Chain-block algorithm, relevance vector machine, machine learning, sparse classification, regression function, fixed basis function, time-and-space complexity, space complexity, initial iteration center, support vector machine.
J. A. Starzyk, H. He	2009	Spatio temporal memories for machine learning: A long-term memory organization	Spatio-temporal memories, machine learning, long-term memory organization, artificial neural structures, machine intelligence, mutual input enhancement, blocking structure, Levenshtein distance method, Markov chain.
Jing et al.	2006	Kinematic analysis of a flexible six-DOF parallel mechanism	Kinematic analysis, flexible six-DOF parallel mechanism, parallel manipulator, object manipulation, fully actuated system, underactuated system, inverse kinematics, forward kinematics, manufacturing industry, robotics.

(Continued)

TABLE 7.2 (Continued)

Details of Research Theme of Artificial Intelligence and Blockchain Technology

Authors	Year	Theme on Blockchain Research	Associated Concept/Topic Focus/ Challenge Area
M. A. Khan, A. R. Cheema, A. Hasan	2008	Improved Nonce construction scheme for AES CCMP to evade initial counter prediction	Nonce construction scheme, AES CCMP, initial counter prediction, IEEE 802.11i standard, integrity services, advance encryption standard, cipher block chaining message authentication code protocol, time-memory trade-off attack.
S. Lee, S. Park, Y. B. Park	2019	Formal specification technique in smart contract verification	Smart contract verification, blockchain technology, ontology, formal specification technique, XML, state information.
T. Artieres, S. Marukatat, P. Gallinari	2007	Online handwritten shape recognition using segmental hidden Markov models	Online handwritten shape recognition, segmental hidden Markov models, incremental learning, Latin characters, Asian characters, command gestures, symbols, small drawings, geometric shapes.
S. Ionita	2018	Modeling human sensory-motor action for vehicle braking based on fuzzy inferences	Mental modeling, sensory-motor changes, artificial intelligence, neurosciences, simulation model, mental functional mode, human action, structural models, basic functional modules, entire sensory-motor chain, suitable models, mental mechanisms.
A. Nemati, S. Feizi	2015	An efficient hardware implementation of a few lightweight block cipher	Hardware implementation, FeW lightweight block cipher, FeW cryptography algorithms, radio frequency identification, RFID, sensor node, resource-efficient cryptographic incipient, security system, FPGA.

In the current scenario of the business environment and with expanding benchmarks, computerization and advances have prompted enormous measures of information getting to be accessible, notwithstanding, business basic leadership procedure has turned out to be confounded. The conventional database framework has not fulfilled users' need for mass information smart examination and gauge.

There is a tremendous enhancement in progress and performance due to the successful integration of AI with many important technologies in different fields, such as blockchain. These advances have been made conceivable because of the emphasis on convincing human points of view. The field of research that has been most productive earlier is what turned out to be known as "AI" units. It's become so indispensable to contemporary AI that the expressions "computerized reasoning" and "AI" are sometimes utilized reciprocally. In any case, it is ideal to consider that AI offers the present best choice in the industry for improved performance. The establishment of AI is done better so that the machines can be modified to figure like human beings. Like humans, they can figure out how to work by watching, arranging, and gaining from its mix-ups.

7.7   CASE STUDY ON AI USING BLOCKCHAIN

Walmart was having trouble providing its customers with high-quality goods. Due to their poor quality, they were dealing with high rates of returns and significant sums of refunds. Fig. 7.4 depicts a case study of Walmart implementing blockchain technology and how their issue was resolved. The Walmart staff could not identify the supply chain's "point of failure," or the location where products were damaged. They looked in the farms, storage, transportation, processing, and distribution center section. However, they were unable to locate the fault.

Then Walmart adopted blockchain technology. With blockchain, the quality of good at each step was permanently inscribed within each block. For example, when a customer complains that a product is damaged, it could be correctly identified at which stage the product was damaged in the entire supply chain. In this way, blockchain helped Walmart identify and fix the problem. This searching technique was based on intelligent logic using artificial intelligence.

Artificial intelligence is the intelligence that is incorporated into systems using different techniques. Various types of artificial intelligence techniques have been proposed in research, and these include neural networks, support vector machines, and fuzzy logic. These techniques have been successfully used for missing data

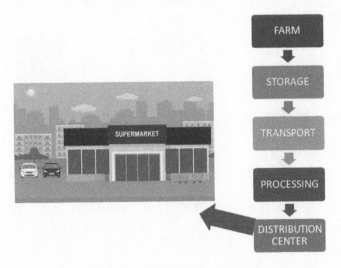

FIGURE 7.4   Case study of Walmart adopting blockchain.

estimation, finite element models, modeling interstate conflict, economics, and robotics. Blockchain records track information about financial payments, movements of products through supply chains, identity verification information, and many other assets. Blockchain denotes an unalterable digital ledger system. One notable feature of blockchain technology is its distributed implementation manner. It originated initially from Bitcoin, which has demonstrated its potential in numerous domains.

7.8   AI IN SMART CONTRACTS AND ITS TESTING

The power of artificial intelligence has been embedded in a smart contract. Smart contracts are lines of code stored on a blockchain and automatically execute when predetermined terms and conditions are met. At the most basic level, they are programs that run as they've been set up by the people who developed them. Smart contract security issues are so that with the popularity of the blockchain concept, smart contracts hold the promise of further decentralizing market environments in many ways. Smart contracts are just like contracts in the real world. The only difference is that they are completely digital.

Fig. 7.5 shows smart contacts within a blockchain, which holds the real power of artificial intelligence. A smart contract is a tiny computer program stored inside a blockchain. A smart contract can perform various operations automatically, e.g., calculations, information storage, funds transfer, etc. In JavaScript, one can view a

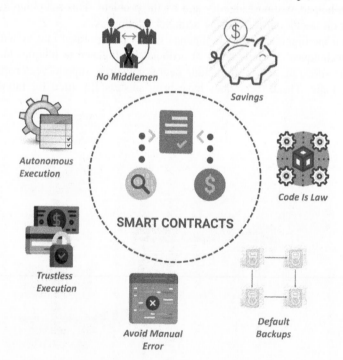

FIGURE 7.5   Smart contract within a blockchain.

contract as a class consisting of state variables, functions, function modifiers, events, structures, and enums. Smart contracts can also support inheritance and polymorphism. In a simple case, a programmer can store the hash of a file and the owner's name as pairs in the code to achieve the functionality of proof of ownership. Similarly, one can store the hash of a file and the block's timestamp as pairs to realize the proof of existence function. Finally, by storing the hash itself, the file integrity can be proven, i.e., if the file is altered, the hash will change correspondingly, and the smart contract is then incapable of finding any such file.

Fig. 7.6 demonstrates a flow diagram of AI-assisted smart contract testing. Two methodologies are used for this purpose: formal verification and search-based software engineering. In its simplest term, formal verification (FV) uses mathematical reasoning to ensure computing systems' correct execution. Generally speaking, the applications of AI in formal verification can be classified as follows: Broad domains: enhance the existing FV tools; and facilitate new FV tools development. Applications areas: automate troubleshooting; debugging and root cause analysis and identification; assist theorem proving; and learning a concept from a concept class. For instance, since writing specifications manually tends to be

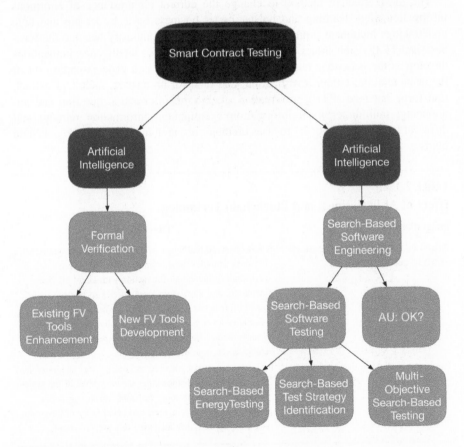

FIGURE 7.6   AI-assisted smart contract testing.

complicated and error-prone, AI can learn specifications from runtime traces. In addition, AI can select a heuristic strategy automatically, that is, choosing a heuristic according to the need-to-prove conjecture's features and the corresponding hypotheses. In principle, search-based software engineering (SBSE) utilizes computational search methodologies to address various software engineering problems, often characterized by their large, complex search spaces. Blockchain (or distributed ledger system) and microeconomics are both large-scale distributed systems, and there are inherent connections between them.

In principle, a blockchain system (including various nodes such as full node, mining node, and lightweight node) and a microeconomic system (including a social system, which consists of producers, consumers, and markets) have many similarities: different interconnected subsystems, decentralized computations, and so on. The broad concern of microeconomics is to allocate scarce resources among various uses to maximize users' utility and producers' profit. Then a unified view of AI-backed blockchain system energy consumption optimization can be established from the large-scale complex systems perspective. Table 7.3 shows an observation of the effect of AI integration with diverse modern technology.

The most effective method to change the current circumstance of enormous information, poor learning and bolster better business basic leadership and help undertakings increment profits and piece of the overall industry become the business and IT division issues of shared concern. Business intelligence innovations develop as the occasions require. Business intelligence is a wide-extending set of the accumulation, union, investigation, and data for an answer, including extract, transform and load (ETL); information stockroom; information question and announcing; multidimensional information examination; information mining; and different innovations. Fig. 7.7 focuses on major research in AI related to blockchain fields.

TABLE 7.3

Effect of AI in Business and Blockchain Technology

Integration of AI	Observation
AI and its incorporation with business analysis and blockchain	It was observed that when AI technology was integrated with business analytics–based applications, the system's performance increased. Interaction with cloud providers increased, and there were more queries so that the system could offer better customer service. The security and reliability level was increased gradually, the API standard became better, and compatibility and performance of the compliances were enhanced.
Applications of AI in data analytics	It was observed that when AI technology was integrated into data analytics applications, the accuracy level of the system increased, they were more realizable, there was better control over the system, there was better usage of the system, and their applicability increased to a greater extent.

Machine-to-machine learning based framework for ad-hoc IoT ecosystems
Secure object tracking protocol for Networked RFID Systems
Parallel architecture for conurent rule match of AI production systems
Extended analysis of motion-compensated frame difference for block-based motion prediction error
Event-B formalization of basic supply chain patterns
Study on distributing pattern of shared data in CC-NUMA system
Detection system for proactive management of raw milk quality: An Australian case study
Inception donut convolution for top-down semantic segmentation
Configuration circuit design for burn-in test of CLB based on structure
Managing inter-organizational business processes using an architecture for M-business scenarios
An analysis of the 2004 supply chain management trading agent competition
Bitcoin price forecast via blockchain technology and artificial intelligence algorithms
Multi-agent based intelligence generation from very large data sets
Parallel match architecture for AI production systems using application-specific associative matching processors

FIGURE 7.7 Major research in AI related to blockchain.

This segment sets out a review of business intelligence, the key innovation of business intelligence, just as the foundation and use of business intelligence systems in various industries. Business subject and measurement structure, ETL device plan, information on the middleware structure, and the fundamental advancement are the key purposes of the framework.

7.9 CONCLUSION

Business intelligence is that incredible logical advanced solution for the financial part of the business. It needs to determine the financial forecast in most of the current banks to handle issues such as how to improve customer administration, control budgetary dangers, improve the bank's working execution, guarantee the continued development in profits, and so on. The current article reviews applications of artificial intelligence in very advanced fields of business and blockchain technology. Our observation concludes that many such critical solution strategies are offered by artificial intelligence and machine language, which intelligently predict business risks up to a higher level and save companies from great loss.

REFERENCES

Adam, O., Chikova, P., & Hofer, A. (2005). Managing inter-organizational business processes using an architecture for M-business scenarios, *International Conference on Mobile Business (ICMB'05)*, pp. 82–88, doi: 10.1109/ICMB.2005.56.

Alfred, R. (2016). The rise of machine learning for big data analytics, *2016 2nd International Conference on Science in Information Technology (ICSITech)*, pp. 1–1, doi:10.1109/ICSITech.2016.7852593.

Artieres, T., Marukatat, S., & Gallinari, P. (2007). Online handwritten shape recognition using segmental hidden markov models, *IEEE Transactions on Pattern Analysis and Machine Intelligence*, 29(2), pp. 205–217, doi:10.1109/TPAMI.2007.38.

Bari, N., Vichr, R., Kowsari, K., & Berkovich, S. (2014). 23-bit metaknowledge template towards big data knowledge discovery and management, *2014 International Conference on Data Science and Advanced Analytics (DSAA)*, pp. 519–526, doi:10.1109/DSAA.2014.7058121.

Broeksema, B., Baudel, T., Telea, A., & Crisafulli, P. (2013). Decision exploration lab: A visual analytics solution for decision management, *IEEE Transactions on Visualization and Computer Graphics*, 19(12), pp. 1972–1981, doi:10.1109/TVCG.2013.146.

Cao, X.-R. (2003). Constructing performance sensitivities of markov systems with potentials as building blocks, *42nd IEEE International Conference on Decision and Control (IEEE Cat. No.03CH37475)*, 5, pp. 4405–4409, doi:10.1109/CDC.2003.1272203.

Casino, F., Dasaklis, T. K., & Patsakis, C. (2019). A systematic literature review of blockchain-based applications: Current status, classification and open issues. *Telemat. Inform, 36*, 55–81.

Cazzanti, L., Davoli, A., & Millefiori, L. M. (2016). Automated port traffic statistics: From raw data to visualisation, *2016 IEEE International Conference on Big Data (Big Data)*, pp. 1569–1573, doi:10.1109/BigData.2016.7840765.

Chie Dou (1994). A highly-parallel architecture for concurrent rule match of AI production systems, *Proceedings of TENCON'94 - 1994 IEEE Region 10's 9th Annual International Conference on: 'Frontiers of Computer Technology'*, 2, pp. 687–691, doi:10.1109/TENCON.1994.369217.

Cook, A., Wu, P., & Mengersen, K. (2015). Machine learning and visual analytics for consulting business decision support, *2015 Big Data Visual Analytics (BDVA)*, pp. 1–2, doi:10.1109/BDVA.2015.7314299.

Cowling, P. I., Devlin, S., Powley, E. J., Whitehouse, D., & Rollason, J. (2015). Player preference and style in a leading mobile card game, *IEEE Transactions on Computational Intelligence and AI in Games*, 7(3), pp. 233–242, doi:10.1109/TCIAIG.2014.2357174.

Das, D. & Sarkar, S. (2018). Machine-to-machine learning based framework for ad-hoc IoT ecosystems, *2018 International Conference on Computational Techniques, Electronics and Mechanical Systems (CTEMS)*, pp. 431–436, doi:10.1109/CTEMS.2018.8769148.

Dou, C. (1993). A highly-parallel match architecture for ai production systems using application-specific associative matching processors, *Proceedings of International Conference on Application Specific Array Processors (ASAP '93)*, pp. 180–183, doi:10.1109/ASAP.1993.397140.

Epishkina, A., & Zapechnikov, S. (2016). A syllabus on data mining and machine learning with applications to cybersecurity, *2016 Third International Conference on Digital Information Processing, Data Mining, and Wireless Communications (DIPDMWC)*, pp. 194–199, doi:10.1109/DIPDMWC.2016.7529388.

Gao, C., Liu, H., Wang, X., & Huang, J. (2015). Configuration circuit design for burn-in test of CLB based on structure, *2015 Prognostics and System Health Management Conference (PHM)*, pp. 1–5, doi:10.1109/PHM.2015.7380071.

Guan, H., Zhang, Z., & Tan, T. (2018). Inception donut convolution for top-down semantic segmentation, *2018 24th International Conference on Pattern Recognition (ICPR)*, pp. 2492–2497, doi:10.1109/ICPR.2018.8545386.

Gupta, A. & Jagadish, S. (2017). Machine learning oriented gesture controlled device for the speech and motion impaired, *2017 International Conference on Data Management, Analytics and Innovation (ICDMAI)*, pp. 294–297, doi:10.1109/ICDMAI.2017. 8073528.

Gupta, S. K., Phung, D., & Venkatesh, S. (2012). A nonparametric bayesian poisson gamma model for count data, *Proceedings of the 21st International Conference on Pattern Recognition (ICPR2012)*, pp. 1815–1818, 1051-4651, 1051-4651. doi: 10.1109/ EMBC.2016.7591246

Harris, D. R., Baus, A. D., Harper, T. J., Jarrett, T. D., Pollard, C. R., & Talbert, J. C. (2016). Using i2b2 to bootstrap rural health analytics and learning networks, *2016 38th Annual International Conference of the IEEE Engineering in Medicine and Biology Society (EMBC)*, pp. 2533–2536, doi:10.1109/EMBC.2016.7591246.

He, X., Chu, L., Qiu, R. C., Ai, Q., & Ling, Z. (2018). A novel data-driven situation awareness approach for future grids using large random matrices for Big Data modeling, *IEEE Access, 6*, pp. 13855–13865, doi:10.1109/ACCESS.2018. 2805815.

Hui, K. & Siu, W. (2007). Extended analysis of motion-compensated frame difference for block-based motion prediction error, *IEEE Transactions on Image Processing, 16*(5), pp. 1232–1245, doi:10.1109/TIP.2007.894263.

Ionita, S. (2018, June). Modeling human sensory-motor action for vehicle braking based on fuzzy inferences, In *2018 10th International Conference on Electronics, Computers and Artificial Intelligence (ECAI)* (pp. 1–7). IEEE.

Jing, F.-S., Tan, M., Hou, Z.-G., Liang, Z.-Z., Wang, Y.-K., Gupta, M. M., & Nikiforuk, P. N. (2006). Kinematic analysis of a flexible six-DOF parallel mechanism, *IEEE Transactions on Systems, Man, and Cybernetics, Part B (Cybernetics), 36*(2), pp. 379–389, doi:10.1109/TSMCB.2005.858409.

Keller, J. M., Buck, A. R., Zare, A., & Popescu, M. (2014). A human geospatial predictive analytics framework with application to finding medically underserved areas, *2014 IEEE Symposium on Computational Intelligence in Big Data (CIBD)*, pp. 1–6, doi: 10.1109/CIBD.2014.7011525.

Khan, M. A., Cheema, A. R., & Hasan, A. (2008). Improved Nonce construction scheme for AES CCMP to evade initial counter prediction, *2008 Ninth ACIS International Conference on Software Engineering, Artificial Intelligence, Networking, and Parallel/ Distributed Computing*, pp. 307–311, doi:10.1109/SNPD.2008.102.

Kiekintveld, C. & Wellman, M. P. (2005). An analysis of the 2004 supply chain management trading agent competition, *NAFIPS 2005 – 2005 Annual Meeting of the North American Fuzzy Information Processing Society*, pp. 257–262, doi:10.1109/NAFIPS. 2005.1548544.

Krause, J., Dasgupta, A., Swartz, J., Aphinyanaphongs, Y., & Bertini, E. (2017). A workflow for visual diagnostics of binary classifiers using instance-level explanations, *2017 IEEE Conference on Visual Analytics Science and Technology (VAST)*, pp. 162–172, doi:10. 1109/VAST.2017.8585720.

Lee, S., Park, S., & Park, Y. B. (2019). Formal specification technique in smart contract verification, *2019 International Conference on Platform Technology and Service (PlatCon)*, pp. 1–4, doi:10.1109/PlatCon.2019.8669419.

Li, G., Xing, S., & Xue, H. (2009). Improved chain-block algorithm to RVM on large scale problems, *2009 International Conference on Management of e-Commerce and e-Government*, pp. 205–208, doi:10.1109/ICMeCG.2009.21.

Maleh, Y., Lakkineni, S., Tawalbeh, L. A., & AbdEl-Latif, A. A. (2022). Blockchain for cyber-physical systems: Challenges and applications. *Advances in Blockchain Technology for Cyber Physical Systems*, pp. 11–59.

Monteiro, S., & Vijaya, B. (2017). Ontology population from complex sentences document, *2017 International Conference on Energy, Communication, Data Analytics and Soft Computing (ICECDS)*, pp. 951–954, doi:10.1109/ICECDS.2017.8389577.

Nauck, D. D., Ruta, D., Spott, M., & Azvine, B. (2006). A tool for intelligent customer analytics, *2006 3rd International IEEE Conference Intelligent Systems*, pp. 518–521, doi:10.1109/IS.2006.348473.

Nemati, A., Feizi, S., Ahmadi, A., Haghiri, S., Ahmadi, M., & Alirezaee, S. (2015, March). An efficient hardware implementation of few lightweight block cipher. In *2015 The International Symposium on Artificial Intelligence and Signal Processing (AISP)* (pp. 273-278). IEEE.

Nguyen, T., Nguyen, V., Nguyen, T., Venkatesh, S., Kumar, M., & Phung, D. (2016). Learning multifaceted latent activities from heterogeneous mobile data, *2016 IEEE International Conference on Data Science and Advanced Analytics (DSAA)*, pp. 389–398, doi:10.1109/DSAA.2016.48.

Nguyen, T., Phung, D., Gupta, S., & Venkatesh, S. (2013). Extraction of latent patterns and contexts from social honest signals using hierarchical dirichlet processes, *2013 IEEE International Conference on Pervasive Computing and Communications (PerCom)*, pp. 47–55, doi:10.1109/PerCom.2013.6526713.

Pan, G., Dou, Q., & Xie, L. (2007). Study on distributing pattern of shared data in CC-NUMA system, *Eighth ACIS International Conference on Software Engineering, Artificial Intelligence, Networking, and Parallel/Distributed Computing (SNPD 2007)*, 3, pp. 9–14, doi:10.1109/SNPD.2007.398.

Patel, H. B., & Gandhi, S. (2018). A review on big data analytics in healthcare using machine learning approaches, *2018 2nd International Conference on Trends in Electronics and Informatics (ICOEI)*, pp. 84–90, doi:10.1109/ICOEI.2018.8553788.

Popescu, D., Ercegovac, V., Balmin, A., Branco, M., & Ailamaki, A. (2012). Same queries, different data: Can we predict performance?, *2012 IEEE 28th International Conference on Data Engineering Workshops*, pp. 275–280, doi:10.1109/ICDEW.2012.66.

Qayumi, K. (2015). Multi-agent based intelligence generation from very large datasets, *2015 IEEE International Conference on Cloud Engineering*, pp. 502–504, doi:10.1109/IC2E.2015.96.

Ray, B., Howdhury, M., Abawajy, J., & Jesmin, M. (2015). Secure object tracking protocol for networked RFID systems, *2015 IEEE/ACIS 16th International Conference on Software Engineering, Artificial Intelligence, Networking and Parallel/Distributed Computing (SNPD)*, pp. 1–7, doi:10.1109/SNPD.2015.7176190.

Rogers, J., Simmons, D., Shah, M., Rowland, C., & Shang, Y. (2019). Deep learning at your fingertips, *2019 16th IEEE Annual Consumer Communications & Networking Conference (CCNC)*, pp. 1–4, doi:10.1109/CCNC.2019.8651868.

Sakiz, B., & Kutlugun, E. (2018). Bitcoin price forecast via blockchain technology and artificial intelligence algorithms, *2018 26th Signal Processing and Communications Applications Conference (SIU)*, pp. 1–4, doi:10.1109/SIU.2018.8404719.

Saksupawattanakul, C., & Vatanawood, W. (2018) Event-B formalization of basic supply chain patterns, *2018 19th IEEE/ACIS International Conference on Software Engineering, Artificial Intelligence, Networking and Parallel/Distributed Computing (SNPD)*, pp. 352–357, doi:10.1109/SNPD.2018.8441070.

Simi, M. S., & Nayaki, K. S. (2017). Data analytics in medical data: A review, *2017 International Conference on Circuit, Power and Computing Technologies (ICCPCT)*, pp. 1–4, doi:10.1109/ICCPCT.2017.8074337.

Sobolevsky, S., Massaro, E., Bojic, I., Arias, J. M., & Ratti, C. (2017). Predicting regional economic indices using big data of individual bank card transactions, *2017 IEEE International Conference on Big Data (Big Data)*, pp. 1313–1318, doi:10.1109/BigData.2017.8258061.

Starzyk, J. A., & He, H. (2009). Spatio Temporal memories for machine learning: A long-term memory organization, *IEEE Transactions on Neural Networks*, 20(5), pp. 768–780, doi:10.1109/TNN.2009.2012854.

Tannahill, B. K., Maute, C. E., Yetis, Y., Ezell, M. N., Jaimes, A., Rosas, R., Motaghi, A., Kaplan, H., & Jamshidi, M. (2013). Modeling of System of systems via data analytics case for bigdata in SoS, *2013 8th International Conference on System of Systems Engineering*, pp. 177–183, doi:10.1109/SYSoSE.2013.6575263.

Tian, Y., Tatikonda, S., & Reinwald, B. (2012). Scalable and numerically stable descriptive statistics in system ML, *2012 IEEE 28th International Conference on Data Engineering*, pp. 1351–1359, doi:10.1109/ICDE.2012.12.

Yetis, Y., Sara, R. G., Erol, B. A., Kaplan, H., Akuzum, A., & Jamshidi, M. (2016). Application of big data analytics via cloud computing, *2016 World Automation Congress (WAC)*, pp. 1–5, doi:10.1109/WAC.2016.7582986.

Yu, L. & Wu, L. (2007). Comments on "A separable low complexity 2D HMM with application to face recognition", *IEEE Transactions on Pattern Analysis and Machine Intelligence*, 29(2), pp. 368–368, doi:10.1109/TPAMI.2007.27.

Zakeri, A., Saberi, M., Hussain, O. K., & Chang, E. (2018). An early detection system for proactive management of raw milk quality: An Australian case study, *IEEE Access*, 6, pp. 64333–64349, doi:10.1109/ACCESS.2018.2877970.

8 Blockchain Solutions for Security and Privacy Issues in Smart Health Care

Pinky Bai and Sushil Kumar
School of Computer & Systems Sciences
Jawaharlal Nehru University, New Delhi, India

Upasana Dohare
Department of Computer Applications, School of
Computing Science & Engineering, Galgotias University,
Greater Noida, Uttar Pradesh, India

CONTENTS

DOI: 10.1201/9781003319917-11

8.1   INTRODUCTION

Smart health care faces security and privacy issues due to the heterogeneity of components and large attack surface area. The medical services are the death questions for the patient, so any vulnerability is very harmful in smart health care. According to a study, volumetric DDoS attacks constitute 73% of all DDoS attacks recorded in 2016. The medical devices and Internet of Medical Things (IoMT) devices, including body sensors, can be stolen, and the information can be exposed to attackers. The attacker can change the real device with the malicious device to get the network's information and possible penetration. Misplacement and un-authorized access to health data cause physical and personal damage. This demands an alternative approach to tackle the challenges of a complex system. Many blockchain-based security solutions have emerged, such as secure data storage, secure data sharing, access control, authentication and authorization, drug supply, remote patient monitoring, and many more in the literature.

The health data must be secure in transit and stored in smart health care. The security solutions for health care need to be more stringent for data storage and sharing of health records due to existing legal requirements like the Health Insurance Portability and Accountability Act (HIPAA), Health Information and Technology for Economic and Clinical Health Act (HITECH), General Data Protection Regulations (GDPR), IT, and many more. The healthcare system needs the health data to follow the CIA (confidentiality, integrity, and availability), and blockchain can help achieve these requirements. Blockchain-based systems maintain the secure storage and sharing of health data among stakeholders. The proposed chapter discusses how blockchain can achieve data security in smart health care.

8.1.1 RESEARCH OBJECTIVES

This chapter aims to provide an overview of security and privacy challenges in the smart healthcare system. Research objectives are the same as follows:

1. Provide a detailed overview of smart health care and component of smart health care.
2. Explore the security and privacy requirement of the smart healthcare system.
3. Present a detailed description of the attack surface in the existing smart healthcare system model.
4. Summarize the existing security and privacy challenges in smart health care.
5. Explore the possible solution for security and privacy with the help of blockchain and computational intelligence.

8.1.2 ORGANISATION

The paper is presented in seven sections and a conclusion. Section 8.2 explains the smart healthcare architecture and components. Section 8.3 elaborates on the security and privacy requirements of smart health care. Section 8.4 describes the security and privacy issues in smart health care and the attack surface. Section 8.5 explains the blockchain and blockchain application in smart health care. Section 8.6 describes mitigating security and privacy issues using blockchain in smart health care. Section 8.7 describes the use case of computational intelligence for smart health care. And Section 8.8 concludes the chapter.

8.2 SMART HEALTH CARE

Use of ICT, including biosensors, wearable devices, Internet of Things (IoT), and body area network devices, reform health care into smart health. Though there is no specific definition of smart health care, the adoption of automation and decision-making capabilities make any system "smart." Baker defines smart health care as an upgraded version of the traditional health system with decision capabilities and automation. Smart health care focuses on empowering the users to self-manage in emergencies. Some researchers define smart health care as per their research in the area of uses. The most relevant vital definitions are as follows.

Solanas et al. define smart health care:

> Smart health (s-health) as the provision of health services by using the context-aware network and sensing infrastructure of smart cities. The main goal of smart health is to promote health to a higher position within society in a distributed, private, secure, efficient, and sustainable way by reusing the principles of m- health and smart cities in a convergent new paradigm of ubiquitous health.

Eysenbach et al. define smart health care as

> an emerging field in the intersection of medical informatics, public health, and business, referring to health services and information delivered or enhanced through the Internet and related technologies. In a broader sense, the term characterizes not only a technical development but also a state of mind, a way of thinking, an attitude, and a commitment to networked, global thinking, to improve health care locally, regionally, and worldwide; by using information and communication technology.

Istepanian et al. explain:

> A probably more important revolution is taking place due to the use of mobile devices (e.g., smartphones): mobile health (m-health), which could be defined as the discipline founded on the use of mobile communication devices in medicine or, more specifically, the delivery of healthcare services via mobile communication devices; or: emerging mobile communications and network technologies for healthcare systems.

Smart health care provides solutions that combine e-health, m-health, and connected health to offer qualitative services to each patient at any place and any time. Smart health care focuses globally on society since everyone will become a patient during their lifetime, and we all participate in healthcare costs (Baker et al., 2017). Smart health care covers the quality of health services, supply chain management, energy conservation, end-user awareness, remote monitoring of the patient, electronically storing health records, mobile accessibility of health services, and many more (Demirkan, 2013). We discuss the components and architecture in the next sections to get more understanding and clarity about smart health care.

8.2.1 COMPONENTS OF SMART HEALTH CARE

Smart health care has the following components:

- IoT and medical devices
- Data management

- Connectivity
- Stakeholders
- Supply chain management
- Services
- Administration

Fig. 8.1 presents the component of smart health care (Eysenbach, 2001; Solanas et al., 2014; Sundaravadivel et al., 2017). The detailed description of components follows.

8.2.1.1 IoT and Medical Devices

Smart health care has different devices for different purposes, such as body sensors or wearables, to monitor patients. The medical devices are used to collect, transmit, analyze, and store the patients' health data. The devices include body sensors, smart wearables, smart measuring devices like a thermometer, smartwatch monitoring, and many more (Baker et al., 2017; Sundaravadivel et al., 2017).

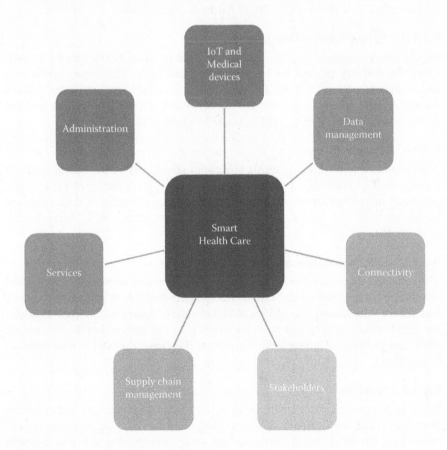

FIGURE 8.1 Smart healthcare components.

8.2.1.2   Connectivity

Smart health care uses connectivity technologies such as wired/wireless communication, cellular network, body area network, and many more to provide seamless connectivity. Remote health monitoring is improved after integrating small medical devices (body sensors) and IoT. For IoT devices, the communication protocols are different and light-weight, such as IPV6, 6LoWPAN, RFID, and many more, to connect in smart health care. Smart health care needs constant Internet connectivity support using WiFi, cellular networks, and Ethernet (Solanas et al., 2014; Abouelmehdi et al., 2018).

8.2.1.3   Stakeholders

Stakeholders in smart health care participate in the system to get the services or provide the services. The stakeholder's primary responsibility is to maintain security, privacy, update data in health care, and use it for better health services. Healthcare stakeholders include patients, doctors, researchers, pharmaceuticals, hospitals, government, business users, regulators, clinical trials, and many more (Eysenbach, 2001; Baker et al., 2017; Aileni & Suciu, 2020).

8.2.1.4   Supply Chain Management

Supply chain management plays an essential role in smart health care by streamlining the delivery process for medical drugs and equipment. Smart health care has scattered ordering systems for medical drugs, equipment, and other critical resources. The patient would directly impact health if supply chain management is compromised (Baker et al., 2017; Sundaravadivel et al., 2017).

8.2.1.5   Administration

Administration looks into the whole process of smart health care and manages all the non-clinical operations such as financial, staffing, budgeting, safety, security, and many more. Administrators manage the planning, directing, and coordination health services and health service providers (Demirkan, 2013; Abouelmehdi et al., 2018).

8.2.1.6   Data Management

The collected data increases exponentially as IoT devices are introduced in smart health care for automation and fast services. Smart health care collects, processes, and shares data among the different stakeholders. Smart health care manages the health data securely and provides privacy to the patient health information (PHI) and publicly identifiable information (PII) (Demirkan, 2013; Abouelmehdi et al., 2018).

8.2.1.7   Services

Smart health care provides health services to improve patient health and eliminate diseases. These services are doctor consultants, nursing care, remote patient monitoring, medical social services, and many more. M-health and e-health are also part of smart healthcare services. Healthcare organizations can provide cost-effective and quality services to patients after adopting the smart healthcare framework (Demirkan, 2013).

8.2.2 SMART HEALTHCARE ARCHITECTURE

We referenced the standard healthcare architecture to study related security and privacy issues, as present in the chapter. The below architecture defines the information flow among different stakeholder in the smart healthcare system (Demirkan, 2013; Baker et al., 2017; Sundaravadivel et al., 2017). Fig. 8.2 shows the information flow in the healthcare system.

8.2.3 RESEARCH METHODOLOGY

This work analyzes the security and privacy issues in smart health care along with the solution for these issues. The participation of blockchain to provide the solution in smart health care is also explored. The work identifies the domain, key objectives, techniques, challenges, and solutions. Many renowned databases, including IEEE, Springer, Elsevier, MDPI, and arXive, were considered to collect the related literature.

Papers were selected using the following methodology:

1. Search closed and open databases.
2. Use specific keywords: Smart health care, security, privacy, security and privacy requirements, authentication, access control, confidentiality, data storage, data sharing in smart health care, and security and privacy solutions using blockchain and computational intelligence to collect the research works.

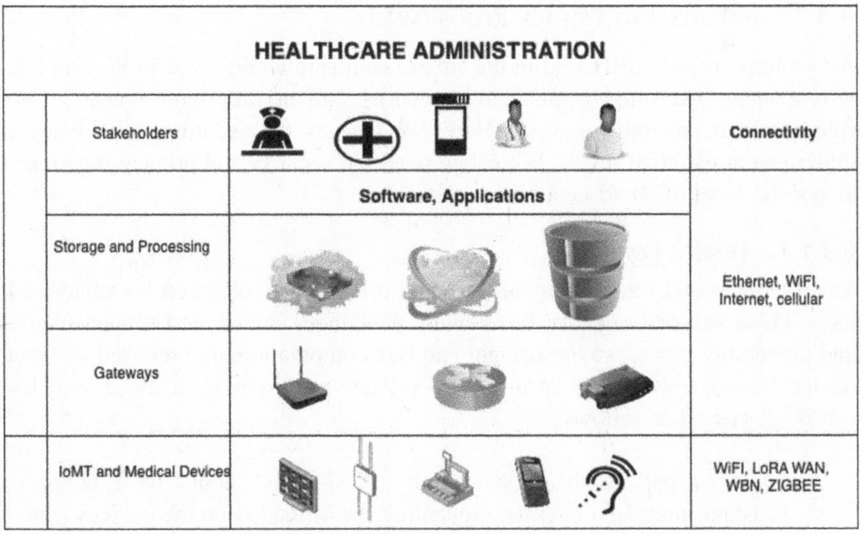

FIGURE 8.2 Basic smart healthcare architecture.

3. Remove the papers that are not peer-reviewed.
4. Remove the papers that are not relevant to the smart healthcare security and privacy.
5. Analyze and classify the papers to get the required results per the research objective.

8.3   SECURITY AND PRIVACY REQUIREMENTS OF SMART HEALTH CARE

The smart healthcare stores, maintains, and transfers large amounts of data to provide quality care to the patients. The security and privacy of massive health data is a highly complicated and critical process for organizations. The disclosure of health data is becoming a common issue due to a lack of security controls.

The security and privacy of health data are significant concerns. Data privacy has the control over personally identifiable information and personal health information in the system. Privacy targets the usage and governance of individuals' personal data, such as establishing authorization requirements and policies to ensure that patients' personal information is collected, shared, and utilized truthfully. Appropriate use of the personal information of the patient comes under privacy.

Meanwhile, security can be defined as protecting the system against unauthorized access and maintaining integrity and availability. Security targets protecting data from malignant attacks and data stealing for profit. Although security is essential for protecting data, it is insufficient for addressing privacy. The system's security is the "Confidentiality, Integrity and Availability" of health data in smart healthcare (Abouelmehdi et al., 2018).

8.3.1   SECURITY AND PRIVACY REQUIREMENTS

As we have already discussed in the smart healthcare architecture in Section 8.2.2, it is evident that smart health care's security and privacy requirement is more rigorous than any other system. Here, we discuss the security and privacy requirement at different levels. We categorized the security and privacy requirement as per the level of smart healthcare architecture.

8.3.1.1   Device Level

Smart devices and sensors play an essential role in data collection for smart health care. These sensors' security faces many challenges due to constrained memory and processing power, so lightweight and less computation are preferred at the end device (sensor) level. The security and privacy requirement at the device level can be discussed as follows:

A. *Tamper-proof*: Medical devices in the systems should have tamper-resistant integrated circuits, preventing codes loaded on the devices from being read by third parties once deployed. An example solution is to use blockchain to enable trusted and auditable computing using a decentralized network (Chanson et al., 2019).

B. *Secure OTA Update*: The different types of sensors or devices are implanted at different locations for the remote monitoring of patients and hospitals in smart health care. The over-the-air update (OTA) method is used to update the firmware, operating system, and security updates of medical devices deployed remotely. The OTA mechanism's secure implementation must be required in smart health care (Zandberg et al., 2019).

C. *Device Authentication*: The malicious device can send false information about the patient's health for diagnosis and care. Further, false information could negatively impact the patient's health. Therefore, device authentication in smart health care must be required. The device or sensors must authenticate themselves on the server before sending the data (Ferrag et al., 2020) (Fig. 8.3).

8.3.1.2   Application Level

A. *User Authentication*: The user variety in smart health care is vast and comes with its own set of vulnerabilities. The system must authenticate users who want to interact with the system and access services. Authentication establishes or confirms the user's claims (Aslam et al., 2017; Kazemi et al., 2020).

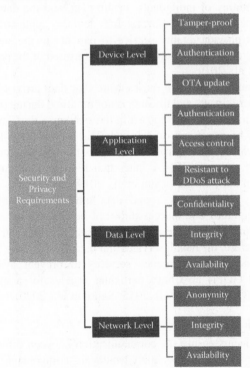

FIGURE 8.3   Smart healthcare security and privacy requirements.

B. *Access Control*: Smart health care stores and processes PHI and PII. Smart health care must ensure control and legitimate access to health data, either public or private. The data collector organization must ask patient's consent before sharing the patient's information with other agencies. Permission-based systems seem difficult to implement, so the medical service provider controls patient information access. Smart health care must deploy an access control policy to manage access to critical information (Kunneman et al., 2017; Rajput et al., 2019).

C. *DDoS Resilient*: Different types of distributed denial of service can be made at different layers like the application layer, network layer, transport layer, and physical layer. Smart health care needs solutions that are resilient to DDoS attacks at each layer. Furthermore, the system must implement DDoS detection, prevention, and mitigation (Salim et al., 2020).

8.3.1.3   Data Level

A. *Confidentiality*: Smart health care collects and stores the patient's information. The collection and storage of health information should comply with privacy and legal regulations such as HIPAA, GDPR, and Personal Data Protection Bill, and many more. The system must ensure the confidentiality of individuals' health data, and the data must be safe from breaches or closure. Several IoT devices, applications, and other stakeholders provide quality service to patients in the smart healthcare domain. Therefore, confidentiality must be ensured of the patient's PII and PHI (Sun et al., 2019).

B. *Integrity*: Smart health care must ensure that data arrives from intended devices or participants and the data is not modified during travel. The data integrity controls must be imposed in the system so that data alteration or stealing can be prevented or detected. The regulations address this differently, such as GDPR Article 5(d) states that the patient data must be accurate and updated. HIPAA states that PHI information cannot be altered without authorization (Sun et al., 2019).

C. *Availability*: Health services and data must be available to patients whenever required. The inaccessibility of health data or services can be life-threatening, such as the inability to generate alerts during an asthma attack. Therefore, the health services and data must always be available to the users and other emergency services to prevent availability loss. HIPAA and GDPR also have particular articles for assurance of data availability (Catarinucci et al., 2015; Salim et al., 2020).

8.3.1.4   Network Level

Networking components ensure the communication between different medical devices and sensors, as well as the smart healthcare components. The networking component and the process are also secure, stable, and available all the time.

A. *Anonymity*: The network devices and communication process/process should not be identified and tracked by the attackers. A mechanism like collision pseudonyms must be ensured in the smart healthcare network.

B. *Integrity*: Network device and protocol configuration must be secure and should not be alerted by unauthorized entities. Effective necessary mechanisms should be used to ensure the integrity of communication.

C. *Availability*: The communication protocol must be free from vulnerabilities like DDoS and always available (Salim et al., 2020; Newaz et al., 2020).

8.4 SECURITY AND PRIVACY ISSUES IN SMART HEALTH CARE

8.4.1 Attack Surface in Smart Health Care

The smart healthcare system is loaded with new technologies (ICT) to provide quality services to patients. As discussed in the earlier section, the current healthcare model components have their security and privacy challenges. Here we discuss the attack surface in smart health care at each layer.

8.4.1.1 Device Layer

The medical devices and Internet of Medical Things (IoMT) devices, including body sensors, can be stolen, and the information can be exposed to attackers. The attacker can change the real device with the malicious device to get the network's information and make penetration possible (Ichikawa et al., 2017).

Medical and IoT devices are gates for attackers to enter the smart healthcare system. Device firmware, device memory, device update, and device physical interface are the most common attack surfaces at the device end. Attackers can get sensitive information like hardcoded credentials, firmware versions, cryptographic keys for different operations, and firmware versions by accessing the firmware. The other attacks are firmware version degradation, stealing the sensitive information stored on a device's memory like encryption keys, device ID, privilege escalation by getting access to the device interface, and many more (Newaz et al., 2020).

8.4.1.2 Network Layer

The network layer manages the communication among devices to application or device or database to pass the health data at different layers to store, process, and analyze. The attackers can use communication means or network services to launch the DoS, buffer overflow, and replay attacks. Over-the-air (OTA) updates, privacy, and integrations breaches are performed from the network interfaces (Sun et al., 2019).

8.4.1.3 Application Layer

Various health applications interact with smart healthcare systems to provide smart health services to patients. The attackers can use vulnerable applications to breach healthcare services. The most common vulnerabilities as per OWASP top 10 at application layers are weak authentication and authorization, SQL injection, privilege escalations, security misconfiguration, broken access control, cross-site scripting, sensitive data exposure, etc. This layer has a broad attack surface and is thus more compromised and vulnerable (Chacko & Hayajneh, 2018; Hathaliya & Tanwar, 2020; Iwaya et al., 2020).

8.4.1.4   Data Layer

Smart health care uses various types of database structures to store the health data like cloud computing storage, relational database system, NoSQL data storage, etc. This storage format comes with its vulnerabilities and becomes an attack surface or gateway to compromise smart health care (Hathaliya & Tanwar, 2020, Iwaya et al., 2020).

8.4.2   Security and Privacy Issues in Smart Health Care

Here we discuss the most common security and privacy attacks in the smart healthcare system. We categorized the security and privacy attack according to the attack surface-wise, as discussed in Section 8.4.1. Table 8.1 presents the security and privacy attacks (Chacko & Hayajneh, 2018; Zhang et al., 2018; Algarni, 2019; Butpheng et al., 2020; Hathaliya & Tanwar, 2020; Iwaya et al., 2020).

A detailed explanation of security and privacy issues follows.

TABLE 8.1

Security and Privacy Attack in Smart Health Care

S. No.	Target Layer	Attack Type	Impacted Data Security Parameter
1	Application Layer	Weak authentication and authorization	Integrity, Confidentiality
		Privilege escalation	
		Outdated operating system	
		Forged firmware updates	
2.	Network/Communication Layer	Eavesdropping	Integrity, Confidentiality, Availability
		Replay	
		Impersonation	
		Denial of service	
		Man in the middle	
3	Physical Layer/Device Layer	Side channel attack	Integrity, Confidentiality, Availability
		Electromagnetic interference	
		Differential power analysis	
		Reverse engineering attack	
		Battery depletion	
4	Storage Layer	Data alteration	Integrity, Confidentiality, Availability
		Data exposure	
		Unencrypted data	
		Unauthorized access	

8.4.2.1 Weak Authentication and Unauthorized Access

The most common security attack on the smart healthcare system is unauthorized access to services. Smart health care is more vulnerable to unauthorized access because of the heterogeneity of components in the ecosystem. The attackers can access the system through many routes like smart medical devices installed at the patient side, the monitoring application, the mobile application, the communication networks, and many more.

8.4.2.2 Outdated Operating System and Firmware

Many medical devices do not upgrade security patches timely, and attackers enter the system with known vulnerabilities in the older operating system, firmware, software, or application. Further, the OTA method introduces many security vulnerabilities in the network, such as malicious sensors forging the update.

8.4.2.3 Eavesdropping and Replay Attack

The flow of information in smart healthcare routes through the large network of smart healthcare components, and the attackers can listen to this information through an open communication channel. Further, the attacker can send modified information to the patient or health service provider for ill purposes.

8.4.2.4 Physical Tampering of Node

The attackers capture the openly deployed sensors and send false information to the receiver. Attackers generate high transmission power and use the compromised node to compromise other components or nodes in smart health care and fail the smart health care.

8.4.2.5 Denial of Service

The compromised/malicious smart healthcare component generates so much traffic that the authorized node does not get the desired service. As the server is busy replying to bogus requests raised by the malicious node, the full network halts, and authorized nodes do not get the services. The medical services are the death questions critical information for the patient, so DDoS is very harmful in smart health care.

8.4.2.6 Social Engineering

The patient or information holders can be influenced to reveal the information for harmful purposes. The GDPR Article provides a provision for deleting the patient's data after the purpose is met. The data collector must mention the purpose of data collection. At the same time, HIPAA focuses on health data collection and protection.

8.4.2.7 Data Modification and Disclosure

Patient health information is a critical and sensitive factor in smart health care. The disclosure of the information may cause financial or health harm to the patients. Similarly, message modification between the health service provider and the patient can be the reason for life threats.

8.4.2.8   Rerouting

The attackers insert a malicious node to reroute the information and change the destination. This rerouting leads to missing critical information and the use of missing information benefits the attackers.

8.4.2.9   Side-Channel Attack

In a side-channel attack, the attacker steals sensitive data like encryption methods, cryptographic keys, and others by analyzing the physical parameters like energy and time without disturbing the ongoing operations. The attackers mainly analyze the circuit working process, processing methods, data, when the device is in use, etc. Smart health care faces side-channel attacks on field-deployed sensors and patient devices.

8.4.2.10   Weak Encryption and Hashing

Smart health care uses breakable or compromised encryption and hashing algorithms while saving and transmitting the information. This results in exposure of patient data and is life-threatening. Smart health care must use standard algorithms like AES 256, ESDSA, and many others.

Researchers worked on the security and privacy issues in health care. They identified that medical devices are most targeted among smart healthcare components; the network layer faces most attacks and integrity is the most impacted parameter (Chacko & Hayajneh, 2018; Zhang et al., 2018; Algarni, 2019; Butpheng et al., 2020; Hathaliya & Tanwar, 2020; Iwaya et al., 2020).

8.5   BLOCKCHAIN USE CASES IN SMART HEALTH CARE

8.5.1   BLOCKCHAIN

A book written by Swan explains blockchain technology in detail. In simple terms, blockchain is a decentralized public ledger technology. A ledger stores the committed transaction in the form of a chain of blocks. The consensus of the participants verifies transactions. Furthermore, the participants share the ledger. We can frame a standard definition of blockchain: "Blockchain is a decentralized computation and information sharing platform which enables multiple authoritative domains which do not trust each other to cooperate coordinate and collaborate in a rational decision-making process."

Although Bitcoin is the most famous blockchain application, blockchain has diverse applications in other areas far beyond cryptocurrencies. Blockchain has applications in several financial services like online payment, tokenization, digital assets management, etc., because blockchain does not need a third party or bank to process the payment. Furthermore, blockchain is also improving other application areas such as smart contracts, public services like digital ID, land registry, etc., Internet of Things (IoT), reputation systems and security services, supply chain, real estate, food safety, stock exchanges, power grid and peer-to-peer energy markets, digital evidence, smart health care, and others in the next generation of Internet interaction systems.

Blockchain technology has key characteristics, such as decentralization, anonymity, trustless network, persistency, and audibility. Blockchain technology has a decentralized environment and integrates with various core technologies such as digital signatures, cryptographic algorithms, and distributed consensus protocols. All the transactions can take place in a decentralized manner with blockchain technology. And this nature of blockchain can save costs and improve the system's efficiency. The main characteristics of blockchain can be summarized as follows:

1. **Decentralization:** In the centralized transaction system, all transactions must be validated by the trusted third/central party, and the central authority becomes a bottleneck in terms of cost and performance. While in the blockchain, the transaction can occur between peers without central authority authentication. And, blockchain can reduce development and operation costs and improve performance.
2. **Immutability:** The alternation or change is not possible on the ledger. Once transactions are stored on a specific block in the change, any change is not allowed in the blockchain.
3. **Persistency:** The transactions are recorded in blocks and distributed over all the participants/nodes in the network, so tampering with a transaction is very difficult or nearly impossible. Additionally, all the transactions are validated before storing the block, and the block also would be validated by the nodes before adding in the chain so falsification can be detected.
4. **Anonymity:** Each user interacts with the blockchain network using a cryptographically generated address instead of a real identity. Additionally, a user can generate many addresses to hide the real identity. The blockchain does not need to store personal information on any central server. The anonymity preserves the privacy of nodes.
5. **Auditability/Transparent:** The user can easily verify and trace the previous records at any distributed node because the transactions are validated and recorded with the transaction generator's digital signature and time-stamp. Each transaction can be traced to a previous transaction iteratively in the Bitcoin network.
6. **Trustless Network:** Blockchain provides a trustless network to the participant. The participants do not need to know or trust each other to run the system. However, the nodes themselves need not be specifically permitted to participate with the additional property. The trust is distributed among the nodes, and no single node needs not to be trusted (Swan, 2015).

8.5.2 Blockchain Applications in Smart Health Care

Blockchain has a use case in health care and other industries like IoT, financial, governance, and others. Health care is one of the regulatory bodies of any nation, and blockchain can improve the healthcare domain's service. Blockchain has a positive impact on health care to solve the traditional system issues; blockchain can provide secure infrastructure to smart health care. Further, blockchain applications exist for secure storage of health records and secure sharing of health records

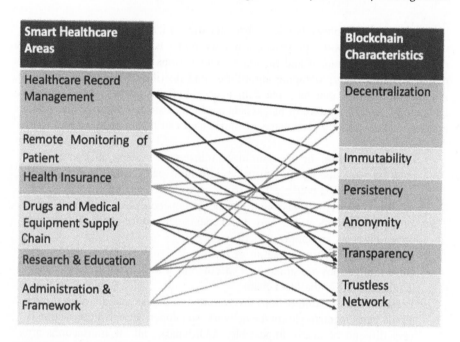

FIGURE 8.4 Blockchain application in smart health care.

among smart healthcare stakeholders. Blockchain provides privacy to the patient while recording, sharing, and analyzing health records; drug supply chain management; fast and efficient health insurance process, etc. We discuss all the applications of blockchain in smart health care further.

Fig. 8.4 maps the smart healthcare area to blockchain characteristics that improve, secure, or increase the smart healthcare process. For example, smart health care record management can be secure, privacy-preserving, auditable, fast, and well maintained by using blockchain's decentralization, immutability, transparency, and persistency.

We can categorize the application of blockchain as follows.

8.5.2.1 Healthcare Record Management

Smart health care has different types of records like patient health records (PHR), electronic health records (EHR), electrotonic medical records (EMR), and prescriptions. We use only the health record term for further analysis and discussion here. Smart health care finds blockchain technology suitable for storing and managing health records because of blockchain's characteristics like decentralization, immutability, smart contract, security and privacy, and auditability. Most blockchain applications are around secure health record storage and sharing.

  a. **Health record storage:** In smart health care, the patient information is captured through the wearable sensor or IoT medical devices, medical reports, clinical/hospital visits, prescriptions, etc. The amount of health records is exponentially increasing as the use of IoT devices increases in health care. Blockchain is a viable choice for managing large storage of health records. MedRec, MedBlock, and SMEAD are some excellent applications of blockchain for the secure storage of health records. Zang et al., Agbo et al., and Griggs et al. present a systematic survey of blockchain applications as storage for healthcare systems (Hölbl et al., 2018; Zhang et al., 2018; Agbo et al., 2019).

b. **Sharing health care data:** The healthcare organization handles critical health records and confidential documents under strict laws. These records are stored in a centralized database in the traditional health-care system. The centralized storing database has security and privacy issues along with a difficult sharing process. The sharing of centralized stored data becomes an issue when overseas or interstate hospitals need particular patient data in the case of medical tourism operations. Here, blockchain can help in distributed storing and sharing of health records. Mettler (2016), Zhang et al. (2018), and McGhin et al. (2019) show that blockchain is a solution for data sharing in smart health care. Many solutions are analyzed in the survey papers.

8.5.2.2   Remote Monitoring of Patients

In remote patient monitoring, the IoT devices and wireless body area network (WBAN) participate in collecting the measures of patients. The data is collected from heterogeneous sources and must be formatted in a single format to analyze and process for providing the service to the patients. At the same time, secure transmission of measurements is also a concern in remote monitoring. Communication is also vulnerable to attacks like man in middle, so data integrity and privacy concern the user. Blockchain provides distributed processing and im-mutable logs between WBAN &IoT and service providers by collaborating with WBAN and IoT. Blockchain ensures privacy and integrity also in the remote monitoring of patients (Griggs et al., 2018).

8.5.2.3   Health Insurance

In smart health care, the insurance process is slow and full of fraud because the insurance companies are using outdated/old models. The most common frauds are customers cheating by applying for insurance from more than one insurance company. The customer gets the benefit very late, and sometimes the insurance company cheats on the customer. So smart health care needs a secure system to remove the middle parties and use the technology to fast the process. Here, blockchain technology interacts with health care and solves fraud, and fastens an insurance claim. The transactions written on the public ledger in the blockchain are not easily modified; hence, insurance companies and customers trace the transaction and detect the fraud. The log maintained on blockchain helps audit the insurance process (Saldamli et al., 2020).

8.5.2.4   Pharmaceuticals and Supply Chain Management

A drug is a counterfeit factor in smart health care because the drugs with improper intergrading are traded illegally, and their authenticity, effectiveness, and provenance are hidden from the system. So, supply chain management is very crucial in smart health care. Here, blockchain has the power to secure supply chain management in smart health care. Blockchain can keep an eye on each stage of the pharmaceutical supply chain, starting from the origin of medicine, its intergrading, and ownership. Each transaction record on a blockchain cannot be modified, and this characteristic is used in fraud detection and allow transparent and secure supply chain management. The drug information on the blockchain is also reused to discover new drugs (Radanović & Likić, 2018).

8.5.2.5   Clinical Trials and Research

Through clinical trials and research, many systems have been developed to diagnose and avoid diseases and pandemics. However, these systems have traditional issues like data integrity, patient privacy, data sharing, etc. Blockchain can help avoid these issues by increasing researchers' and medical staff's transparency, auditability, and accountability. Blockchain participates in different research and clinical trials, like managing trial data, monitoring the trial mechanism, and others. Blockchain enables secure sharing of clinical trial data and increases transparency and reusability of data (Peterson, 2016; Kuo et al., 2017).

8.5.2.6   Administration and Secure Framework

Smart health care uses blockchain technology to manage the administration and non-medical operations. Researchers proposed a secure framework for a smart healthcare system. Blockchain provides a decentralized, secure infrastructure to smart health care to prevent DDoS attacks and other security attacks (Dagher et al., 2018; Xu et al., 2019).

The application of blockchain is not limited to the application mentioned above in smart healthcare. There are many other applications like billing settlement management, prescription management, policy implication, global data sharing for R&D, identity management, policy and standardization, fraud detection, and many more (Peterson, 2016; Kuo et al., 2017; Dagher et al., 2018; Nguyen et al., 2019; Xu et al., 2019; Hasselgren et al., 2020).

8.6   BLOCKCHAIN'S ROLE IN THE MITIGATION OF SECURITY AND PRIVACY ISSUES IN THE SMART HEALTHCARE SYSTEM

We have already discussed the use case of blockchain in the healthcare system in the previous section. Here we discuss the blockchain use case specific to security and privacy. The use cases are categorized as per the healthcare system's security and privacy requirements, as discussed in Section 8.3.

8.6.1   APPLICATION LEVEL

Smart health care provides different services to participants, and they have to authenticate themselves before accessing authorized health services. So smart health care needs proper and robust authentication, authorization, identification, and access control at the service level or application level along with the device level. Device-level authentication and authorization will be discussed in another section. Blockchain can provide authentication, authorization, access control, auditability, anonymity, and non-repudiation in smart healthcare applications.

Blockchain provides distributed authentication and authorization to handle the complexity increased due to the heterogeneity of attributes of participants. Based on trust relations among known certificate authorities (CAs), public key infrastructures (PKIs) can underpin many secure, collaborative platforms. Blockchain smart contracts can provide authentication and user verification. Smart contract–based authentication can work in a trustless environment due to its decentralized nature. Sign encryption and attribute-based authentication are also blockchain-based authentications used in smart health care. Lightweight authentication protocols are also proposed and implemented using blockchain.

The access control policies are programmed in the smart contract, and the smart contract authenticates and verifies each user before providing the service/network entry. The distributed nature can also provide more robust and secure access control as the control policies are distributed to all nodes. Hence, it is challenging to attack and modify the policies. The distributed access control is an energy-saving scheme because computing is distributed among the nodes.

Immutability automatically enables the auditability for smart health care. The transactions are stored encrypted and hard to modify or delete; this enables internal auditing and controls the individual to trace their data. Relevant transactions or data are searched using a back traverse from a specific data pointer to the entire blockchain. A smart contract can add automation for logging off-chain data and store on the distributed ledger; this helps to maintain patient data stored with individuals and off-chain.

The decentralization, tamper resistant, and smart contract nature of blockchain can help achieve non-repudiation in smart health care. Blockchain stores the interactive evidence of patients and service providers via transactions, and these transactions are hard to modify. Thus, smart health care achieves non-repudiation in the network.

Blockchain's anonymity characteristics can deal with privacy, the primary concern of smart health care. The real identity changes with an identifier, and these identifiers are used to authenticate and communicate with the other nodes in the blockchain. The same concept is applied to smart health care, where patients' personal information is hidden while getting healthcare services.

As mentioned, Section 8.6.3 contains the different types of applications to access smart healthcare services. Smart healthcare security from these applications and vice versa can be achieved using blockchain. Other than the application mentioned above, other blockchain applications are designed to secure smart health care like interoperability, non-repudiation, digital signature for authentication, the combination of artificial intelligence and machine learning to achieve an intelligent and sustainable secure environment for smart healthcare services, and many more (Dagher et al., 2018, Ramani et al., 2018; Chen et al., 2019; Yang et al., 2019; Hasselgren et al., 2020).

8.6.2   Data Level

To achieve confidentiality, integrity, and availability (CIA), the data should be secure while traveling, and the rest means at the storage level. Here, we discuss security and privacy at two stages, data storage and data sharing, and how blockchain can help fulfill smart healthcare security and privacy at the data level.

Blockchain is a possible solution for data-level issues like tempering, breaching, and much more secure smart health care. Smart health care can use three essential blockchain characteristics, i.e., immutability transaction ledger, distributed network, and strong encryption, to provide the security and privacy of health data.

The immutable transaction ledger means transactions are stored on a public distributed ledger that is readable to everyone. These transactions are never changed or deleted; hence, ledgers have complete and irreversible transactions. In smart health care, transactions would include the health data specific to the patient's service by smart health care. The health data would be encrypted and stored on the blockchain, and only the patient can decrypt the information with their private key. The patient's health data is connected with the patient ID in the blockchain. The stored data cannot be modified because of immutable characteristics, and updates come with metadata such as location, time, and patient's ID making the changes. Hence, blockchain-based health data will be auditable. In the same direction, Peterson (2016), Fan et al. (2018), and Guo et al. (2020) proposed a secure blockchain-based storage system for smart health care.

Distributed network means that there is no central authority that controls the system. In the blockchain, thousands of nodes participate in the consensus for all the transactions to reach the final decision. Smart health care uses blockchain to replace centralized record-keeping with decentralized infrastructure. The decentralized character reduces the transaction overhead in terms of processing and cost. Along with lower cost, a decentralized infrastructure provides prevention against single-point failure and provides robust and safer infrastructure (Kuo et al., 2017; Mamoshina et al., 2018).

Strong encryption is the key to the blockchain. Blockchain relies on public key infrastructure (PKI) and pseudo-anonymity to prevent content cracking. Blockchain also uses multi-signing (M of N signature) for extra security. The participant signs their transactions with a private key and stores them on the ledger so that only the right user can read the data. In smart health care, the patient uses encryption and signing to prevent the privacy and breaches of health data on the ledger. The pseudo-anonymity keeps the patient's identity secret and replaces the identity with an identifier. Lightweight encryption is also used at the sensor level to provide the confidentiality of patient data at the time of collection (Zhao et al., 2018).

We can say that blockchain's strong encryption and immutability characteristics can help achieve the confidentiality and integrity of health data. Moreover, its decentralized nature improves the availability of health data and health services in smart health care. Data is secure while at rest (storage) and in transit with the help of blockchain technology. Furthermore, the data is invisible to the competent stakeholder (patients, doctors, hospitals, etc.) and increases transparency, security, and health data privacy.

Other than the above that describe the use cases of blockchain in secure data storage and privacy, there are many works use cases and research work also present in the literature like data sharing, access control, key management, accessibility of health data, secure data storage on the cloud, mobile sharing of health data, and many more (Ramani et al., 2018; Nguyen et al., 2019; Xu et al., 2019; Bai et al., 2022).

8.6.3 DEVICE LEVEL

Medical devices and sensors are the core of smart health care as they are deployed to collect patient health data. Collected health data passed to the doctors/hospitals to analyse and health service to the patient. Health data collection and transmission must securely move from device to the service-providing server. As personal data is collected via the sensor, the legal requirement also comes into the picture to protect patients' privacy.

Blockchain can be used at the device level for lightweight authentication of devices, data security on device memory, key management, distribution of computing of resource-constrained devices, patient privacy preservation, and secure communication. Lightweight authentication, lightweight consensus algorithm, smart contract, and distributed computing are the features of blockchain that help smart health care secure the device-level parameters like data and communication (Srivastava et al., 2019; Aileni & Suciu, 2020; Ellouze et al., 2020).

Blockchain use cases to provide security in smart health care at the device level:

- Secure remote patient monitoring as the patient's PII and PHI move via blockchain in an encrypted format.
- The computing and processing at high resources node rather than the sensor and distributed among the nodes.
- Lightweight authentication using a smart contract to authenticate each device in the smart healthcare network.
- Anonymity feature can be used for the privacy of device parameters and related individuals.
- Lightweight consensus algorithms are specially designed for resource-constrained devices.
- Smart contract uses to implant the secure access control policy on devices, and these policies are distributed on the network, so they are hard to modify.
- Secure updating of device's firmware or application.

8.7 SMART HEALTH CARE AND COMPUTATIONAL INTELLIGENCE

Computational techniques are used to tackle large smart healthcare data. Computational techniques mainly include big data analytics, artificial intelligence (AI), cloud computing, deep learning, machine learning, etc. ML, DL, and AI use in the healthcare sector are vital as the data rates are increasing with advanced medical IoT devices. The use case of these techniques in a smart healthcare system is discussed below.

Big data analytics is useful in the healthcare sector to tackle the rising cost of health data maintenance worldwide.

Medical images like X-rays, CT-scan images, MRI images, ultrasounds, and mammography images are vital healthcare data sources. These medical images need long-term data retention, fast decision algorithms, and accurate results to provide good health services. Big data can be applied in different areas of smart health care. However, the main areas are image and signal processing.

Artificial intelligence enables a computer system to perform the task where human intellect is required. AI has a major use case in decision making and object detection and provides a solution to complex problems by high-level computation. AI implements cognitive technology to diagnose based on large medical records. Deep learning and Machine learning have applications across multiple disciplines such as biomedical engineering, medicines, and health informatics of the health sector. The healthcare sector uses deep learning approaches to implement accurate and faster disease detection. Deep learning techniques help with automation and faster computation in the smart healthcare system (Miotto et al., 2018).

Computational intelligence techniques like ML, DL, and AI play an important role in advancing security in smart health care. Mitto et al. presented the state of the art of how deep learning is used for data integration, interoperability, and data security in the medical domain (Miotto et al., 2018).

8.8 CONCLUSION

As sensitive patient data and records increase, smart health care needs a more secure mechanism to transmit, store, share and process health data. Smart healthcare security and privacy attacks are increasing on a daily basis. Cyberattackers are becoming more sophisticated and intelligent every day. This chapter covered all current security and privacy issues present with smart health care. Along with the issues, the attack surfaces in smart health care are also discussed in the chapter to implement the solution.

Further, blockchain application use cases are overall explained in smart health care and specific to the mitigation of security and privacy issues. Computational intelligence use cases are also included in the paper. The paper concludes that blockchain and computational intelligence can be vital solutions to prevent many security and privacy issues in smart health care.

REFERENCES

Abouelmehdi, K., Beni-Hessane, A., & Khaloufi, H. (2018). Big healthcare data: Preserving security and privacy. *Journal of Big Data*, 5(1), 1–18.

Agbo, C. C., Mahmoud, Q. H., & Eklund, J. M. (2019, June). Blockchain technology in healthcare: A systematic review. *Healthcare*, 7(2), 56. Multidisciplinary Digital Publishing Institute.

Aileni, R. M., & Suciu, G. (2020). IoMT: A blockchain perspective. In *Decentralised Internet of Things* (pp. 199–215). Cham: Springer.

Algarni, A. (2019). A survey and classification of security and privacy research in smart healthcare systems. *IEEE Access*, 7, 101879–101894.

Aslam, M. U., Derhab, A., Saleem, K., Abbas, H., Orgun, M., Iqbal, W., & Aslam, B. (2017). A survey of authentication schemes in telecare medicine information systems. *Journal of Medical Systems*, *41*(1), 1–26.

Bai, P., Kumar, S., Aggarwal, G., Mahmud, M., Kaiwartya, O., & Lloret, J. (2022). Self-sovereignty identity management model for smart healthcare system. *Sensors*, *22*(13), 4714. doi:10.3390/s22134714

Baker, S. B., Xiang, W., & Atkinson, I. (2017). Internet of things for smart healthcare: Technologies, challenges, and opportunities. *IEEE Access*, *5*, 26521–26544.

Butpheng, C., Yeh, K. H., & Xiong, H. (2020). Security and privacy in IoT-cloud-based e-health systems—A comprehensive review. *Symmetry*, *12*(7), 1191.

Catarinucci, L., De Donno, D., Mainetti, L., Palano, L., Patrono, L., Stefanizzi, M. L., & Tarricone, L. (2015). An IoT-aware architecture for smart healthcare systems. *IEEE Internet of Things Journal*, *2*(6), 515–526.

Chacko, A., & Hayajneh, T. (2018). Security and privacy issues with IoT in healthcare. *EAI Endorsed Transactions on Pervasive Health and Technology*, *4*(14).

Chanson, M., Bogner, A., Bilgeri, D., Fleisch, E., & Wortmann, F. (2019). Blockchain for the IoT: Privacy-preserving protection of sensor data. *Journal of the Association for Information Systems*, *20*(9), 1274–1309.

Chen, Y., Ding, S., Xu, Z., Zheng, H., & Yang, S. (2019). Blockchain-based medical records secure storage and medical service framework. *Journal of Medical Systems*, *43*(1), 1–9.

Dagher, G. G., Mohler, J., Milojkovic, M., & Marella, P. B. (2018). Ancile: Privacy-preserving framework for access control and interoperability of electronic health records using blockchain technology. *Sustainable Cities and Society*, *39*, 283–297.

Demirkan, H. (2013). A smart healthcare systems framework. *IT Professional*, *15*(5), 38–45.

Ellouze, F., Fersi, G., & Jmaiel, M. (2020, June). Blockchain for Internet of Medical Things: A technical review. In *International Conference on Smart Homes and Health Telematics* (pp. 259–267). Cham Springer.

Eysenbach, G. (2001). What is e-health?. *Journal of Medical Internet Research*, *3*(2), e20.

Fan, K., Wang, S., Ren, Y., Li, H., & Yang, Y. (2018). MEdblock: Efficient And Secure Medical Data Sharing Via Blockchain. *Journal of Medical Systems*, *42*(8), 1–11.

Ferrag, M. A., Maglaras, L., Derhab, A., & Janicke, H. (2020). Authentication schemes for smart mobile devices: Threat models, countermeasures, and open research issues. *Telecommunication Systems*, *73*(2), 317–348.

Griggs, K. N., Ossipova, O., Kohlios, C. P., Baccarini, A. N., Howson, E. A., & Hayajneh, T. (2018). Healthcare blockchain system using smart contracts for secure automated remote patient monitoring. *Journal of Medical Systems*, *42*(7), 1–7.

Guo, L., Li, Z., Yau, W. C., & Tan, S. Y. (2020). A decryptable attribute-based keyword search scheme on eHealth cloud in Internet of things platforms. *IEEE Access*, *8*, 26107–26118.

Hasselgren, A., Kralevska, K., Gligoroski, D., Pedersen, S. A., & Faxvaag, A. (2020). Blockchain in healthcare and health sciences—A scoping review. *International Journal of Medical Informatics*, *134*, 104040.

Hathaliya, J. J., & Tanwar, S. (2020). An exhaustive survey on security and privacy issues in Healthcare 4.0. *Computer Communications*, *153*, 311–335.

Hölbl, M., Kompara, M., Kamišalić, A., & Nemec Zlatolas, L. (2018). A systematic review of the use of blockchain in healthcare. *Symmetry*, *10*(10), 470.

Ichikawa, D., Kashiyama, M., & Ueno, T. (2017). Tamper-resistant mobile health using blockchain technology. *JMIR mHealth and uHealth*, *5*(7), e111.

Iwaya, L. H., Ahmad, A., & Babar, M. A. (2020). Security and privacy for mHealth and uHealth Systems: A systematic mapping study. *IEEE Access*, *8*, 150081–150112.

Kazemi, M., Bayat, M., Haamian, N., Haefi, Z., & Pournaghi, M. (2020). A secure three factor authentication scheme for wireless healthcare sensor networks based on elliptic curve. *Electronic and Cyber Defense*, *8*(1), 147–167.

Kunneman, M., & Montori, V. M. (2017). When patient-centred care is worth doing well: Informed consent or shared decision-making. *BMJ Quality & Safety*, *26*(7), 522–524.

Kuo, T. T., Kim, H. E., & Ohno-Machado, L. (2017). Blockchain distributed ledger technologies for biomedical and health care applications. *Journal of the American Medical Informatics Association*, *24*(6), 1211–1220.

Mamoshina, P., Ojomoko, L., Yanovich, Y., Ostrovski, A., Botezatu, A., Prikhodko, P., Izumchenko, E., Aliper, A., Romantsov, K., Zhebrak, A., & Ogu, I. O. (2018). Converging blockchain and next-generation artificial intelligence technologies to decentralize and accelerate biomedical research and healthcare. *Oncotarget*, *9*(5), 5665.

McGhin, T., Choo, K. K. R., Liu, C. Z., & He, D. (2019). Blockchain in healthcare applications: Research challenges and opportunities. *Journal of Network and Computer Applications*, *135*, 62–75.

Mettler, M. (2016, September). Blockchain technology in healthcare: The revolution starts here. In *2016 IEEE 18th International Conference on e-Health Networking, Applications and Services (Healthcom)*(pp. 1–3). IEEE.

Miotto, R., Wang, F., Wang, S., Jiang, X., & Dudley, J. T. (2018). Deep learning for healthcare: Review, opportunities and challenges. *Briefings in Bioinformatics*, *19*(6), 1236–1246.

Newaz, A. K. M., Sikder, A. K., Rahman, M. A., & Uluagac, A. S. (2020). A survey on security and privacy issues in modern healthcare systems: Attacks and defenses. *arXiv preprint arXiv:2005.07359*.

Nguyen, D. C., Pathirana, P. N., Ding, M., & Seneviratne, A. (2019). Blockchain for secure ehrs sharing of mobile cloud based e-health systems. *IEEE Access*, *7*, 66792–66806.

Peterson, K. (2016). A blockchain-based approach to health information exchange networks. In *Proceedings of the NIST Workshop Blockchain Healthcare*. (Vol. 1. No. 1).

Radanović, I., & Likić, R. (2018). Opportunities for use of blockchain technology in medicine. *Applied Health Economics and Health Policy*, *16*(5), 583–590.

Rajput, A. R., Li, Q., Ahvanooey, M. T., & Masood, I. (2019). EACMS: Emergency access control management system for personal health record based on blockchain. *IEEE Access*, *7*, 84304–84317.

Ramani, V., Kumar, T., Bracken, A., Liyanage, M., & Ylianttila, M. (2018, December). Secure and efficient data accessibility in blockchain based healthcare systems. In *2018 IEEE Global Communications Conference (GLOBECOM)* (pp. 206–212). IEEE.

Saldamli, G., Reddy, V., Bojja, K. S., Gururaja, M. K., Doddaveerappa, Y., & Tawalbeh, L. (2020, April). Health care insurance fraud detection using blockchain. In *2020 Seventh International Conference on Software Defined Systems (SDS)* (pp. 145–152). IEEE.

Salim, M. M., Rathore, S., & Park, J. H. (2020). Distributed denial of service attacks and its defenses in IoT: A survey. *The Journal of Supercomputing*, *76*(7), 5320–5363.

Solanas, A., Patsakis, C., Conti, M., Vlachos, I. S., Ramos, V., Falcone, F., Postolache, O., Pérez-Martínez, P. A., Di Pietro, R., Perrea, D. N., & Martinez-Balleste, A. (2014). Smart health: A context-aware health paradigm within smart cities. *IEEE Communications Magazine*, *52*(8), 74–81.

Srivastava, G., Crichigno, J., & Dhar, S. (2019, May). A light and secure healthcare blockchain for iot medical devices. In *2019 IEEE Canadian Conference of Electrical and Computer Engineering (CCECE)* (pp. 1–5). IEEE.

Sun, Y., Lo, F. P. W., & Lo, B. (2019). Security and privacy for the internet of medical things enabled healthcare systems: A survey. *IEEE Access*, *7*, 183339–183355.

Sundaravadivel, P., Kougianos, E., Mohanty, S. P., & Ganapathiraju, M. K. (2017). Everything you wanted to know about smart health care: Evaluating the different technologies and components of the internet of things for better health. *IEEE Consumer Electronics Magazine*, *7*(1), 18–28.

Swan, M. (2015). *Blockchain: Blueprint for a new economy*. O'Reilly Media.

Xu, Y., Ren, J., Wang, G., Zhang, C., Yang, J., & Zhang, Y. (2019). A blockchain-based nonrepudiation network computing service scheme for industrial IoT. *IEEE Transactions on Industrial Informatics*, *15*(6), 3632–3641.

Yang, Y., Zheng, X., Guo, W., Liu, X., & Chang, V. (2019). Privacy-preserving smart IoT-based healthcare big data storage and self-adaptive access control system. *Information Sciences*, *479*, 567–592.

Zandberg, K., Schleiser, K., Acosta, F., Tschofenig, H., & Baccelli, E. (2019). Secure firmware updates for constrained iot devices using open standards: A reality check. *IEEE Access*, *7*, 71907–71920.

Zhang, P., Schmidt, D. C., White, J., & Lenz, G. (2018). Blockchain technology use cases in healthcare. In *Advances in computers* (Vol. 111, pp. 1–41). Elsevier.

Zhao, H., Bai, P., Peng, Y., & Xu, R. (2018). Efficient key management scheme for health blockchain. *CAAI Transactions on Intelligence Technology*, *3*(2), 114–118.

9 AIC Algorithm for Trust Management in eWOM for Digital Systems

B. H. Khoi, B. V. Quang, and N. V. T. Truong
Industrial Univ of Ho Chi Minh City, Vietnam

CONTENTS

9.1 INTRODUCTION

Vietnam has up to 66% of the population using the Internet, up to 94% of which can easily access the Internet via mobile phones. With a population of over 97 million people, the number of smartphone users is growing rapidly (94%) and the demand for the Internet is increasingly high, and the estimated number of people taking part in online shopping is 44.8 million, Vietnam is considered an attractive market to attract investors in e-commerce. E-commerce sites have simultaneously developed

DOI: 10.1201/9781003319917-12

strongly in Vietnam, such as LAZADA, Shoppee, Sendo, Tiki, and are no longer strangers to consumers in our country.

Electronic word of mouth (eWOM) is a very important and core content in science for micro-consumers, especially in the strong development of the Industrial Revolution 4.0 (Bianchi, 2020). It offers consumers a better way to gather product information and learn from those who have had the experience.

Besides, Vietnam's e-commerce situation has been well developed—a method of buying, selling, and exchanging online in the market. This has sped up the growth of eWOM in Vietnam and brought additional aspects to this digital marketing approach. But not all consumer behavior is influenced by eWOM.

Around the world, there are studies on eWOM affecting economic activities in many industries (Ismagilova et al., 2020; Ngarmwongnoi et al., 2020; Rosario et al., 2020; Roy et al., 2021; Srivastava & Sivaramakrishnan, 2020). We see the impact of eWOM on consumers "intentions and consumers" intentions of use in shopping malls and research in Vietnam. Therefore, we want to explore the subject to supplement the white research space. In the research, electronic word of mouth will be carefully analyzed from a theoretical basis to practice through its effects on the behavior of consumers in shopping malls. Since then, the paper has examined factors influencing the tendency of trust in electronic word of mouth (eWOM) by AIC algorithm in digital systems and cybersecurity management: A case study at shopping malls in Ho Chi Minh City, Vietnam.

9.2 RESEARCH MODEL AND HYPOTHESIS

9.2.1 Trust in eWOM (Electronic Word-of-Mouth)

EWOM is word-of-mouth over the Internet. Today's new form of online WOM communication is called electronic word-of-mouth (eWOM) (Yang et al., 2017). Many researchers have shown optimal power and enhanced eWOM in today's market landscape (Acemoglu et al., 2020; Mahmood et al., 2020). Personal buying patterns improved significantly after the beginning of the Internet. The method of requesting others about the product assessments they are using has been used a lot since consumers have found the internet convenient to refer to a product they have inquired about (Babić Rosario et al., 2016; Kim et al., 2018; Acemoglu et al., 2020). Changes on the eWOM platform are very beneficial to customers. This form of communication is of particular importance with the emergence of online platforms, making it one of the most influential sources of information on the Web (Abubakar & Ilkan, 2016). As a result of these technological advances, these new means of communication have led to changes in consumer behavior (Cantallops & Salvi, 2014), due to the influence they allow consumers to interact with each other by allowing them to obtain or share information about a company, product or brand. In the past, platforms could only communicate one way. Still, after the development of social media, persons and consumers now have contacts to check out who is providing their experience of a real product or service (Abedi & Stovas, 2019; Acemoglu et al., 2020). Electronic word-of-mouth also gives companies an edge over traditional WOM as it allows them to try to understand what motivates consumers to post their opinions online and gauge the impact of their audience to that of others (Cantallops & Salvi, 2014). However, consumers' use of technology to share opinions about products or services (eWOM) can be a liability for companies, as it can become a factor they do not examine (Yang et al., 2017). To combat this, businesses are looking to gain greater control over online customer reviews by creating virtual spaces on their websites where consumers can leave comments and share their opinions on the products and services of the business (García–Gallego et al., 2015). Many researchers have shown the optimization and power of electronic words in marketing (Acemoglu et al., 2020; Mahmood et al., 2020).

Personal buying patterns were launched significantly after the launch of the Internet. Because people find it easier to reference an online search for a product issue, the method of pre-asking others for product reviews is changing (Babić Rosario et al., 2016; Kim et al., 2018; Acemoglu et al., 2020). The changes in the eWOM platform also benefit customers. Previously, platforms had one-way communication, but after the social media launch, individuals now reach out to check out who is providing their experience with real estate products or services (Abedi & Stovas, 2019; Acemoglu et al., 2020). Two-way interactive conversations are one of the advantages of social media over other platforms. It is not only possible to buy or look for certain goods or services from random individuals, but it also provides the ideal opportunity to communicate with friends, colleagues, or family members on a vibrant digital platform (Muszyńska et al., 2018). People often tell one an other about their preferences, likes, and dislikes and all of a sudden because communication is swift (Bashir, 2019; Mahmood et al., 2020). Because of these aspects, information processed on social media is not only fast vision but also individuals who mainly believe in transmitting information (Acemoglu et al., 2020; Oussous et al., 2020). However, this reliability leads to serious problems related to handling fraudulent information on social networks (Lkhaasuren & Nam, 2018). Today's customers want to hear authentic feedback and reviews. They also gradually became warier of the hard-sell method. Reviews come from users, especially those who share their interests, more effectively for brand returns (Pezzelle et al., 2018). Trust is key in electronic word-of-mouth (eWOM) and indispensable for electronic word-of-mouth (eWOM). All eWOM communications are trustworthy and related to trust. Kheng et al. (2017) stated that trust in information sources could affect consumers' attitudes towards products or services.

9.2.2 Information Quality

The utility of information, information quality, and opposition quality are the key values of word-of-mouth, according to a modern study on eWOM (Acemoglu et al., 2020). Information on social media platforms must be of significant value and worth. According to literary sources, information quality is expected to be communicated on online trust-building platforms (Xie et al., 2019). Therefore, the following hypothesis was formed:

Hypothesis 1 (H1): Information quality has a positive impact on the trust in eWOM.

9.2.3 CARE INFORMATION

Laurent and Kapferer (1985) showed that interest comprises four categories: hedonic value, symbolic value, interest, and perceived risk. Fadde and Zaichkowsky (2018) argue that consumers with a high level of interest in products will actively seek care information and evaluate all alternatives, while consumers with high low interest will not do so. So the author has hypothesis H2:

Hypothesis 2 (H2): Care information has a positive impact on the trust in eWOM.

9.2.4 SOCIAL INFLUENCE

The social influence shows the impact of a reference group on consumers' trust in technology use. When an individual's behavior can be positively influenced by the advice, referrals, or support of someone important to that individual, or they can also be influenced by those around or in the community like colleagues, superiors, friends, and community groups (de Sena Abrahão et al., 2016). Therefore, the author proposes the following hypothesis to measure the factor's impact on trust in the intention of using shopping mall goods and services.

Hypothesis 3 (H3): Social influence positively affects trust in eWOM.

9.2.5 PERCEIVED RISK

Some research that identifies risk is considered subjective because its magnitude varies depending on the context (Acemoglu et al., 2020). Acemoglu et al. (2020) argued that consumer behavior is sometimes about taking risks to help businesses thrive. Mahmood et al. (2020) explain that capital and subjective emotions may be shaped through risk perception. The risk associated with the type of product is called essential risk. The significance of the product in the consumer's awareness, its price, its performance, and its characterization is the inherent risk (Pelaez et al., 2019). Alternatively, the risk handled is an inevitable risk related to the product or service, given the abundance of data needed, risk management can be handled (Dabrynin & Zhang, 2019). The shaping of risk effects on belief bias is a thought-provoking aspect that needs to be explored:

Hypothesis 4 (H4): Perceived risk has a positive impact on trust in eWOM.

9.3 METHOD

9.3.1 SAMPLE APPROACH

According to Bollen (1990), the minimum sample size is five samples for one parameter to be estimated. The sample size can be defined as 5: 1 (5 observations

TABLE 9.1

Sample

Characteristics		Amount	Percent (%)
Sex and Age	Male	87	48.33
	Female	93	51.67
	18–24	35	19.44
	25–35	78	43.33
	36–49	46	25.55
	Above 50	10	5.55
Monthly Income	Below VND 3 million	35	19.44
	VND 3 to 7 million	50	27.78
	VND 8 to10 million	58	32.22
	VND 11 to 15 million	28	15.56
	Over VND 15 million	9	5

per 1 variable) (Hair et al., 2006). In this study, there are 21 variables. Therefore, the minimum sample size can be calculated as n = 5 × 21 = 105. Although the minimum sample size requires only 105 surveys, the author submitted 180 survey questionnaires indirectly via the Internet with tools supporting Google forms for users in the city to ensure sample diversity and representativeness. Table 9.1 shows sample characteristic statistics.

Table 9.1 shows that in the total samples collected by the author, the female sex accounts for the highest proportion of 51.67%, and the male accounts for 48.33%. And the age group from 18 to 25 is the highest at 43.33%, followed by 25–35 years old, accounting for 25.55%, followed by under 18 years old, accounting for 19.44%, over 50 years old accounting for 6.11%, the group from 36 to 49 years old, accounting for 5.55%. And it shows that the age group 18–25 has a top level of using shopping mall goods and services. The group of people with the highest income from 7 to 10 million accounts for 32.22%, followed by the group with income from 3 to 7 million, accounting for 27.78%, below 3 million accounting for 19.44%, 10 to 15 million accounting for 15.56%, and over 15 million accounts for 5% and is the group with the lowest rate. For 180 respondents, we utilize a Likert 5-point measure to survey their degree of assent for connected issues. As a result, this paper adopts a 5-point Likert scale to assess the amount of permission for all observing factors, with 1: Totally disagree ... and 5: Totally Agree in Table 9.2.

9.3.2 BLINDING

The length of the preliminary dazed all investigation staff and respondents. The study participants had no contact with anyone from the outside world.

TABLE 9.2
Observations

Factor	Code	Item
Trust in eWOM	Te1	Gives your knowledge/perspective on goods in shopping malls.
	Te2	Helps you easily decide to accept and use shopping mall products.
	Te3	Improve efficiency in making the right goods selection for you.
Information Quality	IQ1	The information you get provides the same thing.
	IQ2	The information you receive is the aim of the sender.
	IQ3	You assume the information is provided from the sender's experience.
	IQ4	The information you receive or find is effective.
	IQ5	The information you receive is presented in a clear and easy-to-understand manner.
	IQ6	You think the information provided has a positive purpose in sharing the experience with other consumers.
Care Information	CI1	You seek information to use goods in the shopping mall.
	CI2	You find product information on many websites.
	CI3	You spend a lot of time searching for information.
	CI4	You look for information given by the consumer and by the vendor.
	CI5	You spend a lot of time refining and aggregating information.
Social Influence	SI1	Many people around me use shopping mall products.
	SI2	The important people thought I should use the product of the shopping mall.
	SI3	People around me support the use of shopping mall products.
Perceived Risk	PR1	The goods are not suitable for finance to spend.
	PR2	Goods not as expected, desired.
	PR3	Food safety risks occur when using goods.
	PR4	There are inherent risks when using the product.

9.4 RESULTS

9.4.1 AIC Algorithm

R program utilized AIC to choose the perfect blockchain information management model. In the theoretical environment, AIC has been used to select models. The AIC technique can also handle many independent variables when multicollinearity develops. AIC can be utilized as a relapse model to appraise at least one ward factor in at least one autonomous factor. The AIC is a crucial and useful metric for determining a full and direct model. A result with a smaller AIC is picked dependent on the AIC data standard. The best model will end when the minimal AIC value is reached (Burnham & Anderson, 2004; Khoi, 2021; Mai et al., 2021). R information displays each progression of looking for the ultimate model. The AIC = −302.17 for Te = f (IQ, CI, SI, PR) step stop with four independent variables.

The p-value for all variables is less than 0.05 (Hill et al., 2018), As a result, they're linked to Ewom Trust in Digital Systems, which is in Table 9.3: information quality (IQ), care information (CI), social influence (SI), and impact trust in eWOM (Te).

9.4.2 Variance Inflation Factor

At the point when the autonomous factors in relapse models have a serious level of connection, the marvel of multicollinearity emerges. At the point when the VIF coefficient is more than 10, Gujarati and Porter (2009) discovered proof of multicollinearity in the model. According to Table 9.4, the independent variables' VIF (variance inflation factor) is less than ten (Miles, 2014). As a result, the independent variables have no collinearity.

9.4.3 Autocorrelation

Since the p-value = 0.2688 is more noteworthy than 0.05, the Durbin-Watson test shows that the model in Table 9.4 has no autocorrelation (Durbin & Watson, 1971).

TABLE 9.3
The Coefficients

Te	Coefficient	SD	t-Value	p-Value	Result
Intercept	0.61491				
IQ	0.37845	0.05155	7.341	0.000	Supported
CI	0.08531	0.04177	2.042	0.000	Supported
SI	0.17875	0.04842	3.692	0.000	Supported
PR	0.21777	0.04767	4.568	0.000	Supported

TABLE 9.4
Model Test

VIF	IQ	CI	SI	PR
	1.410685	1.151047	1.269573	1.023927
Autocorrelation	Durbin-Watson = 1.9121		test for autocorrelation p-value = 0.2688	
Model Evaluation	Adjusted R-Squared 0.5498		F-statistic 46.05	p-value 0.00000

9.4.4 MODEL EVALUATION

Agreeing to outcomes from Table 9.4, information quality (IQ), care information (CI), social influence (SI), and perceived risk (PR) impact trust in eWOM (Te) is 54.98% in Table 9.4. The regression equation below is statistically significant, according to the analyses above (Greene, 2003).

$$Te = 0.61491 + 0.37845IQ + 0.08531CI + 0.17875SI + 0.21777PR$$

9.4.5 DISCUSSION

The outcomes of the AIC Algorithm for the Trust in eWOM (Te) showed that four independent variables information quality (IQ), care information (CI), social influence (SI), and perceived risk (PR) have a positive impact on Te for p-value is bigger than 0.05. The influence of the four factors on trust in eWOM (Te) in descendent instruction is as information quality (0.37845), perceived risk (0.21777), social influence (0.17875), and care information (0.08531).

9.5 CONCLUSIONS

Trust in eWOM (Te) showed that it was influenced by Iinformation quality (IQ), care information (CI), social influence (SI), and perceived risk (PR). As a result, each of the four characteristics listed above has a favorable impact on eWOM trust (Te). In digital systems and cybersecurity management, the AIC algorithm shows the impact of four free factors on the dependent part. The chapter's investigation yielded remarkably comparable results to those of earlier investigations.

9.5.1 LIMITATIONS OF THE RESEARCH AND FURTHER RESEARCH DIRECTIONS

Some of the limitations below are mentioned when doing the research. Hopefully, the authors can research more deeply and solve the problems in previous studies to contribute to the shopping malls. Regarding research capacity and time, the sample selection and sample size are not as expected, so it is only possible to research on Google. The study subjects are quite complete but still have many shortcomings. The variables running in the model are only some influencing factors, not completely the factors that affect the decision to apply the user's belief. The sample size selected for the study is still small compared to the overall study, which may also adversely affect the reliability of the study results.

There are customers who are not very attentive when typing the survey, so there are cases where customers chatter quickly, so the collected opinions make little sense. After statistical data, the test was run, but it was not statistically significant, so it was necessary to re-survey to get good data. There are many factors affecting the trust in eWOM of users that have not been mentioned to explain more clearly about trust in eWOM.

Besides the theoretical and practical contributions drawn from the research results, this research topic has many limitations. It then suggests the following research: Include factors related to trust impact to increase the reliability of the study. We will increase the number of survey samples compared to the overall population to increase the reliability of the study. Expanding the survey in many major cities across the country is recommended in the next research.

ACKNOWLEDGMENTS

This chapter is supported by IUH, Vietnam.

Conflicts of Interest: There are no conflicts of interest declared by the author.

REFERENCES

Abedi, M. M., & Stovas, A. (2019). A new parameterization for generalized moveout approximation, based on three rays. *Geophysical Prospecting, 67*(5), 1243–1255.

Abubakar, A. M., & Ilkan, M. (2016). Impact of online WOM on destination trust and intention to travel: A medical tourism perspective. *Journal of Destination Marketing & Management, 5*(3), 192–201.

Acemoglu, D., Cheema, A., Khwaja, A. I., & Robinson, J. A. (2020). Trust in state and nonstate actors: Evidence from dispute resolution in Pakistan. *Journal of Political Economy, 128*(8), 3090–3147.

Babić Rosario, A., Sotgiu, F., Valck, K. D., & Bijmolt, T. H. A. (2016). The effect of electronic word of mouth on sales: A meta-analytic review of platform, product, and metric factors. *Journal of Marketing Research, 53*(3), 297–318.

Bashir, A. M. (2019). Effect of halal awareness, halal logo and attitude on foreign consumers' purchase intention. *British Food Journal, 121*(9), 1998–2015. 10.1108/BFJ-01-2019-0011

Bianchi, A. (2020). *Driving consumer engagement in social media: Influencing electronic word of mouth.* Routledge.

Bollen, K. A. (1990). Overall fit in covariance structure models: Two types of sample size effects. *Psychological Bulletin, 107*(2), 256.

Burnham, K. P., & Anderson, D. R. (2004). Multimodel inference: Understanding AIC and BIC in model selection. *Sociological Methods & Research, 33*(2), 261–304.

Cantallops, A. S., & Salvi, F. (2014). New consumer behavior: A review of research on eWOM and hotels. *International Journal of Hospitality Management, 36*, 41–51.

Dabrynin, H., & Zhang, J. (2019). The investigation of the online customer experience and perceived risk on purchase intention in China. *Journal of Marketing Development and Competitiveness, 13*(2), 16–30.

de Sena Abrahão, R., Moriguchi, S. N., & Andrade, D. F. (2016). Intention of adoption of mobile payment: An analysis in the light of the Unified Theory of Acceptance and Use of Technology (UTAUT). *RAI Revista de Administração e Inovação, 13*(3), 221–230.

Durbin, J., & Watson, G. S. (1971). Testing for serial correlation in least squares regression. III. *Biometrika, 58*(1), 1–19.

Fadde, P. J., & Zaichkowsky, L. (2018). Training perceptual-cognitive skills in sports using technology. *Journal of Sport Psychology in Action, 9*(4), 239–248.

García–Gallego, A., Mures-Quintana, M.-J., & Vallejo–Pascual, M. E. (2015). Forecasting statistical methods in business: A comparative study of discriminant and logit analysis in predicting business failure. *Global Business and Economics Review, 17*(1), 76–92.

Greene, W. H. (2003). *Econometric analysis.* Pearson Education India.

Gujarati, D. N., & Porter, D. (2009). *Basic econometrics*. Mc Graw-Hill International Edition.

Hair, J. F., Black, W. C., Babin, B. J., Anderson, R. E., & Tatham, R. L. (2006). *Multivariate data analysis* (Vol. 6). Pearson Prentice Hall.

Hill, R. C., Griffiths, W. E., & Lim, G. C. (2018). *Principles of econometrics*. John Wiley & Sons.

Ismagilova, E., Slade, E. L., Rana, N. P., & Dwivedi, Y. K. (2020). The effect of electronic word of mouth communications on intention to buy: A meta-analysis. *Information Systems Frontiers*, 22(5), 1203–1226.

Kheng, V., Sun, S., & Anwar, S. (2017). Foreign direct investment and human capital in developing countries: A panel data approach. *Economic Change and Restructuring*, 50(4), 341–365.

Khoi, B. H. (2021). Factors influencing on university reputation: Model selection by AIC. In *Data science for financial econometrics* (pp. 177–188). Springer.

Kim, S., Chu, K. H., Al-Hamadani, Y. A. J., Park, C. M., Jang, M., Kim, D.-H., Yu, M., Heo, J., & Yoon, Y. (2018). Removal of contaminants of emerging concern by membranes in water and wastewater: A review. *Chemical Engineering Journal, 335*, 896–914.

Laurent, G., & Kapferer, J.-N. (1985). Measuring consumer involvement profiles. *Journal of Marketing Research*, 22(1), 41–53.

Lkhaasuren, M., & Nam, K.-D. (2018). The effect of Electronic Word of Mouth (eWOM) on purchase intention on Korean cosmetic products in the Mongolian market. *Journal of International Trade & Commerce, 14* (4), 161–175.

Mahmood, K., Khalid, A., Ahmad, S. W., Qutab, H. G., Hameed, M., & Sharif, R. (2020). Electrospray deposited $MoS2$ nanosheets as an electron transporting material for high efficiency and stable perovskite solar cells. *Solar Energy, 203*, 32–36.

Mai, D. S., Hai, P. H., & Khoi, B. H. (2021). Optimal model choice using AIC method and Naive Bayes cassification. In *IOP Conference Series: Materials Science and Engineering, 1088*(1), 012001. IOP Publishing.

Miles, J. (2014). Tolerance and variance inflation factor. *Wiley StatsRef: Statistics Reference Online* (N. Balakrishnan, T. Colton, B. Everitt, W. Piegorsch, F. Ruggeri and J.L. Teugels, eds.). 10.1002/9781118445112.stat06593

Muszyńska, B., Grzywacz-Kisielewska, A., Kała, K., & Gdula-Argasińska, J. (2018). Anti-inflammatory properties of edible mushrooms: A review. *Food Chemistry, 243*, 373–381.

Ngarmwongnoi, C., Oliveira, J. S., AbedRabbo, M., & Mousavi, S. (2020). The implications of eWOM adoption on the customer journey. *Journal of Consumer Marketing, 37*(7), 749–759. 10.1108/JCM-10-2019-3450

Oussous, A., Benjelloun, F.-Z., Lahcen, A. A., & Belfkih, S. (2020). ASA: A framework for Arabic sentiment analysis. *Journal of Information Science, 46*(4), 544–559.

Pelaez, A., Chen, C.-W., & Chen, Y. X. (2019). Effects of perceived risk on intention to purchase: A meta-analysis. *Journal of Computer Information Systems, 59*(1), 73–84.

Pezzelle, S., Steinert-Threlkeld, S., Bernardi, R., & Szymanik, J. (2018). Some of them can be guessed! Exploring the effect of linguistic context in predicting quantifiers. *arXiv preprint arXiv:1806.00354*.

Rosario, A. B., Valck, K. d., & Sotgiu, F. (2020). Conceptualizing the electronic word-of-mouth process: What we know and need to know about eWOM creation, exposure, and evaluation. *Journal of the Academy of Marketing Science, 48*(3), 422–448.

Roy, G., Datta, B., Mukherjee, S., & Basu, R. (2021). Effect of eWOM stimuli and eWOM response on perceived service quality and online recommendation. *Tourism Recreation Research, 46*(4), 457–472.

Srivastava, M., & Sivaramakrishnan, S. (2020). The impact of eWOM on consumer brand engagement. *Marketing Intelligence & Planning*, *39*(3), 469–484. 10.1108/MIP-06-2020-0263

Xie, X.-Z., Tsai, N.-C., Xu, S.-Q., & Zhang, B.-Y. (2019). Does customer co-creation value lead to electronic word-of-mouth? An empirical study on the short-video platform industry. *The Social Science Journal*, *56*(3), 401–416.

Yang, W. S., Park, B.-W., Jung, E. H., Jeon, N. J., Kim, Y. C., Lee, D. U., Shin, S. S., Seo, J., Kim, E. K., & Noh, J. H. (2017). Iodide management in formamidinium-lead-halide–based perovskite layers for efficient solar cells. *Science*, *356*(6345), 1376–1379.

10 Study of IoT Security for Blockchain Management: An Application to Data Backup

Cédric Tala Kuate and Franklin Tchakounte
Department of Mathematics and Computer Science,
Faculty of Science, The University of Ngaoundéré,
Ngaoundéré, Cameroon

Jean Claude Kamgang
Department of Mathematics and Computer Sciences
ENSAI, The University of Ngaoundéré, Ngaoundéré,
Cameroon

CONTENTS

DOI: 10.1201/9781003319917-13

10.1 INTRODUCTION

The Internet of Things (IoT) and blockchain (BC) are considered two disruptive technologies in the current world (Tabane et al., 2015) due to the technical innovations they brought in the way of sharing and storing of information. IoT is considered the future in the network domain as it seeks to transform real-world objects into smart virtual objects (Dorri et al., 2016; Rizal, 2018). In fact, according to (Khan & Salah 2018; Panarello et al. 2018), IoT is the evolution of the Internet (the computer network) to cyber-physical and embedded systems called the thing.

IoT devices produce a huge amount of data. Due to the sensibility of data collected by some IoT devices, these data must be stored securely and efficiently. In most developing countries, those data are stored using traditional data backup techniques. The problem is that using traditional backup techniques leads to some security vulnerabilities.

In recent years, there has been a tremendous effort to cope with security issues in the IoT paradigm. According to the industry and research community, blockchain technology has been foreseen as a disruptive technology that will significantly manage, control, and secure IoT devices. A blockchain is fundamentally a decentralized, distributed, shared, and immutable database ledger that stores a registry of assets and transactions across a peer-to-peer (P2P) network (Madakam et al., 2015).

This work aims to demonstrate the effectiveness of blockchain technologies in securing data produced in IoT. The general objective is to investigate the use of blockchain technologies to guarantee the confidentiality, integrity, and availability of data backed up in IoT.

The methodology used for this work follows a design process divided into four phases: Investigation, design, implementation, and evaluation. During the investigation phase, we often did qualitative research using Google and Google Scholar search engines. We investigate research papers concerning IoT by combining keywords in articles of the past five years to make state-of-the-art IoT. Next, we did the same exercise on blockchain technology by emphasizing the security concepts based on blockchain that can be used in IoT. We repeated the exercise, focusing on the literature reviews of the existing solutions that integrate blockchain technology in IoT in the backup domain. The design phase is concerned with elaborating and proposing a blockchain-based architecture for data backup in IoT that uses the interplanetary file system's properties (IPFS) properties. The third phase involves implementing a decentralized application that allows storing files on a blockchain using a smart contract. The last step aims to evaluate our proposed architecture by making a comparison with the traditional client/server architecture based on the criteria: confidentiality, integrity, and availability. The comparison has shown that our model is more efficient.

The overall structure of this paper takes the form of seven sections, including this introductory section. Section 10.2 presents the related works on blockchain-based solutions to address IoT issues. Section 10.3 is concerned with the theoretical background on IoT, and the security requirements and issues are also presented. Section 10.4 deals with the security in IoT based on blockchain technology. In Section 10.5, we propose a blockchain-based architecture for securing data storage. Here, we will present the tools used to realize our simulations and the application's architecture. Section 10.6 presents the results and discussion of the research. Section 10.7 deals with the summary of findings, suggestions for further studies, and the conclusion.

10.2   RELATED WORKS

This section presents a non-exhaustive list of research works related to blockchain and data backup.

In Kumar et al. (2019), the authors proposed an IPFS-based blockchain storage model to solve the storage problem of transactions in a block along with access to transactions of a particular block. In the proposed storage model, the miners' store transactions on IPFS distributed file system storage and got the transaction's returned IPFS hash into the blockchain's block. The feature of the IPFS network and its resultant hash reduce the size of transactions in a block. To secure access to the transaction for a particular block content-addressed (IPFS hash) storage technique has been proposed. They have applied this scheme to a transaction that includes image storage on IPFS and hash storage into the blockchain. In this paper, the authors have also proposed the content-addressed technique in contrast to the location address for the access of transactions.

Kumar et al. (2021) present a detailed study of the IPFS and blockchain-based healthcare secure storage solutions. Their paper analyzes the existing solutions and their architecture, which will further facilitate the future research and development of emerging IPFS and blockchain technologies.

In Sun et al. (2020), based on the cipher text policy attribute-based encryption system and IPFS storage environment, combined with blockchain technology, the authors constructed an attribute-based encryption scheme for secure storage and efficient sharing of electronic medical records in the IPFS storage environment. Their scheme is based on cipher text policy attribute encryption, which effectively controls the access of electronic medical data without affecting efficient retrieval. Meanwhile, they store the encrypted electronic medical data in the decentralized InterPlanetary File System (IPFS), which not only ensures the security of the storage platform but also solves the problem of the single point of failure. Besides, they leverage blockchain technology's non-tamperable and traceable nature to achieve secure storage and search for medical data.

Yang et al. (2019) proposed a management system of the electronic medical records in the blockchain environment. Electronic medical records are first stored in the proposed system's Inter-Planetary File System (IPFS). Then, the system generates the hash value, which will be sent to the smart contract to correlate with the patient's data. After that, if the system confirms the medical staff's medical authority, the smart contract can send back the hash value that IPFS generated. Thus, the system will present the complete electronic medical records.

Zhang et al. (2021) proposed a case study of the traceability of agricultural products to explain a traceability solution for agricultural products supply chain based on blockchain and IPFS. With this model, consumers can know the quality of agricultural products in the shortest time through the evaluation function.

Li et al. (2022) proposed a data sharing platform based on the combination of blockchain and interplanetary file system (IPFS) technology to solve the data sharing and storage. They first constructed the alliance blockchain, used the consensus mechanism of computing power competition to maintain the data written into the blockchain. The IPFS data storage system was established to store data using distributed storage, file splitting, and splicing technologies. Secondly, they built a data sharing platform composed of a blockchain module, IPFS module, encryption and decryption module, and fast retrieval module. The fast retrieval module can quickly locate the required data according to the retrieval conditions in the mass blockchain data; finally, they evaluated the security and storage of the data sharing platform. The research results solve the problem of large data sharing, realize data decentralization, and ensure data storage security.

Liu et al. (2021) realized an efficient data sharing and patient access control of medical data under the condition of guaranteeing the safe storage of bulk medical data. They combined decentralized blockchain technology with distributed file storage platform IPFS. They proposed a federated medical blockchain data storage access model based on IPFS.

As our contribution, to this work, we proposed a blockchain-based architecture that can be used to store the data securely collected by IoT devices. We developed a decentralized application based on the Ethereum blockchain, which will simulate the storage of data collected by IoT devices on a blockchain network. The application will allow to search for a file, send it to an IPFS gateway and get its corresponding hash that will then be stored on a local blockchain using a smart contract. The transaction information will be displayed in the application interface and exported in a CSV file to make a local copy of the blockchain. We will also do a comparative study between client-server and blockchain-based architecture.

10.3   THEORETICAL BACKGROUND ON IOT

10.3.1   DEFINITION OF IoT

The Internet of Things is "An open and comprehensive network of intelligent objects that can auto-organize, share information, data and resources, react in the face of situations and changes in the environment" (Madakam et al., 2015) (Fig. 10.1).

10.3.2   IoT CONCEPTS AND COMPONENTS

The main concepts in the IoT paradigm are those which form its name: "Internet" and "Thing." The "Thing" in IoT can refer to any device comprising any kind of built-in-sensors with the ability to collect and transfer data over a network or internet without manual intervention (Team, 2018). The Internet is the short form of "interconnected network" and is defined as the global system of interconnected computer networks that use a set of protocols known as the Internet protocol suite (TCP/IP) to connect devices worldwide. The three components which make the IoT are the hardware, middleware, and presentation (Gubbi et al., 2013). Fig. 10.2 shows the IoT building blocks.

A generic architecture of IoT can be viewed as three layers: perception, network, and application (Ahmad et al., 2019). Each layer uses specific protocols to ensure an

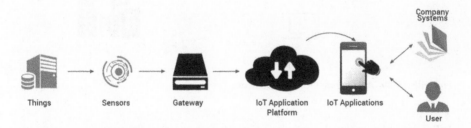

FIGURE 10.1   Functioning of IoT system.

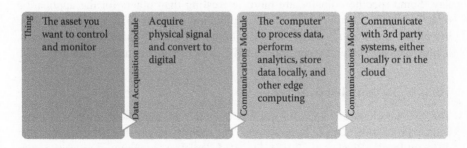

FIGURE 10.2   IoT hardware basic building blocks.

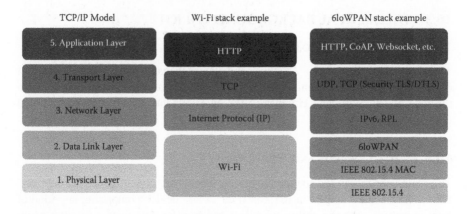

FIGURE 10.3   IoT protocols and standards.

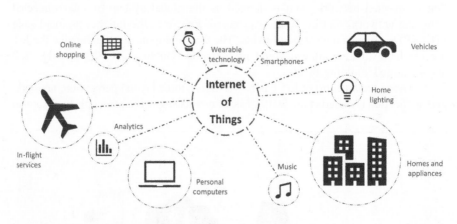

FIGURE 10.4   An overview of IoT elements.

IoT network's smooth functioning. Fig. 10.3 shows the different layers with the associated protocols.

IoT equips multiple domains and millions of devices with connectivity every day. Some specific domains are more interesting than others for the application of IoT. Fig. 10.4 shows some of the application areas of IoT. A non-exhaustive list of IoT applications includes: smart home, wearable, smart city, smart grids, health care, agriculture, transport, supply chain, retail, industrial Internet, etc.

10.3.3   Security Issues in IoT

The IoT paradigm encompasses various devices and equipment, from small embedded processing chips to large servers. The security issues should be addressed at different levels (Rizal et al., 2018). Fig. 10.5 depicts a taxonomy of security issues for IoT.

FIGURE 10.5 IoT issues classification.

10.4 SECURING THE INTERNET OF THINGS

10.4.1 DEFINITION OF BLOCKCHAIN

The blockchain is a peer-to-peer, distributed digital ledger, firstly used in the Bitcoin cryptocurrency for economic transactions. It is tamper-proof and contains only authentic information. A blockchain is not controlled by any single centralized entity (trusted third party) as it is a peer-to-peer system (Khan & Salah, 2018). BC technology was created by a person or a group of anonymous persons known under the pseudonym Satoshi Nakamoto in the 2008. It was designed to address the "double speeding" problem in the Bitcoin network (Nakamoto, 2008; Orr et al., 2018).

10.4.2 EVOLUTION OF BLOCKCHAIN TECHNOLOGIES

Since its introduction by Satoshi Nakamoto in his white paper entitled "Bitcoin: A Peer-to-Peer Electronic Cash System" in 2008, blockchain has evolved as it has been adapted in many other fields in the industry apart from cryptocurrencies. In (Orr et al., 2018), the proposed versions of blockchains are listed. We break down these categories in Table 10.1.

TABLE 10.1

Blockchain Versions

Versions	Description
Blockchain 1.0	Used for cryptocurrencies
Blockchain 2.0	Use the concept of smart contract to automatize transactions within the BC
Blockchain 3.0	Applied beyond cryptocurrency and financial markets, especially in IoT

10.4.3 Types of Blockchains

A taxonomy of blockchains includes public blockchain (or permissionless blockchain), fully private or private blockchain (or permissioned blockchain), and consortium blockchain (or federated blockchain) (Khan & Salah, 2018). Table 10.2 summarizes the comparison of the three types of blockchains.

10.4.4 Key Concepts in Blockchains

10.4.4.1 Block

A block is the "current part" of a blockchain that records some or all of the recent transactions, and, once completed, goes into the blockchain as a permanent database. Compared with an ordinary chain, a block can be considered a link. Each time a block gets completed, a new block is generated. A blockchain is made up of a list of records and those records are stored in blocks. Then, these blocks are in turn linked with other blocks all the linked blocks form a chain, which is the blockchain. Fig. 10.6 shows the block hash calculation.

TABLE 10.2

Types of Blockchains

Property	Public Blockchain	Consortium Blockchain	Private Blockchain
Consensus determination	All miners	Selected set of nodes	One organization
Read permission	Public	Could be public or restricted	Could be public or restricted
Immutability	Nearly impossible to tamper	Could be tampered	Could be tampered
Efficiency/speed	Low	High	High
Centralized	No	Partial	Yes
Consensus process	Permissionless	Permissioned	Permissioned
Types of network analogy	Internet in 1990s	Intranet in 1990s	Intranet in 1990s
Assets	Native	Any asset	Any asset

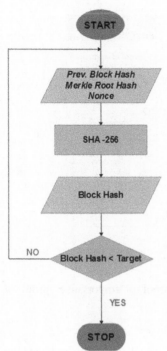

FIGURE 10.6   Block hash calculation.

Hashing is one of the data structure methods and cryptographic fixed output generation techniques used in blockchain applications; it accepts an arbitrary length input and generates a cryptographic fixed output using SHA-2. Since the hash function is a one-way function, its output cannot be converted back to its original form. This makes it more difficult for hackers to crack. The original input will always produce the same result. Still, any changes to the input will produce a different output, making it easy to check for tampering by comparing the digest. A hash represents a blockchain's current state. The input is the history of the blockchain, including every transaction ever recorded. For this reason, blockchain is a reliable security application measure for protecting the validity of the data, as hashing is immutable in that any modification to any component of the input produces a significant change to the output. The overall structure of a blockchain is presented in Fig. 10.7.

10.4.4.2   Consensus Algorithm

The consensus algorithm serves as the heart of the network. It is implemented as part of the node application. It provides the network rules by saying how the system will arrive at a single view of the ledger. The public blockchain, Bitcoin uses the concept of "proof of work." There are other forms of consensus protocols applying the concept of proof of stake (PoS), proof of elapsed time (PoET), proof of existence (PoE), delegated proof of stake (DPoS), proof of activity

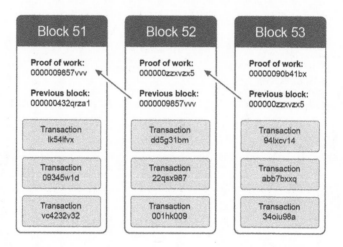

FIGURE 10.7   Structure of a blockchain.

(hybrid of proof of work and proof of stake), proof of importance, proof of storage, etc. (Bach et al., 2018).

10.4.4.3   Smart Contract

Smart contracts are made up of small computer programs that contain, embedded in their code, an agreement between two entities. They were originally introduced by Nick Szabo in 1994 and defined as "a computerized transaction protocol that executes the terms of a contract" (Bach et al., 2018). This contract is distributed across the blockchain network and is responsible for facilitating the execution, verification, and enforcement of an agreement between participants. Fig. 10.8 below shows how a smart contract operates.

Different languages are used to write or develop smart contracts. Here is a non-exhaustive list of most used smart contract development languages: Solidity and the EVM, Serpent, Pact, Viper, Liquidity, Chaincode, Mutan, LLL etc.

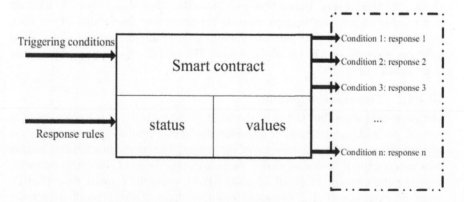

FIGURE 10.8   Operation mechanism of a smart contract.

10.5 BLOCKCHAIN-BASED ARCHITECTURE FOR SECURING DATA STORAGE

This section presents the different tools that have been used to implement the application and the architectural design of the application, which is a fully decentralized application that uses the special properties of IPFS to make the application not relying on a central server. The application takes as input a file containing data collected by an IoT device, in our case a temperature and humidity sensor (DHT 11). The file is then sent to IPFS to collect its hash. The hash of the file is added to a transaction using a smart contract and the transaction is added to a block. The block later run is added to the blockchain.

10.5.1 ARCHITECTURE

The application's architecture can be broken down into four modules: front-end, back-end, blockchain, and file management. The front end is the entry point of our application. It represents the interface used to select the file to be stored on the blockchain and displays the different information about the mined block that will be added to it. The back-end represents the core of the application. It is where the application logic is implemented. We use the truffle framework to build the project structure. This module did all the coding of the application and the smart contract. The blockchain module is where the blockchain has been configured and used. We used Ganache, which is a local blockchain to simulate our blockchain. The metamask extension for chrome was added and configured to enable the smart contracts to be deployed and run on the blockchain. The file management module is based essentially on IPFS. It retrieves the hash of the selected file that will be saved on the blockchain. Fig. 10.9 depicts the architectural design of the proposed solution.

The sequence diagram of the proposed solution is depicted in Fig. 10.10. It shows in detail how the different modules interact in the application. The sequence of messages exchanged between the different modules to implement the application's functionality is shown here.

10.5.1.1 Front-End

The front-end consists of an interface built using html, CSS, and Reactjs library, a JavaScript library for building user interfaces. The web front-end base is the app.js component. It imports the smart contract ABI and the web3js library that allows communicate with the blockchain. The front-end allows selecting a file, sending and saving it to an IPFS network, and recovering its hash. This hash is going to be saved on the blockchain. Storing data on a blockchain is not free and consumes a gas fee according to the size of the data that will be saved; that is where IPFS comes into play. As IPFS is a content-based distributed file system, the hash saved on the blockchain can later be used to retrieve the file. After adding the hash of the selected file to the blockchain, the information of the mined block like: block size, block miner, previous block hash, block hash, block number, hash of the file, the contract address, the transaction hash, the gas used, and the block timestamp are displayed in

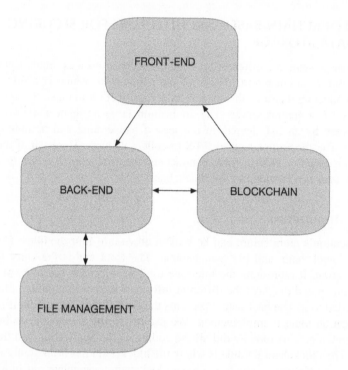

FIGURE 10.9   Architectural design.

the front-end part. The front-end can also interact with the blockchain using the metamask extension we added and configured in our web browser. Fig. 10.11 shows the application interface.

10.5.1.2   Back-End

The back-end module is where all the logic of the application was implemented. We used Truffle, a development environment, testing framework, and asset pipeline for Ethereum, to set up the ReactJs application. Truffle also provides built-in smart contract compilation, linking, development, and binary management. To install truffle, we used the NPM (Node package manager) by entering the command *npm install -g truffle* from the terminal. The project structure of the application will be discussed below. As far as smart contract development is concerned, the smart contract codes were written using the Solidity programming language. The smart contract is going to be discussed in the next sections.

10.5.1.3   Smart Contract

The most important element of our back-end is the smart contract. It acts as the back-end logic and storage. The smart contracts are in charge of reading and writing data to the blockchain. Our smart contract is written in a programming language called Solidity. Below are the pseudo-codes of our main smart contracts that will be deployed on the blockchain and whose aim is to get the hash of the file uploaded on IPFS and save it on the blockchain. The second smart contract is the migration

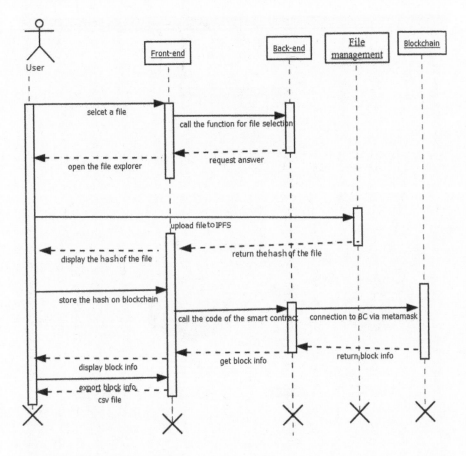

FIGURE 10.10 Sequence diagram.

contract. A migration is a deployment script aiming to modify the state of the application's contracts, moving it from one state to the next.

10.5.1.4 Blockchain

The blockchain module in our architecture represents the simulation network that we used. We used Ganache, a local in-memory blockchain to build our application. We downloaded and installed it from the Truffle Framework website. After installation, it gives us 10 external accounts with addresses on our local Ethereum blockchain. Each account is preloaded with 100 fake ethers.

10.5.1.5 File Management

Storing data on a blockchain is costly depending on the size of the data to be saved; we will save not an entire file on the blockchain, but its corresponding hash. For that purpose, the application uploads a file on IPFS and retrieves its hash that will be stored on the blockchain. To achieve this goal, we started by initializing IPFS. We want to note that there are two ways to do it. The first way consists of using

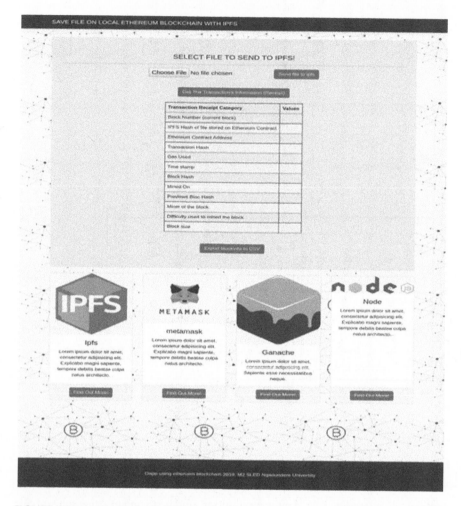

FIGURE 10.11　Application interface.

the local host to start the IPFS Daemon and the second way is by using an IPFS.Infura.io node. In the case of our work, we used Infura since it is popular and easy to integrate.

10.6　EXPERIMENTS, RESULTS, AND DISCUSSIONS

We presented the tools and the application's architecture in the previous section. In this section, on the first hand, after presenting the development environment, we will present the experiments we carried out throughout our work. Second, we will discuss the results obtained and show their limits. We conducted our experiments in two phases. The first can be titled IoT part and the second, blockchain. In the IoT part, we built a temperature and humidity logger that collects the environment's temperature and humidity. The blockchain part is concerned with storing the collected data to a blockchain.

10.6.1 TEMPERATURE AND HUMIDITY DATA COLLECTION

In this part, we realized a temperature and humidity logger. The system uses the DHT11 to measure the temperature and humidity. A real-time clock (RTC) module takes the sensed data time stamps. The collected data are then saved using either an SD card module or a special program that will read the serial com port of the Arduino IDE and export the data in a text file.

10.6.1.1 Circuit and Schematics

Fig. 10.12 shows the interconnection of the different components used for our experiments. Fig. 10.13 shows the electronic connection between the different components.

10.6.2 RESULTS

10.6.2.1 Decentralized Application Based on Blockchain

We used many tools presented in the previous section to develop our Decentralized Application (or simply Dapp). The decentralized application will save the collected data to a blockchain network. The development was done following the steps below.

10.6.2.1.1 Installation of Ganache, Metamask, and Truffle Framework

To be able to run and execute our Dapp, we had to make preliminary configurations. We started installing and running our local Ethereum blockchain **ganache**. The result is shown in Fig. 10.14.

FIGURE 10.12 Circuit.

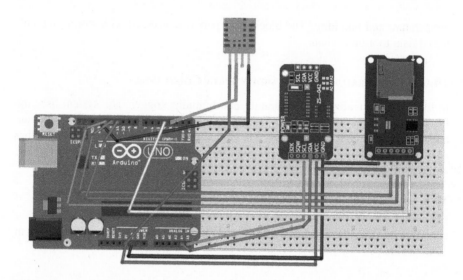

FIGURE 10.13   Schematics.

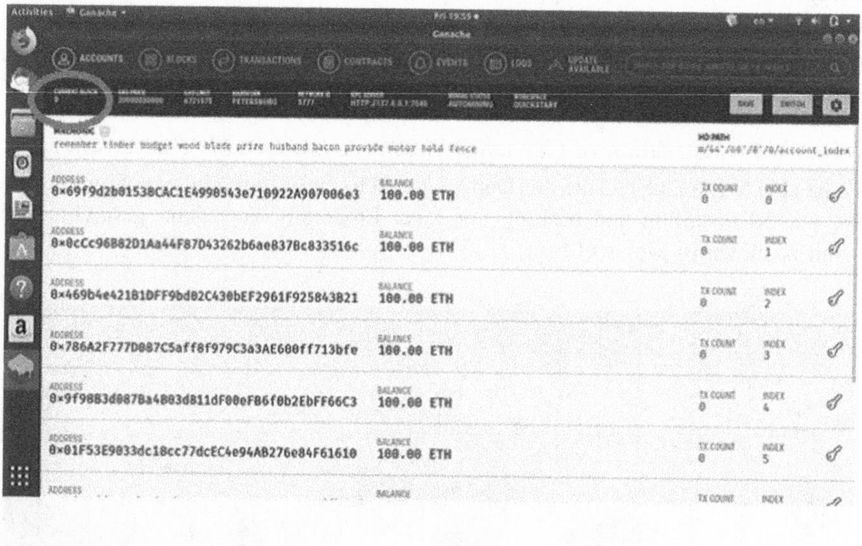

FIGURE 10.14   Local blockchain.

As highlighted in Fig. 10.18, when the Ganache is started for the first time, there is no block mined. After starting Ganache, the next step is to log in into metamask to link it with the ganache blockchain.

10.6.2.1.2   File Importation, Smart Contract Execution, Block Creation, and Addition to the Blockchain

We can now select the file we want to store on the blockchain. The file that will be selected is the one that contains the temperature and humidity data recorded

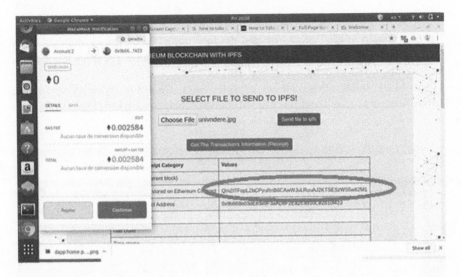

FIGURE 10.15 Hash of the file.

by the DHT11 sensor. After selecting the file, when we click on the button *"send the file to IPFS,"* the file hash will be collected from IPFS, as shown in Fig. 10.15.

Next, we have to confirm the transaction to have the information about the created block by clicking on the button *"get the transaction information (receipt)."*

Once the transaction is confirmed, we can see the transaction hash shown in Fig. 10.16.

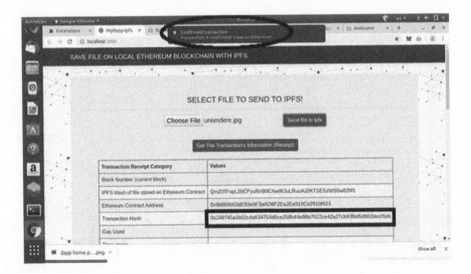

FIGURE 10.16 Hash of the transaction.

10.6.2.1.3 Display Information on the Mined Block and Exportation

The information of the transaction and the new mined block (block number, IPFS hash, contract address, transaction hash, gas used, timestamp, previous block hash, etc.) are displayed as depicted in Fig. 10.17.

The block information can be exported in a CSV file by clicking on the button "*export to CSV*" and the file will be exported as shown in Fig. 10.18.

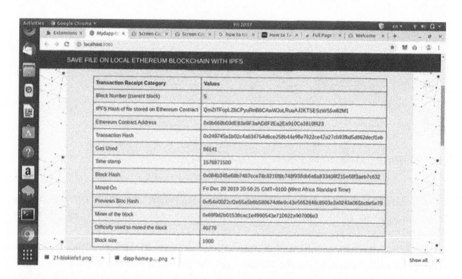

FIGURE 10.17   Information about the new mined block on Dapp.

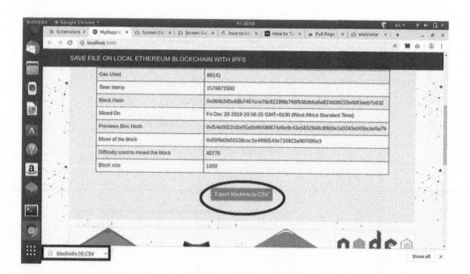

FIGURE 10.18   Exporting the new mined block's information as CSV.

10.6.3 DISCUSSION: COMPARISON BETWEEN TRADITIONAL CLIENT/SERVER ARCHITECTURE AND DECENTRALIZED BLOCKCHAIN-BASED ARCHITECTURE

In this section, we will compare traditional client/server architecture and our proposed decentralized blockchain-based architecture in which each node is an IPFS node. Figs. 10.19 and 10.20 show a traditional client/server architecture and our proposed decentralized architecture.

The criteria on which we based our comparison are confidentiality, availability, and integrity.

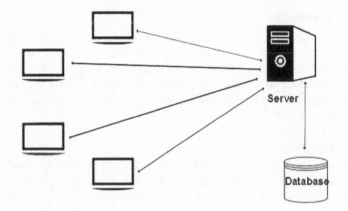

FIGURE 10.19   Traditional client/server architecture.

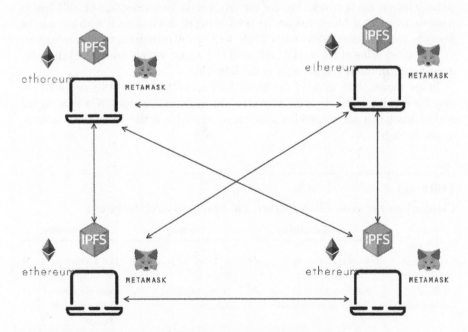

FIGURE 10.20   Proposed decentralized blockchain-based architecture.

10.6.3.1 Confidentiality

Confidentiality in the CIA security triad means data, objects, and resources are protected from unauthorized viewing and other access. In our proposed solution, the information shared among the peer-to-peer network nodes cannot be consulted by someone out of the network. Another reason is that only the hash of a file IPFS is saved in the distributed ledger. As the IP network is private, even if an attacker succinctly reads the information stored in the blockchain, he still has to control the IPFS node to consult the file's content corresponding to the file corresponding to the hash he collected in the ledger.

10.6.3.2 Availability

The criterion availability means that authorized users have access to the systems and the resources they need whenever they need them. Our solution is based on a decentralized network, so there is no single failure point. It cannot suffer from a DDOS attack as the data stored on the network can be accessible from each node. So, if one node is not responding, another node can provide the requested data.

10.6.3.3 Integrity

Integrity means that data is protected from unauthorized changes to ensure that it is reliable and correct. The immutable nature of the blockchain provides the data integrity in our proposed architecture. For an attacker to modify the information stored in our network, he has to control 51% of the nodes. In this case, the attack succeeds as each node is an IPFS node, which implies it maintains the history of all added files on the network. So, for the attacker to be successful, he still has to retrieve the original file stored on the IPFS network and replace it with the one he wants to fool the participants with. Table 10.3 below summarizes our comparison.

The added value of our model compared to existing models using blockchain for data storage in the IoT ecosystem is the following:

In our model, each node of the blockchain network runs an IPFS deamon. So, they form a local private IPFS network. This reduces the risks of a man in the middle attack that can happen if a node has to send a file to the public IPFS network to get its hash.

TABLE 10.3

Comparison between Client/Server and Proposed Architecture

	Confidentiality		Integrity		Availability	
Client/server architecture	Restricts access to authorized users	✓	Uses traditional access control	✗	Has a single point of failure	✗
Proposed architecture	Restricts access to nodes in the network	✓	Uses cryptographic measures	✓	Does not have single point of failure	✓

TABLE 10.4
Symbols Signification

Symbol	Meaning
H_S	The size of the block header
ihash	The size of the hash of the file stored on IPFS
N	The number of blocks in the blockchain
Bc_i	The size of each block in the blockchain

Each node of the network is an Ethereum client. As Ethereum is a programmable blockchain (with the help of smart contract) and uses PoS (proof of stake) as consensus algorithm, our model is less resources consumer (in terms of electricity and computation). Each node of the network can add a new block to the blockchain.

The formula below gives the compression ratio of our model. The symbols used in the formula are explained in the table below (Table 10.4).

$$\frac{Hs + iHash * N}{Hs + \sum_{i=1}^{N} Bc_i}$$

On Ethereum, the size of the block header is 508 bytes. The hash from IPFS takes 46 bytes. Looking at this ratio, it can be estimated that the storage space optimization of the proposed model is very considerable. This will also lead to an economic gain, as writing on the chain is costly according to the size of the data. Compared to others, our model is theoretically more efficient as there is no limitation on the number of transactions per block in Ethereum, which leads to a great variation in the block size. This will give a better storage optimization ratio.

10.7   CONCLUSION

In this work, we first of all made state of the art on IoT. We defined and presented its basic concepts and components. The different communication and messaging protocols used in IoT have different application domains. We also highlighted the main application and use cases related to IoT. After this, we presented the security requirements for IoT and the security issues in IoT.

Secondly, we studied blockchain technology as a security factor to IoT in the backup domain. We started defining what blockchain is. We presented the evolution of BC technology and explained the different types of BC. The key concepts of BC were also presented, like the features it implements. Next, we discussed some BC development platforms after we explained in detail how a BC network works.

After this, we developed a distributed application based on the Ethereum blockchain that enables us to store a data collected by a DHT11 sensor on a blockchain by executing a smart contract deployed on the BC. The Dapp also displays the primary information about each block added to the BC and the information about the transaction it contains. After displaying that information, it can be exported into a CSV file. Later on, the different CSV files representing the different mined blocks can be merged to form the entire blockchain in a CSV file.

Furthermore, we made a comparative study taking as metrics the CIA security triad to show the advantages and performance of a blockchain-based distributed system over traditional client/server-based architecture system as far as data confidentiality, integrity, and availability are concerned. We ended with a comparison of our model with existing ones.

REFERENCES

Ahmad, M., Younis, T., Habib, M. A., Ashraf, R., & Ahmed, S. H. (2019). A review of current security issues in Internet of Things. In *Recent trends and advances in wireless and IoT-enabled networks* (pp. 11–23). Cham: Springer, DOI: 10.1007/978-3-319-99966-1_2

Bach, L. M., Mihaljevic, B., & Zagar, M. (2018, May). Comparative analysis of blockchain consensus algorithms. In *2018 41st International Convention on Information and Communication Technology, Electronics and Microelectronics (MIPRO)* (pp. 1545–1550). IEEE. DOI: 10.23919/MIPRO.2018.8400278

Dorri, A., Kanhere, S. S., & Jurdak, R. (2016). Blockchain in internet of things: Challenges and solutions. *arXiv preprint arXiv:1608.05187.* https://arxiv.org/ftp/arxiv/papers/1608/1608.05187.pdf

Gubbi, J., et al. (2013). Internet of Things (IoT): A vision, architectural elements, and future directions. *Future Generation Computer Systems, 29*(7), 1645–1660. DOI: 10.1016/j.future.2013.01.010

Khan, M. A., & Salah, K. (2018). IoT security: Review, blockchain solutions, and open challenges. *Future Generation Computer Systems, 82*, 395–411. DOI: 10.1016/j.future.2017.11.022

Kumar, R., & Tripathi, R. (2019, November). Implementation of distributed file storage and access framework using IPFS and blockchain. In *2019 Fifth International Conference on Image Information Processing (ICIIP)* (pp. 246–251). IEEE. DOI: 10.1109/ICIIP4 7207.2019.8985677

Kumar, S., Bharti, A. K., & Amin, R. (2021). Decentralized secure storage of medical records using blockchain and IPFS: A comparative analysis with future directions. *Security and Privacy, 4*(5), e162.

Li, W., Zhou, Z., Fan, W., & Gao, J. (2022). Design of data sharing platform based on blockchain and IPFS technology. *Wireless Communications and Mobile Computing, 2022,* 729–784.

Liu, S., & Tang, H. (2021, January). A consortium medical blockchain data storage and sharing model based on IPFS. In *2021 The 4th International Conference on Computers in Management and Business* (pp. 147–153). Singapore: ACM.

Madakam, S., Lake, V., Lake, V., & Lake, V. (2015). Internet of Things (IoT): A literature review. *Journal of Computer and Communications, 3*(05), 164. DOI: 10.4236/jcc.2015.35021

Nakamoto, S., & Bitcoin, A. (2008). A peer-to-peer electronic cash system. *Bitcoin.* https://bitcoin.org/bitcoin. pdf.

Orr, D. A., & Lancaster, D. M. (2018). Cryptocurrency and the blockchain: A discussion of forensic needs. *International Journal of Cyber-Security and Digital Forensics, 7*(4), 420–436. DOI: 10.17781/P002494

Panarello, A., Tapas, N., Merlino, G., Longo, F., & Puliafito, A. (2018). Blockchain and IOT integration: A systematic survey. *Sensors, 18*(8), 2575. DOI: 10.3390/s18082575

Rizal, R., Riadi, I., & Prayudi, Y. (2018). Network forensics for detecting flooding attack on Internet of Things (IoT) device. *International Journal of Cyber-Security and Digital Forensics, 7*(4), 382–390. DOI: 10.17781/P002477

Sun, J., Yao, X., Wang, S., & Wu, Y. (2020). Blockchain-based secure storage and access scheme for electronic medical records in IPFS. *IEEE Access, 8*, 59389–59401. DOI: 10.1109/ACCESS.2020.2982964

Tabane, E., Zuva, T., & Ngwira, S. M. (2015, June). The socio-economic impact of Internet of Things towards smart cities. In *The Third International Conference on Digital Information Processing, E-Business and Cloud Computing (DIPECC2015)* (p. 102). https://www.academia.edu/13580750/The_Socio-Economic_Impact_of_Internet_of_ Things_towards_Smart_Cities

Team, D. (2018, September 11). *IoT tutorial for beginners.* DataFlair. Online [Accessed] 26 Jan 2019: https://data-flair.training/blogs/aws-iot-tutorial/

Yang, W. K., Chen, J. S., & Chen, Y. S. (2019, August). An electronic medical record management system based on smart contracts. In *2019 Twelfth International Conference on Ubi-Media Computing (Ubi-Media)* (pp. 220–223). IEEE. DOI: 10.1109/Ubi-Media. 2019.00050

Zhang, L., Zeng, W., Jin, Z., Su, Y., & Chen, H. (2021). A research on traceability technology of agricultural products supply chain based on blockchain and IPFS. *Security and Communication Networks, 2021*, 1–12.

11 Cybersecurity Management in Cyber-Physical Systems Using Blockchain

Soufyane Mounir and Yassine Maleh
LaSTI Laboratory, ENSAK, Sultan Moulay Slimane University, Morocco

CONTENTS

11.1 INTRODUCTION

The term "blockchain" gained widespread recognition in 2009 with the launch of the cryptocurrency Bitcoin, and only lately has the potential for blockchain use in other fields been considered. A "blockchain" is a term that refers to a method of storing and processing data on computer networks via a chain of blocks. It is not related to any particular type of data (Swan, 2015). Each block in the chain can contain arbitrary data, including production processes, which describes the possibilities of using this technology in production systems (Porru et al., 2017). The growth of cyber-physical systems (CPS) and the Industrial Internet of Things IIoT necessitate

DOI: 10.1201/9781003319917-14

the resolution of several data interchange and processing issues, including storage, access, security, and so on.

Furthermore, there is a contemporary trend toward developing distributed systems rather than centralized ones. One of the essential characteristics of the Internet of Things is its nodes' autonomy and capacity to interact with one another (Teslya & Ryabchikov, 2017). This is a service-based interaction in which specialized nodes deliver services to other nodes in the network. Some blockchain implementations use a smart contract mechanism to enable such interaction. A smart contract is a self-executing script stored with other data on the blockchain. Each smart contract has its algorithm written in a specific programming language and automatically conducts any activities without the involvement of other parties. A smart contract monitors the fulfillment of specified circumstances and, using the given algorithm, takes choices based on them. Because every network member may sign a contract, this mode of engagement extends to Internet of Things nodes. This technique creates a dependable environment for transferring network nodes and makes services visible and uniform. Furthermore, because all contracts are already maintained on the blockchain, there is no need to construct a separate service registry (Christidis & Devetsikiotis, 2016). Blockchain technology is highly general; many applications are now employed in various domains of human activity (Daza et al., 2017).

To effectively use all of the benefits of blockchain technology for developing CPS and the Industrial Internet of Things, it is required to design the ideal blockchain network topology based on the tasks to be done and select the most relevant tools (software and hardware). A cyber-physical system (CPS) results from integrating computation with physical processes. On the other hand, some argue that it is a system that combines environmental elements with the computational part. Data acquired from the environment and actions that correspond to the environmental aspects from the moment there is a translation of data from the environment into the digital world. It is the responsibility of computing to handle this data. CPSs monitor and control the physical world, possibly having sensor networks and associated actuators (Monostori, 2014).

Thus, this type of system depends on the synergy between physical and computational components. On the other hand, and unlike traditional embedded systems, the CPS emphasizes a holistic view of the system, i.e., it is seen as a whole and not only as several isolated modules (Maleh et al., 2022). CPSs have applications in a wide variety of areas, including high-reliability medical and life-support systems and devices, traffic control and safety, advanced automotive systems, process control, energy conservation, environmental control, aviation, instrumentation, distributed robotics (telepresence, telemedicine), defense systems, manufacturing, smart structures, and control of critical infrastructures (e.g., power grids, water resources, and communication systems) (Maleh et al., 2019). So, after a detailed consideration of the concepts of "industrial internet of things" and "cyber-physical production systems," we can go directly to implementing blockchain technology in their structures (Maleh et al., 2019). There are two types of blockchain networks: global and private. The first is the most advanced and is typically employed to tackle global challenges. Global peer-to-peer networks are extremely stable due to their many members, but they are inappropriate for building corporate networks comparable to the industrial networks mentioned above. The fundamental drawback is that all data exchange activities are rigidly bound to the cryptocurrency utilized in one or more global blockchains. Changes in cryptocurrency market exchange prices are nearly impossible to foresee, making the cost of ownership of the planned CPS challenging to estimate. As a result, the architecture now under construction will be built on a private blockchain. The following blockchain functionalities should be implemented in the CPS:

- Organizing a single information space for inter-machine interaction within the CPS;
- Ensuring the cybersecurity of the CPS; Easy scaling and restructuring of the CPS;
- Provisioning equipment and communication channels redundancy;
- Organizing a single data storage facility implementation of "digital twins" technology through the use of smart contracts;
- Ensuring performance of common tasks for the CPS through the use of smart contracts

Blockchain technology has been primarily used to protect storage systems, smart contracts, financial transactions, and notaries. Other applications, like health care, supply chain, transportation, and cybersecurity, swiftly recognized its benefits, as the sector realized it could increase its efficiency by implementing blockchain (Maleh et al., 2021). This has resulted in an active field of inquiry, with researchers and scientists currently looking at various uses for this technology. Among the most commonly mentioned uses are health care, transportation, and cybersecurity. This paper's main contributions are as follows:

- Provide a detailed and in-depth analysis of the applications in CPS systems where blockchain is implemented.
- Identify the various challenges and limitations of blockchain applications.

This paper is organized as follows: Section 11.2 introduces the core concepts of blockchain technology. Blockchain applications in CPS systems, including health care, transportation, and cybersecurity are discussed in Section 11.3. Section 11.4 discusses the limits of the blockchain and offers suggestions for the future. Section 11.5 concludes this work.

11.2 BLOCKCHAIN (BC) FOR CYBER-PHYSICAL SYSTEMS (CPS) APPLICATIONS

There are a lot of conversations going on in the world about blockchain technology. According to Gupta (Gupta, 2017), the blockchain is an information recording system with security features that make it impossible to hack or cheat in the system. Abadi and Brunnermeier (Abadi & Brunnermeier, 2018) indicate a ledger system that decentralizes the records by distributing them across all the blockchain networks. Transactions in the blockchain system are distributed to all the system participants, making it hard to cheat or steal. They further indicate that technology's correctness, decentralization, and cost efficiency make an excellent record-keeping system. Their comparison of the system to the traditional centralized system highlights blockchain's tremendous revolution in the record-keeping industry. One of the blockchain's essential features is the algorithms that permit record-keepers to rewind and undo false reports in the ledger's historical records. Besides the finance industry, the system is quite useful in procurement, Internet apps, and other industries where transparency is highly required. Businesses succeed by improving interaction with their stakeholders.

Blockchain technology achieves this by offering a distributed ledger. The strategy allows businesses to utilize a shared database of transactions. The technology applies encryption mechanisms that focus on authentication and authorization of transactions (Maleh et al., 2022). E-commerce is one of the major industries where the advancement of blockchain has enormously benefited the industry's continuous and overall growth. Blockchain innovation is ready to change the Internet business industry. It offers an unrivaled mix of security, straightforwardness, and cost-productivity. Entrepreneurs hoping to grow their endeavors should accept this turn of events and reclassify how they work. Blockchain technology has positively disrupted finance and e-commerce by offering new and effective payments, smart contracts, sufficient trading execution, and smart contracts. Blockchain technology holds the key to unlocking new possibilities for organizations on a global scale to be more agile, efficient, and efficient while providing an attractive price, security, and security model. Blockchain is a technology enabling digital transactions between a human or an entity and an outside entity. The blockchain is a distributed database that stores information about everything. It stores a wealth of information about users, the networks that connect them, and other connected devices. Each blockchain is called a "wallet" or "blockchain" because of the blockchain's unique identifier. These wallets store information recorded by the network. This information is known as the "transaction." Blockchain provides a framework for decentralized application developers, allowing users to communicate directly and use cryptography to secure their assets. It will enable users to store digital signatures for goods and services securely.

They can also send messages to each other. Some of these messages can be used to make payments, but this is still more than an intermediary service. It is the application-level layer where the application can perform operations. The application can be any operating system or program with a blockchain backend (Ahram et al., 2017). It is considered that blockchain can create a new way to control transactions and data flow on multiple layers without the need to have an exchange infrastructure and data centers. It allows the developers to add features to it as an efficient, trusted, and efficient solution. It is interesting to understand why and how blockchain works. The concept of blockchain differs from traditional banks as they are created by the people and are made to transact and manage their assets by themselves to avoid risk and make money. Blockchain is a platform that helps create a central resource that will automatically act as a ledger where these resources and the records can be verified to validate the information. Blockchain is undoubtedly a significant innovation. I have seen massive growth in the application of blockchain to the industry. Not only has it led to the transformation of companies like Airbnb and Dropbox, but many others. This change in the way businesses operate will help drive growth and improve the business's efficiency.

It will also help the government employ more people, thus improving the service quality. It has played an essential role for businesses by providing a cost-effective and efficient alternative to cash payments. Blockchain technology allows the payment system to function. It is also useful in several applications, including digital identity, e-commerce, insurance, property management, e-payments, and crowdfunding. The fact that it facilitates the flow of data and information is the ability to verify every transaction made on a network. The ability to do impossible things in conventional financial institutions and businesses can be achieved in less than two seconds. The speed at which companies and industries can create new products and services. Blockchain technology is all about consensus, which is where the blockchain works. Blockchain has had a significant impact on businesses and industries in several industries. For example, the largest IT company in America, Accenture, said they are exploring a blockchain implementation to build blockchain-based applications. As with any technology, blockchain has a variety of applications, such as enabling automated, low-latency bidding through automated contract systems or systems of record for large, complex businesses, or making certain types of transactions more secure and efficient.

This paper focuses primarily on emerging blockchain applications for cyber-physical systems, namely medical records, transportation, e-commerce, finance, and cybersecurity. Table 11.1 lists the various systems covered in the study and their respective application domains.

11.3 BLOCKCHAIN APPLICATIONS IN CYBERSECURITY

The current techniques available in cybersecurity offer a centralized storage system to authorize access (Koh et al., 2020). However, blockchain uses distributed ledger technology, giving it the additional power of not getting compromised quickly. By applying cryptographic and mathematical algorithms, blockchain achieves trust among its users and does not depend on any third party. The characteristics of blockchain technology like authenticity, transparency, and immutability make it applicable to various other sectors. For example, it is applied in the financial sector, medical, IoT, education, and cybersecurity. Further discussed are some of the cybersecurity problems addressed by blockchain.

Secure Domain Name Service. The centralized Domain Name Service (DNS) is susceptible to attacks as the core functions of resolving the domain name, etc., are located in a centralized location. A map can be established between DNS and hash using blockchain. Users can register, transmit, and revise domain names. Each block represents domain owners' public and private keys and resolved domain names. Since the information is distributed across the nodes, there is no centralized location to attack. Unlike a centralized DNS system, even if a node is

TABLE 11.1

CPS Application Domains

Systems	Applications	Benefits
Transportation	Automobile electronics, rail systems, road networks, aviation, and airspace management	• Facilitation of complex flow and equipment compliance management • Simplification of payment procedures • Traceability of flows • Reverse logistics
e-commerce	Monitoring and tracking of the supply chain to ensure openness in the market, redesign of the payments system, secure e-commerce platform, product testimonials for the real deal	• Alternative payment methods • Better order processing • Enhanced payment security • Faster transactions
Healthcare	Automobile electronics, rail systems, road networks, aviation, and airspace management	• Medical data management • Clinical trial optimization • Drug traceability and anti-counterfeiting
Finance	Fraud prevention, financial inclusion, money laundry prevention, trade finance, smart assets, and smart contracts	• Uberization of banking services • Facilitation of fund transfers • More secure and efficient transactions
Cybersecurity	Keyless signature infrastructure, user anonymity, validate transactions in cyber-physical systems, data authentication	• Permanent data security • Decentralization on a blockchain could replace certification authorities • Advanced authentication

attacked, there is no harm to other nodes in the network (Ming Huang Shun & Chan, 2013).

Keyless Signature Infrastructure. Authentication schemes relying on keys suffer from key distribution, updating, and revocation. Recent blockchain research resolves this problem using key signature infrastructure (KSI). Each node in the blockchain stores the state of the data, network, and hash. KSI will constantly monitor the hash value with a timestamp. Any change in the data changes the hash value and helps detect unauthorized access. When employing a timestamp-based monitoring system, there is no need to distribute, retain, or revoke keys. In England, nuclear power plants and flood control systems use KSI-based security protection systems.

Secure Storage. Information regarding finances and medical records is usually stored in a centralized location, and unauthorized access brings various problems for the organizations and the users. The data can be stored efficiently using the blockchain's hash value concept. Apart from the areas discussed, there are other IoT equipment certification areas such as cloud data desensitization and secure data transmission (Maleh et al., 2018). Though there are advantages to using blockchain in cybersecurity, gaps are identified.

Gaps and Resolutions of Security Issues in Blockchain. The frauds that happen in a cryptocurrency network are increasing. The increase in fraud each year is slowing down the cryptocurrency market. Weak security systems and a lack of government regulations are blamed for it. Another gap is the increase of quantum power. An increase in quantum power will make hackers break the key used for encryption in the blockchain. It is therefore feared to be a cybersecurity threat.

Similarly, one more gap identified is that of inexperienced users in the blockchain networks. Users who are unaware of safe practices in the blockchain are prone to get attacked by scammers. Therefore, they provide insecure access to the blockchain network. Further discussed are three solutions to handle the security gaps identified in the blockchain (Maleh et al., 2020).

Quantum Computing. The gap related to quantum computing can be overcome by using a key with a higher number of bits, because quantum computers can quickly crack keys with a lower number of bits. Therefore, it is better to offer 64-bit, 128-bit, and 256-bit cryptography packages so that users can choose depending on their requirements.

Dealing with Inexperienced Users. Proper training must be provided for inexperienced users not to give away their keys to the scammers. Similarly, it is better to add two or three layers of authentication for verification purposes. Another solution is to track transactions using network features, alerting users and confirming access to their systems.

User Anonymity. The identity of the user is hidden in the blockchain network. Scammers and hackers are taking advantage of this. When a public key gets flagged, there should be a possibility to track the user's identity. The tracing should also be enabled for government agencies that deal with cybersecurity. This feature would create fear among scammers, so the probability of fraud might be reduced. Although the blockchain has many features to improve cybersecurity, some attacks happen on the blockchain.

11.3.1 APPLICATION OF BLOCKCHAIN TECHNOLOGY TO VALIDATE TRANSACTIONS IN CYBER-PHYSICAL SYSTEMS

A relatively new trend in cybersecurity is the development of protection mechanisms and systems based on blockchain technology. The blockchain ensures transaction integrity in the absence of a reliable central hub. System users' tangible and intangible assets are subject to transactions specified as specific activities taken from a predetermined list. Blocks containing transaction information are linked together using hashing to build a chain. To make it more difficult for an attacker to undermine the blockchain, a specific method known as a consensus algorithm is employed to distribute identical copies of the blocks to all system members. The main advantage of blockchain, which makes the technology attractive for various data protection applications, is the difficulty of violating the integrity of stored transactions. Any change to a single block might have disastrous consequences for the rest of the chain, and it will have to be rebuilt from scratch. However, the computational complexity of this task minimizes the probability of blockchain hacking (Nakamoto, 2008).

Blockchain technology is currently actively used in cyber-physical systems for various purposes. As previously stated, the primary benefit of this technology is the ability to verify various transactions that would otherwise be impossible in an untrusted environment. According to several studies, blockchain technology is crucial for the next fourth industrial revolution (Industry 4.0) (Alladi et al., 2019; Fernández-Caramés & Fraga-Lamas, 2019). Furthermore, blockchain is being promoted alongside other promising technologies of our time as part of Industry 4.0 (Aceto et al., 2019). The Internet of Things (Fernández-Caramés & Fraga-Lamas, 2018), big data (Zhaofeng et al., 2020), fog computing (Baniata & Kertesz, 2020), and augmented reality (Fernández-Caramés & Fraga-Lamas, 2019) are examples. In the Industrial Internet of Things, blockchain is widely regarded as a key technology, helping transform traditional factories into modern smart factories that use the latest breakthroughs in digital technology. Let us mention some current research examples that offer specific scientific and technical solutions to applying blockchain technology to solve security problems in cyber-physical systems. The secure management of diverse assets, including those in cyber-physical systems, is an important element of the existing work. Blockchain technology was initially used in conjunction with Bitcoin. Therefore, this is what happened. With the advancement of blockchain technology, the cryptocurrency industry grew and today plays an essential part in society's daily activities. Over time, the number of applications of blockchain technology has expanded considerably. For example, a recent paper (Bhushan et al., 2020) analyzes the utility of blockchain in solving the security problems of the smart city, which is an example of a large-scale cyber-physical system. The authors consider such components of smart city functioning as transportation, health care, smart grids, financial systems, supply chain management, and data center networks, and discuss blockchain technology capabilities in relation to these components and suggest future research directions.

In general, blockchain technology research may be classified into numerous main categories. The first group of studies is related to blockchain technology's supply chain management. This group is primarily general research, which does not focus on a specific area or a specific class of cyber-physical systems, but instead offers a general solution for secure blockchain-based supply chain management and discusses some aspects of the problem. In some cases, the proposed solutions are designed for use in cyber-physical systems for different purposes. Sometimes they are not explicitly specified with such a scope of use. Thus, Saberi et al. (Saberi et al., 2019) presented the classification of barriers that prevent blockchain technology implementation in supply chain management. Aceto et al. (Aceto et al., 2019) discussed some of the challenges of overcoming these roadblocks. The precise asset is not provided in either scenario. A wide range of supply chain services and items are also included in this research set. Kshetri et al. (Kshetri, 2018) described real-world applications of blockchain for tracking raw materials, ingredients, or spare parts in various industries. In many cyber-physical systems, the emphasis is on leveraging blockchain technology combined with Internet of Things technologies. If not to be classified in more detail, the first group includes studies devoted to related tasks arising in the organization and management of production. For example, the work (Yu et al., 2020), presented an architectural solution for data integrity protection in cyber-physical production systems used in co-production. The second group of studies aims to tackle the risk-free management of a particular asset or service, including supply chain management of the associated assets. Today, there is a plethora of such applications to choose from. Blockchain is used to control the sales or distribution of electricity (M. Li et al., 2020), fuel (Lu et al., 2019), computing resources (Seitz et al., 2018), and software. The previous studies have one thing in common: they all involve trading commodities for money. As a result, blockchain-based solutions borrow heavily from cryptocurrency concepts. The next group includes research devoted to the problem of the organization of trusted interaction between multiple devices. The specific tasks related to ensuring the integrity of some or other data operated by such devices may differ. Many papers deal with the interaction of arbitrary IoT devices without reference to specific types of cyber-physical systems. Some examples of recent work in this direction are Chi et al. (2020), Koshy et al. (2020), Luo et al. (2020). Most of these studies focus on the energy efficiency of architectural solutions intended for use in IoT systems, and propose various ways to achieve this property. Regarding tasks to be completed, the works under consideration can be divided into those that only ensure transactional integrity. Those that do that also ensure the confidentiality of the data contained in transactions. For example, in a study (D. Li et al., 2020), data on the location of Internet of Things devices is considered the object of protection. The authors point to the need to ensure the confidentiality of this data, so in the scheme they propose, blockchain is combined with encryption. Turning from general solutions for the application of blockchain technology for data protection in cyber-physical systems, which are based on the Internet of Things technology, to particular cases, it is necessary to note such a class of cyber-physical systems as connected vehicles, including unmanned vehicles (Cebe et al., 2018; Qian et al., 2020; Rathee et al., 2019). In 2019–2021, there is an "explosive" growth in the number of journal publications devoted to relevant research, so we can say that the security of this class of cyber-physical systems using blockchain technology is an example of a promising direction in the problem area under consideration.

11.3.2 Data Authentication in Cyber-Physical Systems

Digital evidence may be subject to an entire forensic process, encompassing the following stages: identification, collection, examination, analysis, documentation, and presentation (Evsutin et al., 2019). Preservation of digital evidence is an essential principle that should be considered in all stages of this process. For this purpose, blockchain plays an important role in ensuring the collected evidence's integrity and proof of origin. On the other hand, the complexity existing in the operation scenarios of cyber-physical systems imposes, on the security solutions and methods used, restrictive non-functional requirements concerning scalability, computational performance, and use of the communication network, among others. Several blockchain techniques have been proposed to provide data authentication and prevent cyber-physical attacks. Evsyutin et al. (O. O. Evsyutin, A. S. Kokurina, 2019) provided an overview of strategies for embedding information into digital data in the Internet of Things at the end of 2018. As a result, this review focuses on new research that has arisen in recent years. At the same time, we should stress that only digital watermark embedding methods will be addressed in the context of this study.

In contrast, digital steganography methods are often unrelated to data integrity. At the outset, it is vital to distinguish between several research projects focused on developing methods and algorithms for concealing information in digital photographs (as well as other digital objects) to ensure the security of sensitive data in cyber-physical systems. Examples of work in this area are Qian et al. (2020) and Prasetyo et al. (2020).

Even though their authors claim that their solutions aim to ensure data security in the Internet of Things, they do not provide any examples of how their algorithms could be used in other domains. In much of this research, the authors are worried about the security flaws in telemedicine systems. Because such studies are so prevalent, they should be classified as a different class. However, the works in this class do not go beyond traditional embedding into multimedia data and will not be studied further. The following set of works also includes traditional data embedding into multimedia products. The authors identify unique data transmission situations specific to such systems and explain the limits associated with them while stressing the applicability of their solutions in cyber-physical systems. This group's works are not as extensively represented, but they should be separated from those in the first group. A solution for secure picture transmission in telemedicine systems is also presented in Peng et al. (2020). Encrypted confidential pictures are placed in photographs with non-confidential material. In addition, the secret picture's fingerprint (perceptual hash) is included in the image container for further authentication. The tracking of the picture transmission sequence is a distinguishing characteristic of this approach. To that end, the authors offer the concept of a picture fingerprint chain by analogy with blockchain technology. The research of Zhang et al. (Pu et al., 2019) is fairly unique because it entails embedding secret attachments in graphics used in printed items.

On the other hand, this research explicitly describes the potential applications of the proposed approach in IoT systems and the associated situations. These scenarios include, for example, offering data authentication to protect products from being counterfeited. There should be an emphasis on the endurance of digital watermark embedding in the authors' discussion on steganographic embedding. The following works are unrelated to multimedia and deal with inserting digital watermarks in data created and transferred through cyber-physical systems. A substantial portion of the work in this group is concerned with inserting digital watermarks in wireless sensor network data for integrity control.

A comparable approach is proposed, among other places, by one of the authors of this review's papers (Evsutin et al., 2019). This approach's ability to alter the degree of distortion generated by embedding is a distinguishing characteristic. As a result, it applies to sensor data of many physical types. Hoang et al. (Hoang et al., 2020) incorporate digital watermarks into wireless sensor network data to protect against cloned sensor node attacks. The embedding is based on a gamming-like modification of the binary alphabet. It is argued that the light-weight algorithm provides an advantage. The algorithms embed the digital watermark components into the sensory data consistently and independently since they are not dependent on the values of the sensory data or some of their features. While traditional digital watermarking methods and algorithms and the problem of wireless sensor networks and the Internet of Things can create a digital watermark based on protected data, the notion is exceedingly broad. In the simplest example, digital watermark components are created based only on the values of sensor data elements.

The embedding approach provided in Xiao & Gao (2019) is one example. This approach generates the digital watermark bit inserted in the next sensor value depending on previous sensor values. Separate embedding of digital watermark components has several advantages; however, timing is an issue with this technique. The digital watermark extraction will be hampered even if there isn't an active intruder on the communication channel. Wang et al. (Wang et al., 2019) offer an answer to this dilemma. Sensor data is divided, depending on the key, into variable-length groups, as proposed by the authors in their paper. Digital watermark chains are produced and implanted for pairs of adjacent groupings.

A series of digital watermarks are used to verify the sensor data. The second digital watermark chain provides separation and data synchronization, which encodes group separators. In a more complex scenario, it is possible to create a digital watermark that contains sensory quantity values and some of their characteristics. For example, see Ferdowsi et al. (Ferdowsi & Saad, 2019), Internet of Things device authentication. Data streams' stochastic features might be extracted and used to create digital watermarks. Spectrum expansion is a technique for incorporating digital watermarks into data streams. Hameed (Hameed et al., 2018) also addresses how to create a digital watermark using several aspects of the acquired data, such as data length, frequency of occurrence, and time of capture. Nguyen et al. (Nguyen et al., 2019) create a digital watermark based on CSMA/CA protocol collisions to deter sensor node clone attacks. Furthermore, the way the sensor data is portrayed is a distinguishing characteristic of the study. They are combined to make a matrix resembling a digital image.

In general, such a system enables the adoption of methodologies that have proven successful when dealing with digital pictures with sensory data. All of the algorithms in the mentioned studies work using digital watermarks that represent binary sequences. Watermarking analog transmissions (mainly modulated signals) to solve signal source authentication is also a field of study. The answers discovered in those pieces are ideally comparable to those found in digital watermarking. The distinction is solely in the manner in which the signal is represented and, as a result, in the manner in which it is processed. Sender authentication in systems matching the NB-IoT (Narrow Band Internet of Things) standard focuses on research (Zhao et al., 2019).

The notion of a radio-frequency watermark is used in the investigation. Rather than using binary sequences for future embedding, the watermark is first created as a digital one and then converted to modulated signals. The main benefit of the suggested technique is that it is more reliable since the useable signal and the watermark signal do not conflict with one another. Watermarks can be used to deter certain sorts of assaults in some instances. Rubio-Hernan et al. (2018) suggested an adaptive control-theoretic technique for detecting cyber replication attempts on networked control industrial systems. This refers to an intruder's effort to tamper with system control by replicating previously intercepted data sequences. The main contribution of this work is not the embedding technique taken from previous publications, but rather the approach for using this algorithm to protect against an intruder.

Huang et al. (Huang & Zhang, 2019) offer a technique for embedding reversible air signs in signals conveyed in "hard" real-time industrial control systems. The authors chose ship control systems as the most important field of application. A secret key must be delivered in advance through a secure communication channel before embedding can begin. The approach described here can detect attacks that aim to cause signal delay and distortion. Finally, experiments integrating blockchain with digital watermark technology have emerged, as outlined in the preceding section. Different security concerns in cyber-physical systems are addressed by blockchain and digital watermarks. Their combined use may produce better security than each of these methods alone.

This concept has previously been explored in prior works, but mostly in one aspect, namely the issue of digital rights management (Qian et al., 2020; Zhao et al., 2019). The collaborative implementation of these technologies in other areas (Iskhakov & Meshcheryakov, 2019; Maleh et al., 2019; Sadeghi et al., 2015) is a promising research field whose advancement will benefit cybersecurity. Table 11.2 summarizes the many blockchain uses in cybersecurity.

11.3.3 Blockchain in Cryptocurrency and Finance Industry

Many financial networks exist, including banks, brokers, bonds, and real estate. If they have a car or vehicle and buy fuel, this happens on a blockchain where they own the supply and use a blockchain. In cars with their drivers and their distributed ledgers, anyone on the network can verify anything that goes on there, and they will sell it and repurchase it at a fair price as if it was not there. It is a technology that takes the underlying information that has been used to create the payment system from the banking system and distributes that information to millions of potential customers without any intermediaries that the bank can hold the lead. They can do so using blockchain to create a consensus mechanism. This has made this whole technology, and it is a vast revolution. It allows anyone to transact anything with anybody in any block or chain using an Ethereum smart contract. So, in banking and finance, the payment of funds is possible. It may be the next thing to move banks and companies from analog to digital technology (Eyal, 2017).

Banks are attempting to provide digital customer service and financial information. Banks are trying to replace old banks and financial information with

TABLE 11.2

Blockchain Applications in Cybersecurity

Application Domain	Applications	Contributions
Quantum-Inspired Blockchain (Abd El-Latif et al., 2021)	Smart edge utilities in IoT-based smart cities	Resist potential assaults from digital and quantum computers.
Lightweight Blockchain-based Cybersecurity (LBC) (Abdulkader et al., 2019)	IoT environments	Address intensive computational requirements and bandwidth consumption overhead.
Blockchain Empowered Cooperative Authentication (Abdulkader et al., 2019)	Vehicular edge computing	Protect and preserve the privacy and confidentiality of data while also ensuring mutual authentication is in place (e.g., reply attack, etc.).
BloCyNfo-Share (Badsha et al., 2020)	Cybersecurity information exchange (CYBEX)	Describe how to share private information with other organizations or provide private information to other organizations access.
BBDS (Xia et al., 2017)	Electronic medical records in cloud environments	Aim to disseminate medical data outside of the protected institutions' cloud.
Ancile (Dagher et al., 2018)	Electronic medical records	Preserve the privacy of patients' sensitive information.
Secure and decentralized sharing (Patel, 2019)	Image sharing across domains Personal health data may be processed in a batch using a hyperledger fabric tree-based system.	Allowing parties to agree without relying on a single authority.
BlockChain (Dorri et al., 2017)	Interconnected smart vehicles	Address the security and privacy threats that smart vehicles face, such as location tracking and remote vehicle hijacking.

blockchain technology. The banking sector is looking for blockchain solutions to solve its economic problems. The banking and finance industry is about business, technology, and managing money. In the banking and finance industries, the term "blockchain" refers to dealing with information or a system of transactions that can move money. When they talk about blockchain technology, they can be sure of being part of the banking and finance industry. Blockchain technology creates a secure and reliable system of payments or electronic transactions. This technology is for money generation. It involves ledger-like records. One can read and see the information by using a device called a device with chips. There is no need for any financial information to be stored in a ledger using this technology. They can keep all of the transactions or the blockchain data, and it is not required to have any financial information in the catalog. This technology is related to banking and finance businesses; information is more straightforward than a ledger system.

The processes are done automatically on blockchain technology. The server carries out the network to verify all transactions and the data with a chip. It is not required to take the money received, and the information is kept in the blockchain data. As the blockchain data is transparent, there is no need to keep records in a ledger system (Eyal, 2017).

Advancing blockchain is about increasing speed, safety, and availability for financial and banking users. Blockchain is the most scalable, tamper-proof, and secure way to transfer money anywhere. It has already revolutionized how our money is held in the cloud and has been the most disruptive technology for the digital economy. The latest industry is applying this future to the real world. As part of blockchain technology, it provides a framework that facilitates transactions to and from accounts. As a result, a person or entity of the financial institution may act as an intermediary between the bank and a customer at one point in the process. As a bank, if any person completes a transaction, it can act as a transaction broker simultaneously. This way, the person or entity acts as a transactor, and the account's funds are released in one or two transactions that would otherwise be delayed. As an institution that wants to develop new technologies, it is working to become a blockchain platform provider. It is a good business strategy.

Technology can facilitate technology companies. It provides a framework for banking companies to create a blockchain and provide transparency and record-keeping. Banks need to adopt Bitcoin with these changes. Blockchain is making significant progress in the banking and finance industries. Moreover, everyone has the technology to build smart contracts that operate entirely on blockchain. Banks can now offer their customers financial products they can make without a central bank. So, this process is accelerating. The pace of change in this process is improving every day.

Moreover, multiple sectors have already started working on what blockchain can be and how to implement it in various industries, where blockchain cannot be used for this purpose. For example, the banking industry, which has a huge problem, is working on smart contracts to manage credit and debt to give customers better banking. Both the credit and debit are stored in a specific virtual account.

The advancement of the blockchain in the banking and finance industry is due to many reasons, including high transaction volume, efficient use of the network, rapid pace of payment settlement, and low costs. For the banking industry, there are several advantages, like a single ledger of account details provides transparency and ease of access; automated settlement helps in making large transactions quickly and costs less; the rapid scale of payments in financial services makes transactions possible in less time than before; and the fast growth of business in financial services makes it easier for new ideas to advance. Each register is an encrypted archive in a distributed ledger called the "distributed ledger of payment details," a data storage system. These two information systems are complementary. They are separate from each other, which is why they are complementary. However, one may prefer to use one over the other. It is a different phenomenon compared to the familiar concept of the ledger of account details.

They contain a copy of the ledger of account details, but these two copies exist on separate machines with their state. It is not easy to know how they are synchronized since they are not synchronized. One may prefer to use a ledger of payment information in the banking and finance industry, reducing transaction speeds and making transactions cheaper. The difference between banks and finance firms is noticeable.

A blockchain is an online, distributed ledger that can record everything that has ever happened to something. A blockchain ledger, or a distributed ledger, is like a digital currency. Instead of using physical money, one uses computers to create a virtual currency to pay for goods and services. A block is a file that can be written to and read from the blockchain. The blockchain is a record of files, including all Bitcoin network records, the personal Bitcoin wallet, and any changes they have made to it, like transactions or minting coins. The blockchain is a platform that allows for a distributed, transparent, decentralized, and secure computing platform for managing all financial information. It offers a peer-to-peer platform for managing digital assets and transactions. It is a secure mechanism by which transactions are recorded and acts as a centralized trust to manage digital assets.

This industry deals with a lot of currency, and with the slip of a finger, millions of transactions are happening worldwide. The blockchain advanced how financial operations occur; most individuals needed cash, but it was no more complete. The blockchain has introduced more cryptocurrency technologies, but the most well-known one is Bitcoin (Calvão, 2019). In traditional transactions, organizations and companies can invest as much as possible; there is no limit to how much can happen. The traditional transaction has limitations and can not allow the user or organization to have a certain amount of money in one transaction. However, the blockchain has changed this industry as they can transact as much as possible and there are no limitations.

Peer-to-peer global financial transactions are made possible. The traditional transaction has many limitations, one of which concerns the boundaries. A third party that carries out the transaction has limits to the boundary of the nation-state of its origin. For example, a transaction in the United Kingdom cannot be completed for a bank account in France or Spain (Knezevic, 2018). The traditional transaction system works in the country and works for neighboring countries only in the case of advancement. The blockchain has advanced the transitions from the sender to the receiver directly without a third party. It makes the transaction process easy and fast, reducing the time taken to wait for verification. It does not require any third party to validate the process, hence confidentiality in the transaction.

Blockchain is useful for protecting market communications from dissimilar clients, strategy holders, and insurance companies. It is useful to exchange, purchase, and record insurance policies. Making a complete transaction is traditionally expensive; the sender must pay the sending fee and the receiver must pay a withdrawal fee. Blockchain has taken the financial industry to another level. Making transactions with the blockchain requires less transaction fees; to some extent, there is no fee to complete a transaction. It has increased cryptocurrency adoption because it allows users to compete for the transaction rather than the traditional way, which is unreliable.

The stock market is another advancement in the financial industry as a result of blockchain technology. Different nation-states have different currencies and are not a problem regarding the exchange stock. The seller may sell the currency to the buyer at a higher price, but the buyer ends up selling it at a lower price due to a lack of currency standardization. Blockchain has transparency, and the currency remains the same globally. The price of Bitcoin currency remains standard in all nations; if it rises, the impacts apply when there is a drop. It has made the transaction permanent and reduced the cyber activities concerning traditional transactions.

Blockchain technology is essential to all industries and critical in stimulating productivity. This technology is very secure when using it due to the encryption mechanisms in cryptography. Only those with perfect encryption keys will be able to decrypt the information. There is no limit to blockchain technology as a way to complete your transaction. It is available all the time, provided there is an Internet connection. Indeed, the financial industry has evolved due to blockchain technology, allowing you to save as much as you have.

There are a lot of conversations going on in the world about blockchain technology. According to Gupta (2017), the blockchain is an information recording system that has been customized with security features that make hacking attacks and system cheating impossible. Abadi et al. (Abad & Brunnermeier, 2018) indicate a ledger system that decentralizes the records by distributing them across all the blockchain networks. Transactions in the blockchain system are distributed to all the system participants, making it hard to cheat or steal. They further indicate that technology's correctness, decentralization, and cost efficiency make an excellent record-keeping system. Their comparison of the system to the traditional centralized system highlights blockchain's tremendous revolution in the record-keeping industry. One of the blockchain's essential features is the algorithms that permit record-keepers to rewind and undo false reports in the ledger's historical records. Besides the finance industry, the system is quite useful in procurement, Internet apps, and other industries where transparency is highly required. My focus will be on the finance industry, exploring technology's advancements in the industry.

11.3.3.1 Fraud Prevention

The blockchain has tremendously contributed to the finance industry's reduction in fraud. The financial organizations dealing with money and asset transactions are highly exposed and susceptible to experiencing losses brought about by fraud or crime. The financial sector has previously depended on a centralized system for record-keeping. Hackers and criminals are well-versed in this type of design, and it is simple for them to manipulate it, as access to such a system would grant them complete control over the system. Blockchain is a secure, non-corruptible technology that relies on a hard, decentralized network for attackers to manipulate or penetrate. Each transaction is recorded and stored in the form of a cryptographic mechanism. The mechanism has an almost impossible way of being corrupted; if corrupted, there are easy ways to trace the attackers. The difficulty is linking all blocks so that if one breach is detected, they all detect and show the change. The linked blocks also reduce the time of tracing the breach, reducing the time for the attackers to conduct any illegal business in the system.

11.3.3.2 Financial Inclusion

The current banking regulations and restrictions highly prevent banks' use by many people who are left looking for an alternative solution. Financial inclusivity is the ability and opportunity for everyone to use a formal financial system for economic growth and development. The low cost associated with blockchain gives start-ups a chance to compete with central banks. The start-ups rely on the alternative that comes with digital identification and mobile devices to access financial services. The hassle-free system has a competitive opportunity for innovators willing to serve small bankers, achieving financial inclusivity.

11.3.3.3 Money Laundry Prevention

With the anti-money laundering regulations taking place in most developed and developing economies, knowing your customer's policy has made registering a customer in a banking institution quite expensive. Financial institutions are estimated to spend between USD$0.60 million and USD$500 million enrolling a customer in their records. They are required to conduct a background check or what is commonly known as customer due diligence. The process is undertaken to reduce or eliminate global money laundering and curtail criminal organizations such as terrorists and drug groups. Due diligence by one bank or institution on a customer makes the information about the customer access to other financial institutions in the blockchain system. The workload is reduced tremendously, and efforts from the same industry are not repeated. This advantage of the blockchain system highly motivates business leaders in the financial sector to acquire and join the blockchain system to reduce their operations costs, and optimize their organization's profits (Gupta, 2017).

11.3.3.4 Digital Currency

The digital currency known as cryptocurrency is the new wave of financial assets as the blockchain system increases financial inclusivity and allows innovators. The cryptocurrency heavily relies on the blockchain system to increase its credibility and security features. The currency is now used in different parts of the world as an alternative to traditional money. Although the cost of accessing digital currency is currently high, companies are working to reduce the barrier by providing a continuous exchange of money.

11.3.3.5 Trade Finance

Trade finance has been made easier on the blockchain system. Transactions involving complex trading in the traditional system are considered a long and tedious process that involves a lot of paperwork and can also be costly. In blockchain technology, trade finance is an essential application that eliminates lengthy processes and involves experts conversing with the system. The experts' role is to engage the traders involved in the complex transaction by signing them into the system and exporting and importing needed ledgers. Once agreed upon, the transaction automatically completes the rest of the task in an impressively short time. All the parties are privy to the activities being conducted in the system. In a practical example, the Barclays Bank in Israel completed a transaction record of four hours. In traditional design, the transaction would have taken seven to ten days to complete.

11.3.3.6 Smart Assets and Smart Contracts

Smart assets and smart contracts are features in the blockchain system that are automatically executed. A smart asset application on the blockchain is used to store records of asset transactions and eliminate the long process of buying and selling paperwork documentation. Once the transfer of assets is done, the blockchain system holds this information digitally, updating any information or activity conducted on the system. On the other hand, smart contracts are an application that facilitates the ease of agreements. It enables financial transactions by increasing the speed and simplifying the process of reaching or completing a transaction. The application ensures that the information transferred is accurate, and its approval is dependent on the written code. This application's errors and execution time are significantly reduced at the extreme level, and all parties involved are aware of the transaction.

Blockchain technology is quite a handful of tasks to understand but, once understood, reduces financial fraud in the finance industry, reduces activities by criminal organizations such as terrorists, makes trading finance a light task, increases cryptocurrency trading, allows financial inclusivity, and transfers assets and the achievement of contracts an easy task. Although there are challenges associated with the system as it is based on peer-to-peer transactions where everyone in the network is privy to the information and allowed to add data, blockchain is a solution to most of the challenges experienced in the financial industry. It has experienced adoption globally, and its scalability is expected to open up more opportunities to innovators and financial consumers. The universal adoption of blockchain means the system will open up cross-border money transfers and scale-up trade across the board.

Cryptocurrency is not just one asset but many asset classes. Cryptocurrencies, like credit cards and stock markets, have different characteristics in many ways. They are different types of asset classes that provide services to specific groups. Fiat currencies are used in many cases to control prices, but the money is not limited to that role. Like stocks, crypto can become an asset like a bank payment system. The blockchain is a network of digital records, immutable digital copies of all electronic transactions, including paper money. The history of all Bitcoin transactions in the peer-to-peer networks is stored in a blockchain database. The blockchain records all of the transactions in Bitcoin. To create a digital asset, one needs to hold Bitcoins in an exchange, which is similar to a bank account, so that a user can

It is worth mentioning that many people may not know about it due to the market's low visibility and its lack of development. Since there is nothing wrong with the idea of a blockchain platform, it would be good to write a blog about it. It would help people understand the ecosystem better as it is very technical and might even make them rethink their views. They might start using the services that it provides. Crowdfunding has been a great way to fund projects, and this has helped people with cryptocurrency needs. Since we are beginning the coin economy based on the blockchain, we aim to increase adoption and decrease entry barriers for anyone interested in cryptocurrencies and technology. We are already working on the coin economy to create a platform to allow anyone with a computer or smartphone to earn tokens by creating projects. Many people have launched their cryptocurrency projects, but with the current market structure, it takes them. Ripple, Bitcoin, and Bitcoin Cash are now the most popular cryptocurrencies in the market. They were even the most significant currencies in the world. Many people are interested in Bitcoin, and it seems people are ready to make some progress with it in the future (Aste et al., 2017).

The blockchain industry is rapidly growing because of its simplicity, ease of use, and flexibility. This technology could be applied to several sectors, such as IT, manufacturing, finance, banking, real estate, insurance, education, real estate, health care, transportation, retail, and more. Blockchain technology enables smart contracts to be validated, making it easier to do business and track and manage digital assets from start to finish. It also allows for the transfer of digital assets through the Internet and creates a new era of investment in digital assets. Blockchain technology has enabled much innovation in the development of the cryptocurrency market. The community has gone so far as to put in the necessary resources to allow technology development.

One exciting aspect of the blockchain is that it allows for a decentralized peer-to-peer financial system. Unlike traditional financial networks, where parties rely on their networks, no central authority provides them with services. As a result, the peer-to-peer network that creates a blockchain has no financial institutions. There have been few breakthroughs in cryptocurrencies since the beginning. It has been in this space for quite a while before it caught onto Bitcoin, before it caught onto the crash of the Bitcoin bubble that went after its price, and finally, it caught onto the Ethereum Bubble. Blockchain has already taken many coins in the space, giving them significant growth that will surely go bigger. The world over, blockchain solutions have been used to build real-time settlements, make real-time payments, provide the backbone for the banking system, verify digital identities, enable financial contracts, and allow digital transactions among people who know each other. With blockchain, it is becoming increasingly apparent that real-time solutions are the currency's backbone. The technology itself provides more applications than just cryptocurrency (Hashemi Joo et al., 2020).

There have been few breakthroughs in cryptocurrencies since the beginning. It has been in this space for quite a while before it caught onto Bitcoin, before it caught onto the crash of the Bitcoin bubble that went after its price, and finally it caught onto the Ethereum Bubble. Blockchain has already taken many coins in the space, giving them significant growth that will surely go bigger. The world over, blockchain solutions have been used to build real-time settlements, make real-time payments, provide the backbone for the banking system, verify digital identities, enable financial contracts, and allow digital transactions among people who know each other. With blockchain, it is becoming increasingly apparent that real-time solutions are the currency's backbone. The technology itself provides more applications than just cryptocurrency.

11.4 BLOCKCHAIN LIMITATIONS AND FUTURE DIRECTIONS

Despite their wealth, blockchain promises continue to face many security issues, as seen by the numerous breaches and fraud that have been reported. This is a paradoxical snare to fall into for a system whose key touted attributes are dependability and inviolability. Computer assaults, on the other hand, are carried over to all types of interactions with other systems—primarily markets, which are vulnerable to the classic flaws of centralized systems, like banks (Tasatanattakool & Techapanupreeda, 2018).

In general, the speed, throughput, secrecy, scalability, and interoperability issues with blockchains have been shown and well documented. Mining issues, at the heart of the proof of work on which the Bitcoin consensus is based, are also the subject of much debate. On the theoretical level, it is a matter of rigorously defining the conditions that will protect against malicious validation nodes. The level of 51% of the computing power held by a malicious entity is certainly considered the reference level. However, this value is the subject of controversy in the research community. The number and distribution of nodes is also a sensitive issue. Economic issues are also beginning to mobilize researchers (Chang et al., 2020). In addition to the monetary and financial aspects (competition between currencies, and monetary systems), the themes concern the economics of mining, with the question of cooperative incentives for miners or the evolution of mining capacity. And the debates do not stop at Bitcoin, since many depend on the consensus model chosen to replace the centralized decision-making system. Whatever the case, the technological environment for distributed registries will continue to evolve significantly.

The time it takes to complete a transaction on the blockchain is a significant drawback. Due to the vastness of the Bitcoin network, this process might take many hours to complete. Using a blockchain like Hyperledger Sawtooth helps reduces this latency since it allows the PoET (Proof of Elapsed Time) consensus process to be used, which is among the fastest and least resource-hungry in terms of reaction time, making it better suited to our current context, which includes networked object data and services (Da Xu et al., 2021). Second, not everyone should have access to blockchain data. This challenge may be solved by utilizing private blockchains, which can govern blockchain access privileges and transaction execution rights. Second, the blockchain's consensus algorithms, notably the PoW (proof of work), are extremely energy-hungry in terms of calculations.

Additionally, the redundant data and redundant calculations necessary to decide whether or not a new block may be added to the blockchain are energy-hungry. The blockchain, in the end, represents a sea change in thinking. In other words, the network is becoming decentralized instead of centrally controlled.

Other limitations of blockchains are regularly invoked, particularly the tension between transparency and confidentiality, and between anonymity and identification of stakeholders (see box above on the "dilemmas of blockchain for the financial sector"). Because the register is widely disseminated, stakeholders may easily access the plain language information it includes. When it comes to tracing transactions, this is a benefit, but when it comes to corporate confidentiality, such as in banking or health care, it's a redhibitory problem. The market looks for ways to reliably disguise information while engaging in activities that require disclosing some and the protection of others (Hashemi Joo et al., 2020).

Another limitation is the high amount of energy required. Using blockchain necessitates a lot of power-hungry verification, validation, and cryptography procedures. If this technique is widely used, it might have significant negative environmental externalities.

Despite the widespread interest in blockchain, it must be recognized that distributed registries are not a panacea. Blockchain is not yet suitable for the fast processing of large amounts of data, especially video and audio, and use in a fast-changing environment. Blockchain is ideal for the long term and as reliable as possible for storing information that changes infrequently. Therefore, the technology is promising for capturing customer data from banks, medical institutions, insurance, and logistics companies (Kolb et al., 2020). A distributed transaction registry will benefit patent offices and cadastral offices. Technology is suitable for law enforcement and tax authorities to record personal data. Brokerage and investment firms will benefit from blockchain as a registry of transactions. The technology's current capabilities are just an in-between. The continuous improvement of blockchain opens up prospects for its application in new and new industries. In its evolution, any technology must overcome distrust by conservatives and not be used to change quickly. Blockchain has already passed that stage and, therefore, it will continue to evolve.

11.5   CONCLUSION

Rapid advances in computational and communication technologies drive the scientific community's interest and industry in cyber-physical systems. Using sensor, computational, and networking capabilities, cyber-physical systems contribute to a new generation of scientific and technical solutions that provide automatic decision-making processes in various fields, from the automation of small domestic processes to the transportation of materials, factories of the future, and mission-critical industries.

An overview of various applications of blockchain in cyber-physical systems control protocols is presented. Although each industry has advantages in using blockchain, challenges are also involved. However, blockchain is well known and adopted for its various benefits in various industries.

This paper contributes to the thematic area by providing information on a poorly documented topic in the scientific literature. It became clear during the development of the work that it deserved further theoretical investigation. The analysis of the results shows that the theme addressed has grown annually and has become relevant for emerging and developing new applications using blockchain for cyber-physical systems. It is still too early to say whether blockchain technology is more appropriate in cyber-physical system applications and compare it with other technologies already used.

REFERENCES

Abadi, J., & Brunnermeier, M. (2018). Blockchain economics. *National Bureau of Economic Research (No. W25407)*.

Abd El-Latif, A. A., Abd-El-Atty, B., Mehmood, I., Muhammad, K., Venegas-Andraca, S. E., & Peng, J. (2021). Quantum-inspired blockchain-based cybersecurity: Securing smart edge utilities in IoT-based smart cities. *Information Processing & Management, 58*(4), 102549. 10.1016/j.ipm.2021.102549

Abdulkader, O., Bamhdi, A. M., Thayananthan, V., Elbouraey, F., & Al-Ghamdi, B. (2019). A lightweight blockchain based cybersecurity for IoT environments. *2019 6th IEEE International Conference on Cyber Security and Cloud Computing (CSCloud)/ 2019 5th IEEE International Conference on Edge Computing and Scalable Cloud (EdgeCom)*, 139–144. 10.1109/CSCloud/EdgeCom.2019.000-5

Aceto, G., Persico, V., & Pescapé, A. (2019). A survey on information and communication technologies for industry 4.0: State-of-the-art, taxonomies, perspectives, and challenges. *IEEE Communications Surveys & Tutorials, 21*(4), 3467–3501. 10.1109/COMST.2019.2938259

Ahram, T., Sargolzaei, A., Sargolzaei, S., Daniels, J., & Amaba, B. (2017). Blockchain technology innovations. *2017 IEEE Technology & Engineering Management Conference (TEMSCON)*, 137–141. 10.1109/TEMSCON.2017.7998367

Alladi, T., Chamola, V., Parizi, R. M., & Choo, K. R. (2019). Blockchain applications for industry 4.0 and industrial IoT: A review. *IEEE Access, 7*, 176935–176951. 10.1109/ACCESS.2019.2956748

Aste, T., Tasca, P., & Matteo, T. Di. (2017). Blockchain technologies: The foreseeable impact on society and industry. *Computer, 50*(9), 18–28. 10.1109/MC.2017.3571064

Badsha, S., Vakilinia, I., & Sengupta, S. (2020). BloCyNfo-Share: Blockchain based cybersecurity information sharing with fine grained access control. *2020 10th Annual Computing and Communication Workshop and Conference (CCWC)*, 317–323. 10.1109/CCWC47524.2020.9031164

Baniata, H., & Kertesz, A. (2020). A survey on blockchain-fog integration approaches. *IEEE Access, 8*, 102657–102668. 10.1109/ACCESS.2020.2999213

Bhushan, B., Khamparia, A., Sagayam, K. M., Sharma, S. K., Ahad, M. A., & Debnath, N. C. (2020). Blockchain for smart cities: A review of architectures, integration trends and future research directions. *Sustainable Cities and Society, 61*, 102360. 10.1016/j.scs.2020.102360

Calvão, F. (2019). Crypto-miners: Digital labor and the power of blockchain technology. *Economic Anthropology, 6*(1), 123–134. 10.1002/sea2.12136

Cebe, M., Erdin, E., Akkaya, K., Aksu, H., & Uluagac, S. (2018). Block4Forensic: An integrated lightweight blockchain framework for forensics applications of connected vehicles. *IEEE Communications Magazine, 56*(10), 50–57. 10.1109/MCOM.2018.1800137

Chang, V., Baudier, P., Zhang, H., Xu, Q., Zhang, J., & Arami, M. (2020). How blockchain can impact financial services – The overview, challenges and recommendations from expert interviewees. *Technological Forecasting and Social Change, 158*, 120166. 10.1016/j.techfore.2020.120166

Chi, J., Li, Y., Huang, J., Liu, J., Jin, Y., Chen, C., & Qiu, T. (2020). A secure and efficient data sharing scheme based on blockchain in industrial Internet of Things. *Journal of Network and Computer Applications, 167*, 102710. 10.1016/j.jnca.2020.102710

Christidis, K., & Devetsikiotis, M. (2016). Blockchains and smart contracts for the internet of things. *IEEE Access, 4*, 2292–2303. 10.1109/ACCESS.2016.2566339

Dagher, G. G., Mohler, J., Milojkovic, M., & Marella, P. B. (2018). Ancile: Privacy-preserving framework for access control and interoperability of electronic health records using blockchain technology. *Sustainable Cities and Society, 39*, 283–297. 10.1016/j.scs.2018.02.014

Da Xu, L., Lu, Y., & Li, L. (2021). Embedding blockchain technology into IoT for security: A survey. *IEEE Internet of Things Journal, 8*(13), 10452–10473. 10.1109/JIOT.2021. 3060508

Daza, V., Pietro, R. Di, Klimek, I., & Signorini, M. (2017). CONNECT: CONtextual NamE disCovery for blockchain-based services in the IoT. *2017 IEEE International Conference on Communications (ICC)*, 1–6. 10.1109/ICC.2017.7996641

Dorri, A., Steger, M., Kanhere, S. S., & Jurdak, R. (2017). BlockChain: A distributed solution to automotive security and privacy. *IEEE Communications Magazine, 55*(12), 119–125. 10.1109/MCOM.2017.1700879

Evsutin, O., Meshcheryakov, R., Tolmachev, V., Iskhakov, A., & Iskhakova, A. (2019). Algorithm for embedding digital watermarks in wireless sensor networks data with control of embedding distortions. In V. M. Vishnevskiy, K. E. Samouylov, & D. V. Kozyrev (Eds.), *Distributed computer and communication networks* (pp. 574–585). Springer International Publishing.

Evsyutin, O. O., & Kokurina, A. S., R. V. M. (2019). A review of methods of embedding information in digital objects for security in the internet of things. *Computer Optics, 43*(1), 137–154.

Eyal, I. (2017). Blockchain technology: Transforming libertarian cryptocurrency dreams to finance and banking realities. *Computer, 50*(9), 38–49. 10.1109/MC.2017.3571042

Ferdowsi, A., & Saad, W. (2019). Deep learning for signal authentication and security in massive internet-of-things systems. *IEEE Transactions on Communications, 67*(2), 1371–1387. 10.1109/TCOMM.2018.2878025

Fernández-Caramés, T. M., & Fraga-Lamas, P. (2019). A review on the application of blockchain to the next generation of cybersecure industry 4.0 smart factories. *IEEE Access, 7*, 45201–45218. 10.1109/ACCESS.2019.2908780

Fernández-Caramés, T. M., & Fraga-Lamas, P. (2018). A review on the use of blockchain for the internet of things. *IEEE Access, 6*, 32979–33001. 10.1109/ACCESS.2018.2842685

Gupta, S. S. (2017). Blockchain. *IBM Onlone* (Http://Www. IBM. COM).

Hameed, K., Khan, A., Ahmed, M., Goutham Reddy, A., & Rathore, M. M. (2018). Towards a formally verified zero watermarking scheme for data integrity in the internet of things based-wireless sensor networks. *Future Generation Computer Systems, 82*, 274–289. 10.1016/j.future.2017.12.009

Hashemi Joo, M., Nishikawa, Y., & Dandapani, K. (2020). Cryptocurrency, a successful application of blockchain technology. *Managerial Finance, 46*(6), 715–733. 10.1108/ MF-09-2018-0451

Hoang, T., Bui, V., Vu, N., & Hoang, D. (2020). A lightweight mixed secure scheme based on the watermarking technique for hierarchy wireless sensor networks. *2020 International Conference on Information Networking (ICOIN)*, 649–653. 10.1109/ ICOIN48656.2020.9016541

Huang, H., & Zhang, L. (2019). Reliable and secure constellation shifting aided differential radio frequency watermark design for NB-IoT systems. *IEEE Communications Letters, 23*(12), 2262–2265. 10.1109/LCOMM.2019.2944811

Iskhakov, A., & Meshcheryakov, R. (2019). Intelligent system of environment monitoring on the basis of a set of IOT-sensors. *2019 International Siberian Conference on Control and Communications (SIBCON)*, 1–5. 10.1109/SIBCON.2019.8729628

Knezevic, D. (2018). Impact of blockchain technology platform in changing the financial sector and other industries. *Montenegrin Journal of Economics, 14*(1), 109–120.

Koh, L., Dolgui, A., & Sarkis, J. (2020). Blockchain in transport and logistics – paradigms and transitions. *International Journal of Production Research, 58*(7), 2054–2062. 10.1080/00207543.2020.1736428

Kolb, J., AbdelBaky, M., Katz, R. H., & Culler, D. E. (2020). Core concepts, challenges, and future directions in blockchain: A centralized tutorial. *ACM Comput. Surv.*, *53*(1). 10.1145/3366370

Koshy, P., Babu, S., & Manoj, B. S. (2020). Sliding window blockchain architecture for internet of things. *IEEE Internet of Things Journal*, *7*(4), 3338–3348. 10.1109/JIOT. 2020.2967119

Kshetri, N. (2018). Blockchain's roles in meeting key supply chain management objectives. *International Journal of Information Management*, *39*, 80–89. 10.1016/j.ijinfomgt. 2017.12.005

Li, D., Hu, Y., & Lan, M. (2020). IoT device location information storage system based on blockchain. *Future Generation Computer Systems*, *109*, 95–102. 10.1016/j.future. 2020.03.025

Li, M., Hu, D., Lal, C., Conti, M., & Zhang, Z. (2020). Blockchain-enabled secure energy trading with verifiable fairness in industrial internet of things. *IEEE Transactions on Industrial Informatics*, *16*(10), 6564–6574. 10.1109/TII.2020.2974537

Lu, H., Huang, K., Azimi, M., & Guo, L. (2019). Blockchain technology in the oil and gas industry: A review of applications, opportunities, challenges, and risks. *IEEE Access*, *7*, 41426–41444. 10.1109/ACCESS.2019.2907695

Luo, J., Chen, Q., Yu, F. R., & Tang, L. (2020). Blockchain-enabled software-defined industrial internet of things with deep reinforcement learning. *IEEE Internet of Things Journal*, *7*(6), 5466–5480. 10.1109/JIOT.2020.2978516

Maleh, Y., Baddi, Y., Alazab, M., Tawalbeh, L., Romdhani, I. (2021). *Artificial intelligence and blockchain for future cybersecurity applications*. Springer. 10.1007/978-3-030-74575-2

Maleh, Y., Ezzati, A., & Belaissaoui, M. (Eds.). (2018). Security and privacy in smart sensor networks. *IGI Global*, 1–441. 10.4018/978-1-5225-5736-4

Maleh, Y., Lakkineni, S., Tawalbeh, L., & AbdEl-Latif, A. A. (2022). Blockchain for cyber-physical systems: Challenges and applications. In Y. Maleh, L. Tawalbeh, S. Motahhir, & A. S. Hafid (Eds.), *Advances in blockchain technology for cyber physical systems* (pp. 11–59). Springer International Publishing. 10.1007/978-3-030-93646-4_2

Maleh, Y., Shojafar, M., Alazab, M., & Romdhani, I. (2020). *Blockchain for cybersecurity and privacy: Architectures, challenges, and applications*. CRC Press. 10.1201/978042 9324932

Maleh, Y., Shojafar, M., & Darwish, A. (2019). *Cybersecurity and privacy in cyber-physical systems*. CRC Press. https://www.crcpress.com/Cybersecurity-and-Privacy-in-Cyber-Physical-Systems/Maleh/p/book/9781138346673

Ming Huang Shun, J. & Chan, B., L. D. (2013). An efficient key management scheme for data-centric storage wireless sensor networks. *IERI Procedia*, *4*, 25–31. 10.1016/ J.IERI.2013.11.005

Monostori, L. (2014). Cyber-physical production systems: Roots, expectations and R&D challenges. *Procedia CIRP*, *17*, 9–13. 10.1016/j.procir.2014.03.115

Nakamoto, S. (2008). Bitcoin: A peer-to-peer electronic cash system. *Decentralized Business Review*, *21260*.

Nguyen, V., Hoang, T., Duong, T., Nguyen, Q., & Bui, V. (2019). A lightweight watermark scheme utilizing MAC layer behaviors for wireless sensor networks. *2019 3rd International Conference on Recent Advances in Signal Processing, Telecommunications & Computing (SigTelCom)*, 176–180. 10.1109/SIGTELCOM. 2019.8696234

Patel, V. (2019). A framework for secure and decentralized sharing of medical imaging data via blockchain consensus. *Health Informatics Journal*, *25*(4), 1398–1411. 10.1177/ 1460458218769699

Peng, H., Yang, B., Li, L., & Yang, Y. (2020). Secure and traceable image transmission scheme based on semitensor product compressed sensing in telemedicine system. *IEEE Internet of Things Journal*, *7*(3), 2432–2451. 10.1109/JIOT.2019.2957747

Porru, S., Pinna, A., Marchesi, M., & Tonelli, R. (2017). Blockchain-oriented software engineering: Challenges and new directions. *2017 IEEE/ACM 39th International Conference on Software Engineering Companion (ICSE-C)*, 169–171. 10.1109/ICSE-C.2017.142

Prasetyo, H., Hsia, C., & Liu, C. (2020). Vulnerability attacks of SVD-based video watermarking scheme in an IoT environment. *IEEE Access*, *8*, 69919–69936. 10.1109/ACCESS.2020.2984180

Pu, Y., Zhang, N., & Wang, H. (2019). Fractional-order spatial steganography and blind steganalysis for printed matter: Anti-counterfeiting for product external packing in internet-of-things. *IEEE Internet of Things Journal*, *6*(4), 6368–6383. 10.1109/JIOT.2018.2886996

Qian, Y., Jiang, Y., Hu, L., Hossain, M. S., Alrashoud, M., & Al-Hammadi, M. (2020). Blockchain-based privacy-aware content caching in cognitive internet of vehicles. *IEEE Network*, *34*(2), 46–51. 10.1109/MNET.001.1900161

Rathee, G., Sharma, A., Iqbal, R., Aloqaily, M., Jaglan, N., & Kumar, R. (2019). A Blockchain framework for securing connected and autonomous vehicles. *Sensors*, *19*(14). 10.3390/s19143165

Rubio-Hernan, J., De Cicco, L., & Garcia-Alfaro, J. (2018). Adaptive control-theoretic detection of integrity attacks against cyber-physical industrial systems. *Transactions on Emerging Telecommunications Technologies*, *29*(7), e3209. 10.1002/ett.3209

Saberi, S., Kouhizadeh, M., Sarkis, J., & Shen, L. (2019). Blockchain technology and its relationships to sustainable supply chain management. *International Journal of Production Research*, *57*(7), 2117–2135. 10.1080/00207543.2018.1533261

Sadeghi, A., Wachsmann, C., & Waidner, M. (2015). Security and privacy challenges in industrial Internet of Things. *2015 52nd ACM/EDAC/IEEE Design Automation Conference (DAC)*, 1–6. 10.1145/2744769.2747942.

Seitz, A., Henze, D., Miehle, D., Bruegge, B., Nickles, J., & Sauer, M. (2018). Fog computing as enabler for blockchain-based IIoT App marketplaces – A case study. *2018 Fifth International Conference on Internet of Things: Systems, Management and Security*, 182–188. 10.1109/IoTSMS.2018.8554484

Swan, M. (2015). *Blockchain: Blueprint for a new economy*. O'Reilly Media.

Tasatanattakool, P., & Techapanupreeda, C. (2018). Blockchain: Challenges and applications. *2018 International Conference on Information Networking (ICOIN)*, 473–475. 10.1109/ICOIN.2018.8343163

Teslya, N., & Ryabchikov, I. (2017). Blockchain-based platform architecture for industrial IoT. *2017 21st Conference of Open Innovations Association (FRUCT)*, 321–329. 10.23919/FRUCT.2017.8250199

Wang, B., Kong, W., Li, W., & Xiong, N. N. (2019). A dual-chaining watermark scheme for data integrity protection in internet of things. *Computers, Materials & Continua*, *58*(3), 679–695. 10.32604/cmc.2019.06106

Xia, Q., Sifah, E. B., Smahi, A., Amofa, S., & Zhang, X. (2017). BBDS: Blockchain-based data sharing for electronic medical records in cloud environments. *Information*, *8*(2), 1–16. 10.3390/info8020044

Xiao, Y., & Gao, G. (2019). Digital watermark-based independent individual certification scheme in WSNs. *IEEE Access*, *7*, 145516–145523. 10.1109/ACCESS.2019.2945177

Yu, C., Jiang, X., Yu, S., & Yang, C. (2020). Blockchain-based shared manufacturing in support of cyber physical systems: Concept, framework, and operation.

Robotics and Computer-Integrated Manufacturing, *64*, 101931. 10.1016/j.rcim. 2019.101931

Zhao, B., Fang, L., Zhang, H., Ge, C., Meng, W., Liu, L., & Su, C. (2019). Y-DWMS: A digital watermark management system based on smart contracts. *Sensors*, *19*(14), 1–17. 10.3390/s19143091

Zhaofeng, M., Lingyun, W., Xiaochang, W., Zhen, W., & Weizhe, Z. (2020). Blockchain-enabled decentralized trust management and secure usage control of IoT big data. *IEEE Internet of Things Journal*, *7*(5), 4000–4015. 10.1109/JIOT.2019. 2960526

Index